D0389575

⊘ Waste Management

⊛ Waste Management

An American Corporate Success Story

Timothy C. Jacobson

**GATEWAY
BUSINESS
BOOKS**

Library of Congress Cataloging-in-Publication Data

Jacobson, Timothy C., 1948–
    Waste management : an American corporate success story / Timothy Jacobson.
      p.   cm.
    Includes index.
    ISBN 0-89526-511-7 (alk. paper) : $21.95
    1. Waste Management Inc.   2. Refuse disposal industry—United States.   I. Title.
HD9975.U54W375   1992
338.7'61363728'0973—dc20   92-28617
                                             CIP

Published in the United States by
Gateway Business Books
A Regnery Gateway Subsidiary
1130 17th Street, NW
Washington, DC 20036

Distributed to the trade by
National Book Network
4720-A Boston Way
Lanham, MD 20706

This book is printed on recycled, acid-free paper.

Manufactured in the United States of America

10 9 8 7 6 5 4 3 2 1

For Christopher and Anne:

Better drowned than duffers;
If not duffers, won't drown.

Acknowledgements

THE PORTRAIT of Waste Management, Inc. presented in this book derives from time spent with its people. At last count, they numbered some 65,000 worldwide, and it is beyond possibility to know them all. From the hundreds I have known, however (many of whom cannot be named here), I have made inferences about the character of their company that I believe are reasonable and that capture some useful truths about it. People from top to bottom talked freely. I hope they will find that my interpretation of what they have said is faithful to their meaning, and that they will approve my probing of their particular understandings for general patterns of thought and action.

To Chairman Dean Buntrock, President Phil Rooney, Senior Vice President Harold Gershowitz, and the company's other officers at home and abroad I am grateful for time spent and doors opened. Individuals to whom those doors have led and whose experience of early years has helped me to portray them include H. Wayne Huizenga, Peter Huizenga, Rosemarie Buntrock, Larry Beck, Don Flynn, John Melk, Fred Weinert, Peter Vardy, Rich Evenhouse, Dave Blomberg, Harold Smith, Harold Vandermolen, Tom Tibstra, Ben Essenberg, Odie Lenderink, Kay Hahn, John Blew, John Bitner, and Jack McCarthy.

Journeys in the field, where the company does its daily work, yielded acquaintance with dozens of others who talked, guided, and helped this stranger to understand the business by seeing it: Deborah J. Adams, David M. Beavens, Michael J. Berg, Marco Bijl, William Y. Brown, Bill Burrows, Harold P. Cahill, George Chacon, Floyd Cherry, Siuwang Chu, Stu Clark, Douglas W. Coenen, Steve David, Don Demkovitz, Becky S. Eatmon, M. Jennifer Edwards, Robert Faber, Ed Fierro, Francis C. Flynn, Karlheinz Freesen, Ivan D. Good, Richard G. Harbrukowich, George E. Hurst, Beth Davison Hyde, Caitlin M. Gallagher, Sinon M. Galvin, Alan Griffiths, William H. Grube, Nick Harbert, Gregory C. Harris, Jim Herak, Vernon T. Ichimura, Jan C. Ingwersen, Jackie Jacobi, Frits Jellema, Jorgen W. Jernsen, Mukhtar A. Khaku, Robert P. Keller, Jr., Donald S. King, Reinard Kortmann, Bruce Manning, Don McClenahan, Jim McGrath, Cam Moretti, Sven Nerell, Ing. Uwe-Jens Ohlsen, Barbara Zeitman Olsen, Steve Osborne, John M. O'Sullivan, S. S. Pasha, Klaus Petersen, Charles P. Pietsch, Mike Popowich, Charles E. Powell, S. Prasad, Tom Puckett, Cherie Collier Rice, Bill Rose, Crawford Ross, Linda A. Sapienza, Bob Van Schaik, Tony Shabarat, Lennart Sivertsson, Paul Spann, Peter Staberow, James P. Staehr, Jerry Stevens, Mark J. Taylor, B. Teichert, Rajan Thomas, Hans Witteborg, and Skip Wray.

Staff in Oak Brook, Vice President Bill Plunkett, and particularly Darlene Chesky, tended to countless details. Deborah Gabriel in Milan expeditiously turned Italian to English and vice versa. To Martin Marty in Chicago, for pointing out Waste Management to me in the beginning, and to publisher Alfred S. Regnery and editor Trish Bozell in Washington, for bringing us to the end, go special thanks.

TIMOTHY JACOBSON
All Souls, 1992
Winnetka, Illinois

Contents

Preface

DRIVE AROUND America, and if you are at least forty or so, see the difference. The roadsides and the countryside are cleaner than in days of youthful summer vacations when litterbags, like seatbelts, were novelties. The fact surprises. Millions more populate the land now, than then. The style of their civilization continues to produce refuse in abundance. Where did it go, and why?

Two images have helped me into this subject. The first is ubiquitous. You will confront it at country crossroads, at interstate interchanges, in urban alleys all across America. Steel containers, both small and great, made for hoisting aloft by the mechanical arms of the great trucks that haul the trash away. They are to the waste business what the boxcar was to the railroads fifty years ago: the maid-of-all-work, the fundamental tool of the trade, the symbol of a reusable business resource. Chances are, the container you see will be painted a discrete burgundy and bear the "WM" logo of Waste Management, Inc. Or it may bear the markings of its several large corporate competitors, or of the still-numerous smaller companies who remain in the business. Whosoever, their numbers are immense, their simple steel shape a powerful visual commonplace on the landscape of our times.

The second image is more particular. The open dump in a small

Northwoods village where I visit is now a grassy sward. As a result, there is one less opportunity for summering city children to see the bears. The bears, deprived of an easy feed-lot, are a greater nuisance than ever before. The trash, once so casually disposed of from the back of the stationwagon on the way into town, now is husbanded for the caretaker who keeps it in a container for a hauler who trucks it miles away for disposal in an up-to-date sanitary landfill in accordance with the regulations of the United States Environmental Protection Agency and the Wisconsin Department of Natural Resources.

When you look at all those containers, it is impossible not to be struck by the great scale. The "problem" here must be immense, and so therefore the enterprise that can solve it. This is not a subtle idea. It is rather like looking at the vast number of grocery stores and convenience markets and thinking how daunting is the number of people who need to eat. The challenge either makes the heart sink or the blood race.

When you look at the dump that ceased to be a dump, it is just as difficult not to be struck by the fact of great change. That you can no longer toss the garbage onto a smoldering heap in the woods reflects, to put it mildly, a changed cultural attitude. Among ingredients of the good life, as they are widely understood at the end of the twentieth century, the environment ranks equal with democracy, free markets, and human rights. Twenty-five years ago, no one knew the word. Today, young schoolchildren come to attention and grow somber at its mention. Twenty-five years ago, no one knew Waste Management. Today, it has grown to become one of the world's most valuable concerns. What follows is an essay into the character of that company.

⬬ Waste Management

1

The Job

DEAN BUNTROCK has a vision. It is a vision of the future, for his company and for his time. It is a vision with power to motivate thousands of people today. It is a vision of a world different from the past, but soundly built upon it.

Few people at Waste Management, the company Dean Buntrock founded, think much about the past. Theirs is a high-velocity growth company ever anticipating the next business hurdle, ever striving for the next growth target, waiting for the daily judgment of the institutions and thousands of individual investors that have made the company among the most valuable in the world. The reasons for their success are numerous and rooted in history. Throughout runs the power of consistency. In twenty-five years, Dean Buntrock's vision has broadened but not changed. His company has anticipated and accommodated change—in the marketplace and in the culture—with deftness but without endlessly reinventing itself. At Waste Management, they stick to their knitting. Today, Waste Management people—the men and women in the middle, between the past and the future—reach hard and high, but they stand on steady ground.

The Environment Is Our Future

The vision is this: to make Waste Management the world's most important provider of environmental services and one of the world's great companies. Today, in 1992, that vision is arguably attained. The company's new organization and new name confirm it. WMX Technologies, Inc., the new parent holding company formed late in 1992, embraces the businesses that define environmental services today: Waste Management, Inc. (solid waste management and recycling in North America), Chemical Waste Management, Inc. (hazardous waste management), Wheelabrator Technologies, Inc. (waste-to-energy, clean air and clean water technologies), Waste Management International plc (solid and hazardous waste management, including recycling, worldwide). An eighth unit, Rust International, Inc., consolidates a variety of environmental remediation, engineering, and industrial services, formerly spread throughout the company, to improve management efficiency and enhance shareholder value: the value of the new whole will exceed the simple sum of the old parts.★ The new name charts an evolution in both corporate substance and self-perception. As the market and the culture have come to demand new services and new sensibilities, new words have risen up to describe them. "WMX Technologies, Inc." captures this shift, from a waste company performing a time-honored task, to a complex technological enterprise poised before an age of environmentalism.

★ For the sake of historical consistency, the text that follows and which ends with 1992 adheres to the company names that were in place prior to the end of 1992, when the WMX Technologies, Inc. reorganization took place.

4

No company in this business, anywhere in the world, can match Waste Management's range of experience and store of technology, its financial prowess and management skills. Many companies everywhere envy its balance sheet. Investors revel in the value their company has created. But it is capitalism's way to let no record stand, to let no winner pause for breath. If it is possible, they work even harder at Waste Management today than in the first uncertain years. They must. The risks are greater; the competition is keener; the expectations are higher. The work they have chosen for themselves has never been more controversial. What was achieved today, can be lost tomorrow.

Today, more than ever before, the two halves of Buntrock's vision make a unity. This is because, in the age of the "information revolution," more people everywhere want the same things and expect, realistically or not, to obtain them. The range of capabilities that Waste Management's family of companies offers today represents a wish-list of services for the environmentally awakened end of the twentieth century. It includes collecting, disposing, and reusing solid waste in sanitary landfills, incinerators, and through recycling; managing all forms of hazardous wastes through treatment, incineration, and recovery processes; remedying chemical waste pollution; managing medical waste; transporting and securing disposal of low-level nuclear wastes; generating a scarce commodity, energy (chiefly electricity), from an abundant one, garbage, in waste-to-energy incinerators and through methane gas recovery from landfills; and programs to encourage waste-reduction and recycling—that greatest of all environmental crusades.

It is a list that abounds with superlatives, which are important less as a boast than as an indicator of scale. Waste Management, Inc. is the nation's largest handler of solid and chemical waste; the largest asbestos-abatement company; the largest private wastewater treatment company; the largest low-level radioactive waste management company; the largest waste-reduction consultancy; the third largest engineering firm; one of the largest managers of

5

medical waste. The company is the largest buyer of trucks and containers, whose burgundy color is recognized in cities and towns everywhere.

Eighty percent of the company's revenues comes from the solid waste operations of Waste Management of North America, Inc., the company's first home and the foundation upon which it has all been built. Their scope, in an enterprise just twenty years old (30,000 employees, and 12 million residential and 1 million commercial and industrial customers, in all 500 of the United States' top markets), reflects an intensely growth-oriented culture and foreshadows growth to come, here and elsewhere. Its Recycle America and Recycle Canada programs recover nearly 2 million tons annually of materials from the solid waste stream. Fifteen tire-shredding facilities deal with that particularly troublesome commodity. Energy harnessed from decomposing garbage in landfills yields 94 million watts of electricity and 7 million cubic feet of medium BTU gas every day (power sufficient for 100,000 homes and the equivalent of 1.6 million barrels of oil). Eleven treatment facilities deal with the wastes of hospitals and medical laboratories. Its Port-O-Let and Modulaire service centers manage 123,000 portable toilets for the construction and special events industries.

Chemical Waste Management, Inc. (Chem Waste), a 76 percent-owned subsidiary, is the nation's largest provider of comprehensive hazardous waste services, with 25,000 customers and 11,400 employees. Chem Waste operates seven hazardous waste landfills, seventeen hazardous waste incinerators, recovery, and treatment facilities. Its environmental remediation service (ENRAC) has nineteen divisions. Chem-Nuclear Systems, a Chem Waste Subsidiary, is the only private provider of low-level nuclear waste disposal east of the Mississippi River. With proprietary technologies like X★TRAX™ (thermal separation of contaminants from solids and sludge), PO★WW★ER™ (waste treatment for both organic and inorganic contaminants), and Chem-Matrix (waste stabilization systems), Chem Waste leads the industry in the recycling, treatment, and disposal of hazardous materials. Chem Waste also holds a majority interest in the Brand Companies, which offer asbestos abatement and numerous industrial services in all fifty states.

Waste Management, Inc. holds a 58 percent interest in Wheelabrator Technologies, Inc., which operates fourteen waste-to-energy plants serving four hundred communities and producing 585 megawatts of electricity annually from 8 million tons of garbage. It provides a range of technologies and services to clean the air and treat water and wastewater. Through capabilities provided by Rust International Corporation and SEC Donohue, Inc., Wheelabrator ranks among the world's leading environmental engineering firms. It employs four thousand.

Abroad, the fourteen thousand employees of Waste Management International plc orchestrate many of the same services for thousands of customers and millions of households. An 80 percent-owned subsidiary (12 percent each is held by Chem Waste and Wheelabrator, with Waste Management holding 54 percent), the company conducts operations in Europe, the Middle East, South America, Australia, New Zealand, and East Asia. Its operations are managed on a country basis from headquarters in London and focus on collection, treatment, and disposal services. In Europe alone the company serves 4 million households through 1,500 municipal contracts, plus an additional 9,400 hazardous waste customers. In South America, the company is the leading provider of waste services in Argentina. In the Pacific, the company is a major provider in Sydney and Brisbane, Australia. In Hong Kong, it is building with local partners Asia's first comprehensive hazardous waste treatment facility. In Indonesia, it will shortly begin work on the second.

Tote it all up: at this writing, 65,000 employees, 900 operating divisions in 48 states and two dozen foreign countries; revenues approaching $10 billion, income approaching $1 billion, assets of $12.5 billion. Although the value of its stock has been subject to the volatile perceptions of a frequently emotionally charged business,

Waste Management's record of growth and growing value has been without fundamental interruption.

Such vast "environmental services" represent far more than just a new, more sophisticated response to the old problem of garbage. They result from a genuine demand, unstimulated by advertising, that human beings rework the nature of their relationship with the earth, the seas, and the sky that surround them. The phrase is not marketers' hype. Indeed, it conveys an urgency about matters that are not at all discretionary. The garbage business has always been attractive for that very reason: the stuff was always there and always had to be gotten rid of somehow, somewhere. But today, two facts transform the old problem, putting it in radically new relief. There is both more waste (more waste-producers living their lives very differently from the way people used to), and the waste is deemed by them to be more harmful.

More is at work here than heightened fastidiousness about garbage as a hazard to public health and as a general source of pollution. It is that for sure, but since the 1960s when solid waste was first dubbed "the third pollution" (after air and water pollution), a revolution has occurred in many though not all countries (Japan being a notable exception) in the way we think about these things and in the words we use to describe them. The result is nothing less than a new moral dispensation on the subject of humanity and the environment: an environmental ethic. The peppering of our public and private conversation with phrases like sustainable development, global warming, deforestation, and ozone-depletion measure its pervasiveness. The word "green," once a color, now a cause, visually symbolizes it. The old term, "waste," conveyed meanings that were precise, concrete, something that could be identified and managed. The word "environment," by comparison, evokes ideas that are boundless in their capacity to consume our attentions, energies, and resources. Dangers abound when moral enthusiasms collide with finite economic and political realities, and the full market-costing of this particular enthusiasm is still in its early stages. Happily for a company like

Waste Management, one immediate consequence of the green revolution has been the creation of an enormous market for "environmental services" beyond the dreams of any mere garbageman.

But Dean Buntrock has a vision, not a dream: "the environment is our future." It is also what millions of customers want.

Service

"Environmental services" is a relatively new phrase at Waste Management, or anywhere else for that matter. It reflects the changing perceptions and sensibilities of our times on all matters to do with "waste." Under its umbrella are gathered activities of great technical sophistication that only yesterday had hardly been thought of. It is, in this sense, a good and serviceable phrase. It accurately describes a business, and helps make the intelligent distinction between the nature of that business today and what it once was. It is a dangerous phrase only if, amid high-tech bright lights of modern "environmental services," one forgets the basics. Twenty-five years ago, fifty years ago, a hundred years ago, the basics of the waste business were these. Pick it up. Put it down. Pull out in between anything that might be saved, that had a market and might be used again. These are still the basics today, although they are performed on a greater scale and with greater care than yesterday's garbageman could ever have imagined.

The core of Waste Managements operations today, and the heart of its short history, is the removal, disposal, and recycling of nonhazardous solid waste: simple trash, rubbish, garbage. This is the business of its largest subsidiary company, Waste Management of North America (WMNA). Here is most easily observed the extent to which this is a service business: it makes nothing, but moves almost everything. To get its job done, day after day, takes a lot of men and a lot of trucks.

It is a cliché that "a service business is a people-business." At Waste Management, much is made of "our people." But they

9

speak the phrase less by rote than from conviction. While it is not literally true that the company's biggest assets go down the elevator at the end of the day, as in a consulting firm or an ad agency, it is fair to say that if you should subtract even the assets represented by the company's real estate holdings, by its fleets of rolling stock and its high-technology waste treatment facilities, you would still have thirty thousand people in North America who know the basics and practice them. Their skills are where the value lies.

You will find them at eight hundred operating locations across the United States and Canada, organized into four major groups. A group president—Bill Hulligan in Bensalem, Pennsylvania; Jim O'Connor in Ft. Lauderdale, Florida; Jerry Girsch in Westmont, Illinois; Jerry Caudle in Irvine, California—is in charge of each. Each is a man of long seniority with the company and much experience. Each reports directly to President Phil Rooney at corporate headquarters in Oak Brook, Illinois, outside of Chicago. It is a straightforward organization designed to keep this, the continent's largest provider of solid waste services, close and responsive to its customers. It is an organization intended to ground growth on the basics.

Twelve million households (served through 1,700 local government contracts) and 1 million businesses are the objects of this attention. They want, in a modern "waste-services provider," essentially what people have always wanted from the "garbageman." They want the trash picked up neatly, on time, and at a price they can afford to pay. As large as Waste Management of North America has become, it operates in an open marketplace with other substantial national and regional companies who offer similar services, and with hundreds of local competitors. It is a business atmosphere that keeps a man alert.

Alertness is abetted by streamlined corporate structure—few layers between bottom and top and a culture that encourages employees at all levels to make decisions and take responsibility for them. It also derives from the character of individuals. WMNA operates the world's largest waste collection system. To do so, it maintains a fleet of some 13,000 vehicles (most of them trucks) and employs 11,000 drivers, who in 1991 logged 650 million miles. Count on the numbers to keep rising. But when they were half their present level, or when they are double it, it is the constancy of each man's performance on which the whole enterprise depends.

From his earliest days in the business, Chairman Dean Buntrock had a concept that quickly became a bedrock business principle at Waste Management: "Every truck is a profit center." And at the center of every truck is a driver. It is remarkable how many managers at Waste Management once did, and still can, drive a truck. The company takes great care of its drivers—who gets to be one, how they are trained, what reward and recognition they receive.

Each year, drivers from Waste Management regularly are recognized for their safety and performance records. In 1991, they were Bob McConnell of Waste Management of Oregon, Marion Clemmons Wright of Southern Sanitation in South Florida, Richard Hernandez of Waste Management of Tucson, Dale Watson of Waste Management of Northern Michigan, Rafael Navarro of Waste Management of San Fernando Valley, Jimmy Burnett of Waste Management of Santa Clara County, and Fausto Gutierrez of Waste Management of San Diego. Each year, at the annual shareholders meeting in Oak Brook, Chairman Buntrock and President Rooney single out one driver for something extraordinary that he has accomplished in the course of an ordinary job, like spotting a car spun off the road and rescuing its driver from the burning wreckage. The driver's family usually attends (at the company's expense), to watch him receive the ritual plaque and the tangible shares of Waste Management stock. This sort of occasion is not unique to Waste Management, although it is handled with a certain simplicity and lack of slickness that is unusual in the world of carefully orchestrated corporate events. "Wholesome" is the word that I would choose to describe it, and I use it literally, without innuendo, in the sense of promoting health or well-being of mind, spirit, and body. Buntrock and Rooney choose their own word, calling this individual precisely what, to them, he is: a hero.

The Trucks

It is on thousands of routine days, however, that these "heroes," named and unnamed, prove their alertness in ordinary, highly repetitive jobs. Watch such a day begin. It almost always starts before dawn, in the probably not-too-pretty part of town that is home to the truckyard of a Waste Management hauling company. The company works in many cities under large municipal contracts that run for varying terms and sometimes are, or (due to the vicissitudes of local politics and the marketplace) are not renewed. If the scene is a city of even modest size—San Jose, Brownsville, Boston—you will be struck by several things.

When it was awarded late in 1985, the seventy-six month, 186,500 residential-unit collection contract in San Jose, California, was the largest ever of any American city. There the day begins at the Tenth Street Facility (a truckyard, garage, and a few offices). A guard has been on duty all night. The mechanics clock in at 5:00 A.M. The drivers come half an hour later in order to have their trucks off the mark at 5:45. The trucks—one hundred burgundy-painted Volvo-White side-loaders—sit idling, lights on, poised diagonally, facing forward, ready to go. The managers—the general manager, the operations manager, the safety director, the route supervisors—are all on the site attending, as it were, the day's "launch." A wiry driver, forty-eight years old with thirty years of garbage behind him, pauses to relate to a visitor how the one-man truck is a good life:

"You don't have to depend on anybody else. You know what you have to do and you go and do it. It's simple honest work. I take care of myself, and it's a healthy life. The garbageman sees everything, you know: wrecks, fires, violence. But when you put it all together, it's really interesting. I still like the garbage after all those years. I do my job and go home . . ."

A supervisor interrupts (it is now 6:00): "Sam, that garbage is calling you." And Sam too is off.

An hour later, the last crew has left its monthly safety meeting, is out the gate and on the street, hefting twelve to sixteen tons of trash. The dust settles, and the yard grows as quiet as the school-yard at recess. Mechanics work their repairs; they keep the operation running with only three spare trucks. The trucks will return around midday, hoppers empty, their job done. Supervisors will do their productivity reports and other paperwork and attend to customer complaints (just twenty-five a day for 36,000 homes serviced). It all happens every working day, over and over again.

Two things about it are remarkable. First is the scale: modern life generates vast waste that requires vast resources to manage. But there is also the crispness. Part of this for sure is just that beginning-of-the-day quality: men and machines are rested and ready for work. It is not, obviously, a military operation, but the comparison inevitably suggests itself and is meant as a compliment. There is no top sergeant with swagger stick shouting orders; indeed the atmosphere is largely first name, slap-on-the-back egalitarianism. But the morning "launch" of a large Waste Management collection operation is a bit like watching the troops mount up: officers delivering the "here's the objective, men, we've got a big job to do and everybody's part is important" speech, the plain soldiers well trained and ready to put their backs into it. Like the objective "Take That Hilltop!" the objective in the solid waste business is an unambiguous "Pick Up The Trash!" In this particular company, mobilizing for that straightforward task has been developed into a minor art form.

The Street

To watch that happen, sit beside a driver after he leaves the gate. He is a man under orders, with a specific route to follow. He is off the base, far from camp, and in a uniform and a vehicle that advertise the firm he represents. How well he performs, at that moment, determines the welcome he receives, and whether or not the firm will be invited back. From Ace Disposal, a Waste Management company in Chicago, he will follow his commercial route through the apartment houses, clubs, and restaurants of the Near North Side. By himself, he works a massive rear-loading compactor truck up and down the alleys of the old city, tight with cars and his (and other) company's steel waste containers. He is an expert "in reverse." At fifty or sixty stops, he must position the rear hoist of his truck using side mirrors and a small video monitor on the dashboard that shows what lies behind him. He seldom fails to get in position on the first try. He is in and out of the cab endlessly, rolling the heavy often reeking containers (restaurants pack the most odiferous garbage) the last few feet up to the back of the truck, yanking the lever that hydraulically dumps the bin and activates the steel compactor blade, and then rolling the container back again. It is noisy, dirty work. Lids bang. Engines roar. "This-vehicle-is-backing" beepers beep. Trash crashes. The heavy lifting on such commercial routes is all mechanized, but no machine is perfect. Containers are routinely packed to overflowing, and something frequently spills. The Waste Management driver is responsible for that too; his job is to empty the bin and leave the place neat. Strapped to the side of his massive truck are two timeless tools of his trade: a shovel and a broom.

Of all the vehicles ever mounted on rubber tires, none rides rougher than a garbage truck. Suspensions are tight to support heavy loads over hefty potholes. Drivers ride in cabs directly over the front wheels and right beside the engine. At Ace on Chicago's North Side, if it takes a man four or five hours to collect his load, it might take another hour or two to get rid of it. The company's CID Landfill in Calumet City is far to the southeast and a long ride down the expressways or, if they are not available, down older arteries like Western Avenue. Safety is a constant concern. Garbage trucks do not maneuver or stop like cars. With steel containers hoisted high in the air, if something slips, a man can be crushed in a flash. Drivers are drilled endlessly on how to drive and work defensively in order to avoid danger to themselves and the public. Care has consequences. For every Louis Flaschenriem, "Driver of the Year" in 1989 who has logged a million accident-free miles in thirty-two years behind the wheel in Minnesota, there are hundreds of others building records the same basic way, by checking everything twice and then checking it yet again.

The Neighborhood

Checking is basic at Waste Management, from the driver on up. It is how you know the job got done and how you know what still needs doing. As in all companies, there is a chain of command, but in this one it is better described as a chain of accountability. It is not a fancy management idea, but simply a common sense approach driving responsibility downward in the organization. Make a man accountable, and you will make him behave responsibly. Only if he behaves responsibly will he work productively for himself and his company. A driver is accountable to a supervisor who is accountable to an operations manager who is accountable to a general manager and so on up the chain. To ride beside a supervisor, whose job is checking, is to witness the kind of detail on which accountability is built.

George Chacon, a route supervisor at Waste Management in the San Fernando Valley in southern California, trails his trucks every day, checking and helping out if help is needed. He covers a diverse territory: quiet working-class neighborhoods in the city of San Fernando, gang-infested Las Palmas Park, apartment houses along Langdon notorious for drugs, respectable delis south on Sepulveda, swank clubs and eateries on Ventura, elegant Sherman Oaks, the sound stages and back lots of Universal Studios (where even dreams make trash, and lots of it; the company services 150 containers there every day).

Waste Management has a contract with the city of San Fernando to collect residential garbage, recyclables, and green yard waste;

Chacon follows a trail of empty cans. He checks in with city hall for any complaints the city might have received about service, and to leave off any of his own drivers' reports of a can put in the wrong place or of hazardous materials set out with the trash (illegal). He looks down one street and sees unemptied yellow cans at three houses, which tells him that the driver, who is new on that route, has missed the street—if it were a full can in front of only one house, he would conclude that the residents had gotten the trash to the curb too late for the pickup. But they are in front of three houses, which tells him that the new driver missed a turn and thus the whole street. He will go back and do it again that same afternoon.

The city prides itself on getting rid of its graffiti, and Waste Management is responsible for painting the stuff out on any of its bins. "I have bins that constantly get marked up, and I've been confronted by a gang member about why I'm taking his markings ("Lobo") off the can. I tell him it's Waste Management property, I'm a part of this company, and I'm taking it off. It's not a big confrontation but next day, sure enough, old Lobo's back on the bin and I keep wiping it off till he gets tired of it—and he does." At Las Palmas Park, where the city had to outlaw the wearing of gang colors, the Waste Management men never have a problem: "You see, we're not a threat to them; we service their families, just like the gas man and postman."

He cruises the old main street, still alive with largely Hispanic small retail shops. The problem here is that shopowners are tempted to use the public trash containers for their own commercial waste. It's a driver's job to spot this, and the city's to reprimand the offenders. The yellow recycle bins contain glass, aluminum, and newspaper. The green ones are for yard waste only but not for anything fibrous—none of the palm leaves and cornstalks common in neighborhoods in this part of the country. "The woodchipper just won't chip it; so the drivers sort it out before it goes into the truck."

On the boundaries with Los Angeles, he has to be careful of

people who slip the unwanted sofa across the street onto the San Fernando side next to someone else's trash and say, " 'Now it's your problem.' So I'll take a picture, give it to city hall, and they'll clear the street off." Chacon always has to watch out for cardboard: "See that? It's supposed to be flattened and tied. That isn't. That's illegal. It's off the sidewalk, it's on the street, it's not supposed to happen. The city tells us to go ahead and pick it up, give them a green tag [a notice of the improper procedure], and put the cans back on the parkway. If we don't, we're in violation of the city ordinance. There goes truck 201, the driver is Luis, who's been with us five months . . ." Chacon knows all their names.

He notices three paint cans stacked in front of a house that has already been picked up. "The driver set those out because they're hazardous and he can't take them. But he should've tagged them." He's on the radio to the driver who explains he did leave a green tag, spoke with the residents who said they would get rid of it some other way. The driver also remembered they gave him a cold glass of water.

On the commercial routes, he visits a locked container where someone needs a key. He investigates a request to change the location of a container in a cramped apartment house parking lot. Both the radio and the carphone stay busy. In the different world of Sherman Oaks, he checks containers servicing contractors who are adding on to homes of Steven Spielberg and Tony Danza (whose father, Chacon has discovered, was a trashman in New York City). He calls Dana, the driver on Route 51, to make sure the Danza container gets emptied. Dana is one of two female drivers in this Waste Management company and is in charge of the "Stinger," a small pick-up with a hydraulic lift on the back used to pull boxes out from tight spots so the big truck can grab them. She wants to move up to a front-loader.

He moves east past the eateries along Ventura, many of them Waste Management accounts: Jerry's Drive-In, and Joe's, and Mel's, and Moscow Nights, "where the trash is always real wet and heavy." At Universal Studios, the Waste Management men are a daily presence, packing away the tons of plywood and other once-used trash that movie make-believe is made of. They are in by 3:00 A.M. and usually out by 10:00, when production work gets underway. Like everyone else in this city-unto-itself, they keep a sharp eye out for the illuminated red lamp outside every sound stage that announces "Shoot in Progress": Kill that engine!

And When the Truck Is Full?

Every driver, at the end of the day, dumps the trash. It is an old ritual with a bright future. But the distinction between where it was dumped in the past and where it is dumped today is sharp and offers another example of the tendency in modern life for technological advance to outpace public understanding of it. Typically, language reflects the lag.

On the pages of a newspaper as business-friendly as the *Wall Street Journal*, the places where trash-haulers deposit the trash are called "dumps." On the pages of Waste Management annual reports and other official literature, they are called "sanitary landfills." Little riles Waste Management managers more than this discrepancy of language. The discrepancy is vast. "Dump" is an old word, from Dutch and Old English, and, properly used, a perfectly good one. "Sanitary landfill" is an industry neologism: six syllables to do the work of one. Conscientious wordsmiths recoil. But precision as well as felicity measure the power of language, and the Waste Management managers insist that "dump" is no longer precise. Far from it; it maligns the work they do. It works neither as noun nor verb.

"An accumulation of refuse or other discarded materials?" Well, yes, of course, a sanitary landfill is that (although an accumulation of a rather special and expensive sort).

"A disorderly, slovenly, or dilapidated place?" At Waste Management, never!

This old connotation of carelessness is what the company finds most offensive. "To let fall in a heap or mass; to get rid of unceremoniously or irresponsibly?" Anyone not careless himself and who has observed the construction and operation of a Waste Management "sanitary landfill" will grasp the enormous gap between the old word and the new thing.

Waste Management of North America operates 130 sanitary landfills in the United States and Canada and has forty others under development. They represent an important, if partial, solution to the problem posed by the mountains of municipal solid waste that Americans and Canadians toss out, enough to fill 63,000 garbage trucks every day, 154 million tons every year. Such quantities would be daunting in any age. Coupled with the expectations of our own environmentally fastidious age, and the problem takes on the aura, if not necessarily the substance, of "crisis." It is a problem that has evoked, from those who make waste management their business, increasingly technological solutions. Just as Waste Management people shudder at the negative connotations of "dump," so they warm to the positive ones of "landfill technology," which they have made the newest "basic" of their old business.

In this, ever-greener government regulations spur them onward. The United States Environmental Protection Agency's "Subtitle D" rules, scheduled for implementation in October 1993, are an example. They represent the first national standards for the siting, operation, closure, and postclosure care of the nation's estimated six thousand municipal solid waste landfills (many of them dumps). They establish stringent requirements for liner and leachate collection systems, for groundwater monitoring and methane gas recovery, and they will force the closure of thousands of sites that cannot meet them. As a matter of environmental policy, Waste Management welcomes the new rules. It has invested heavily in the technology necessary to satisfy and indeed exceed them. From a business perspective, it regards them as a healthy leveller—upward—of the field on which all waste management companies henceforth must compete.

"Leachate collection?" "Methane gas recovery?" Not exactly everyday argot of garbagemen in the not very distant past, they are today the product of complex systems that lie at the core of responsible solid waste management, and that justifies the use of new words to describe it. A modern landfill design is as sophisticated a piece of civil engineering as one will find anywhere. Its aim—to stabilize and contain garbage so that it poses no threat to human health or the environment—is met with deliberateness akin to the preparation that attends a pharmaceutical company's bringing a new drug to market. Investments are enormous; mistakes can be few.

First, a capacity goal is determined to meet current and future disposal needs. Geologic surveys are conducted of local subsoil and groundwater conditions to ascertain permeability of the natural strata separating the waste from the underlying aquifers. Using computers, engineering drawings are prepared of the planned site, which will include a variety of linear systems, leachate collection and gas management systems, landfill caps, litter control, landscaping and perimeter security. Designed to be inert—to hold their contents in perpetuity, as it were—modern sanitary landfills are designed to be monitored heavily. Collection systems of gravel and perforated pipes gather naturally occurring leachate from the bottoms of waste cells and pump it to leachate treatment plants. Sites are surrounded with specially dug wells to check the performance of the liners that prevent leakage of leachate into groundwater below. Each year, some fifteen thousand groundwater test samples from more than five thousand monitoring points are sent for analysis to Waste Management's own $30 million environmental monitoring laboratory in Geneva, Illinois, west of Chicago, the largest groundwater testing facility in the world. Civil and environmental engineers, hydrogeologists, soil engineers, surveyors, and monitoring technicians abound, during planning and construction, and during operations. No liquid or hazardous waste is accepted at a Waste Management sanitary landfill. Each day's garbage is compacted and covered with a layer of topsoil to reduce pests and prevent litter.

The idea is for much to go in, but as little as possible to go out. A sanitary landfill is not a huge compost pile, and in its deliberately sealed, largely oxygen-free environment, not much degrades. Depending on temperature and moisture levels, organic solids do, however, decompose slowly, producing methane. Waste Management's larger North American landfills are designed with gas collection wells to harvest this by-product, which is used to feed electricity generating turbines on-site, or is cleaned and sold to industrial customers and public utilities (a technology first developed by Waste Management in Wisconsin in the early 1970s). All landfills eventually reach permitted capacity; they fill up. All Waste Management landfill plans call for either turning the capped site back to its natural contours, or for working with local planners to put the property to some community use. Golf courses, ski hills, athletic fields, and nature preserves all now rest comfortably atop yesterday's trash.

Down in the ... Landfills

Unless you were vacationing in the North Woods and wanted to show the children an extra bear or two (and perhaps a rat or two for your trouble), the "dump" used to be a place you avoided. A Waste Management sanitary landfill is a place that invites visitors. You will see no rats and remarkably little trash. It is worthwhile to seek one out and take a tour. No credentials other than "interested citizen" are necessary. The staff may arrange for you to join a scheduled tour, or they may just ask you to sign the guest book, give you a badge and hard hat, and show you around. You can find these landfills in all sorts of settings all over the country, which is not to say that the company sites them whimsically, but only that the varied geology in a nation this vast allows for the intelligent placement of such facilities in strikingly different locales. To see the locales is to learn something about the business.

Move west to east. In the West, with few trees and much sky, the landscape is striking in a way that bowls over the Easterner used to horizons hedged in with green. The shape of the land is easier to see, and that shape is not always as nature made it. In Los Angeles, the hand of man has left very little unmolested. One such site in Sun Valley, a dozen miles north of downtown, is the scar of an immense rock quarry, which became a Waste Management landfill in 1989. Engineered to meet Subtitle D requirements by next year, Bradley Sanitary Landfill plays a key role in handling Los Angeles's immense volume of municipal solid waste; even so, it will not last for long. The hole left by the quarriers is very deep. Looking down into it is rather like gazing into the Niagara or the Yellowstone gorge without the river at the bottom. It sits in an exceedingly heavy duty landscape of rail lines, rock-crushing operations, and cement factories, where the southern California sun must filter through a fine gray dust, in addition to the usual smog. But part of it is certainly the traffic: to the eye, Bradley seems the busiest landfill of the large lot visited by this writer.

The company probably has a measure for these things, but whether it is in fact the busiest matters less than the message conveyed by that image: with luck, and with good engineering, there are (for a short time longer) safe ways to dispose of a city's trash, close-in. The parade of rear-loaders, front-loaders, roll-offs, and semis roaring in and out of Bradley's resembles something out of a "D-Day-plus-five" movie, when all the tanks and trucks and APCs the Allies could float across the Channel got flung ashore at Normandy. Here as there, now as then, they know which way they're going despite the scrambler appearance. To learn that in a few years this place will be "full" is hard to believe, just looking at the hole in the ground. It is not at all hard to believe looking at the traffic—and the sprawl of Los Angeles all around.

Three hundred miles north one finds Waste Management's Kirby Canyon landfill. Approached over a two mile access road off of Interstate 101, the place suggests another sort of movie—this one a Western. High brown hills and intervening canyons reach off to the east. Up a narrow draw looms what looks like a small version of Hoover Dam, which defines the beginning of Kirby's first active disposal area, Cell No. 1. The 827 acre site (of which only 327 acres will be used for actual waste disposal) is designed for a service life of fifty-five years from its opening in 1986, at a rate of 1,500 tons of refuse per day, and will ultimately consist of a series of thirteen cells across several canyons. An adjacent "stockpile" or "excavation" cell, where refuse is not currently being placed, provides soil for the 6 inches of daily cover for the working waste cell. The "dam" is actually a toe berm at the base of the landfill, which is a system of a grout curtain, an extraction well, and several monitoring wells. Injecting chemical grout into the ground fills any voids where water might flow and forms an underground wall preventing potentially contaminated water from moving downstream and polluting groundwater. A system of natural and man-made channels and storm drains directs rainwater away from refuse areas and into a 9 million gallon sedimentation basin. The site sits entirely on serpentine rock, a rock created by stresses associated with earthquake faulting, and is highly impermeable to water. An old geologic fault separates the serpentine formations from the alluvial soils to the west and creates a natural hydraulic barrier between any potential seepage from the landfill and the groundwater supply in the valley.

The permitting process for Kirby Canyon entailed review by twenty-one local, regional, state, and federal agencies, and occasioned Waste Management's now famous meeting-up with the Bay Checkerspot Butterfly. It turned out that Kirby Canyon's foothill site was the natural habitat of the "mother population" of this delicate creature, with a lifespan of approximately two weeks, which was just then being proposed for listing as a threatened species due to development in the San Francisco Bay area. Permitting for the landfill therefore had to work through the Endangered Species Act, a well-known but then little-used provision of which allowed for negotiation with the U.S. Fish and Wildlife Service (which administers the act) of a "habitat conservation plan." Once agreed to, such a plan becomes a binding agreement between developer and the government. In this instance, Waste Management set aside a 250 acre preserve high on the ridge above the landfill and established a $500,000 trust fund to support study of the butterfly. To help maintain the Checkerspot's Serpentine Grassland habitat, the company arranged for grazing of the remaining portion of the site (more than half the total acreage) not currently in use for disposal operations.

The reason for this has to do with the history of settlement here over a century ago and its effect on the local vegetation. When the Easterners went West with their cattle, or as naturalist John Muir dubbed them, their "hooved locusts," and their non-native grasses, the smaller Serpentine plants that are the butterfly's habitat had a hard go of it. Controlled grazing by today's "hooved locusts" helps keep the non-native plants down, makes room for the natives, and helps preserve the Checkerspots. Even the *Wall Street Journal* was impressed by all this and contrasted Waste Management's enlightened choice for preservation with United Technologies's efforts to fight the Checkerspot's "endangered listing" for fear it would restrict testing of rocket motors at their 5,200 acre facility adjacent to Kirby Canyon. The *Journal* reported the episode on the front page, graciously calling Kirby Canyon a landfill, not a dump.

Today, Kirby Canyon is the only landfill with an insect for a mascot, with roads adorned with bright yellow signs cautioning: "Butterfly Crossing." Programs are also in place to protect the California Red-legged Frog and the Mount Hamilton Thistle. In the context of other more notorious nature-versus-development controversies (think of snail darters and spotted owls), the case of the Bay Checkerspot and Waste Management is particularly felicitous. And years hence (ca. 2041), when the fill is full, its 4 foot deep soil cover will be seeded with a mix of native plant species including the California Poppy, the state wildflower—all this atop the serpentine, the California state rock.

In some places it makes most sense to fill canyons with trash. In other places it is better to make mountains out of it. Let the local "environment" govern; best to use the conditions that nature provides. Three thousand miles east of Kirby Canyon, in South Florida, the local environment leaves rather less to work with. But the garbage problem is no less urgent. Central Disposal Sanitary Landfill handles much of it.

This landfill covers six hundred acres abutting the Florida Turnpike in Northern Broward County, northwest of Ft. Lauderdale. Two social forces—population growth and intensified environmental consciousness—account for it. Between 1950 and 1990, Broward County's population rose from under 100,000 to 1.3 million. Its residents, business, and visitors currently generate 1.6 million tons of solid waste every year, and most of it is landfilled. Open dumping, once a common practice here as elsewhere, was curtailed when municipal incinerators were introduced in the 1950s. Landfills were developed for bulky and bypassed wastes and were relied upon more and more heavily as air-pollution laws shut down old incinerators in the mid-1970s.

Since 1971, Waste Management's Central Disposal Sanitary Landfill has provided safe, monitored disposal of solid wastes for Broward and southern Palm Beach counties. Southern Sanitation, a Waste Management hauling company, brings in a majority of the daily intake of approximately four thousand tons of municipal and construction waste. Once unloaded, it is compacted in place at some 1,300 pounds per cubic yard and buried with all the fanfare that modern environmental engineering can give it: a synthetic membrane liner atop a low permeability clay sub-base, a leachate collection system, a protective drainage layer, 6 inches of daily cover, and a final cap of topsoil and landscaping. Monitoring wells test for leakage into the shallow Biscayne Aquifer. Gas recovery wells collect methane which is converted to electrical power at an on-site turbine generating station and sold to the local utility, Florida Power & Light.

The site is laid out in three cells. The northeastern cell, which is currently active, is being filled from the perimeter toward the center. The resulting high outside berm effectively screens the active landfilling—the trucks, compactors, bulldozers, and the garbage—and makes the site more attractive to the neighbors, who see not a hole in the ground filling up with trash, but a pleasant green hill rising in the flat Florida landscape. The southwestern quadrant is undeveloped and slated for future waste burial; part of it is in fact still cultivated by local truck-farmers. The northwestern sector, the oldest, has reached its permitted capacity and has been closed out and capped off. It is the high point, literally and otherwise, for the many visitors who seek this place out. Florida's high water table has forced construction of such facilities to go vertical. The peak, at 210 feet, was determined by the Federal Aviation Administration; the site lies in the landing path of a nearby airport. It is high enough to afford an impressive view: north and south across pervasive development, east to the Atlantic, west to the Everglades. Model airplane clubs fly remote-control craft there on weekends, and school and civic groups are given lunch there in a demonstration of the park-like potential of well-interred garbage.

The view also suggests the problem: pressing population, a fresh water supply that must be protected from intrusion by salt, rich subtropical wildlife in vulnerable habitats chock-a-block with golf courses and shopping malls. In the early 1980s, Broward County initiated its Resource Recovery Project in order to find a long-term solution. The comprehensive program, developed by government and the private sector over twelve years, called for the expansion of landfill capacity, for curbside separation of waste for recycling, and for the promotion of composting. Authorities also undertook to develop two trash-to-energy facilities to be privately owned and operated, and instituted an interlocal agreement among twenty-five municipalities to create the Broward Solid Waste Disposal District.

"Waste-to-energy"—the incineration of garbage to generate electricity in steam turbine power plants that use garbage rather than coal, oil, or natural gas for fuel—though a technology vastly different from landfills, addresses the same social problem. At Waste Management, it is a plausible part of the same basic business, and the company completed its first plant, the 1,000 ton per day MacKay Bay facility in Tampa, Florida, in 1985. Today at Waste Management, this technology is conducted by its 58 percent-owned subsidiary, Wheelabrator Technologies, Inc. Wheelabrator developed the country's first private trash-to-energy plant in Saugus, Massachusetts, in 1975, serving Boston's north shore, and today operates fourteen. Wheelabrator and Waste Management submitted their proposals for the Broward County project in 1984, and contracts were approved in 1986. The South and North Broward Resource Recovery Facilities, as the plants are called, were built by Rust International (a Wheelabrator subsidiary) and began changing trash to power in 1991.

Hot Recycling

From the 210 foot peak of the topped-off cell of the Central Disposal Sanitary Landfill, the only other tall point is the 209 foot stack of the new North Wheelabrator plant. It is designed to consume 2,250 tons of garbage per day and turn out 550 kilowatt hours of electricity for every ton burned up. The process, which is the same as at Wheelabrator's dozen other similar plants, is highly engineered but not conceptually complicated. Though Greens adamantly refuse to regard it as such, it is a form of recycling, and, unlike most other forms of recycling, it is simple. Trucks deliver trash to an enclosed receiving area and dump it into a large pit. Mammoth overhead cranes lift it to the feed hoppers of the boilers. The trash is then moved onto reciprocating grates where it is burned (without assist from other fuels, except when fires are being started) at temperatures exceeding 2,500 degrees Fahrenheit. Air from the receiving area is blown in above and below the grates to ensure a complete combustion process in the furnace and to maintain negative pressure, preventing the spread of dust and odors outside the building. A waterwall boiler above the grates produces superheated steam, which drives a turbine generator, which produces electricity for the plant's own needs and for sale to the local utility. A dry scrubber and fabric filter clean stack gases, exceeding all local, state, and federal environmental requirements. The process reduces waste volume by 95 percent. Ash goes to a dedicated cell in the landfill.

It is simple, and it is also safe. Much is made in Florida today about pollution of the Everglades by air-borne contaminants, particularly mercury which has been measured in distressing quantities in wildlife, and the state has imposed a moratorium on further trash-to-energy plants. It is a topic where emotions run high and where intelligent distinctions are sometimes in short supply. When anything is burned, gases are produced, which today (for a price) can be controlled. The air-emissions requirements imposed on trash-to-energy plants are stricter than those on conventional power plants and other industrial facilities.

Wheelabrator's facilities are among the cleanest in the world and commonly emit stack gases cleaner than the ambient outside air. Wheelabrator is the company that pioneered modern air-pollution control systems. It developed the world's first dry flue-gas scrubbers for the electric utility industry, and it has built some of the world's largest fabric filter and electrostatic precipitator installations. The fear (and fear is the word) about poisonous, particularly metals-laden, emissions that is focused on trash-to-energy plants is misdirected. The amount of mercury occurring in municipal solid waste, largely from batteries and fluorescent lights, is minute, about .004 pounds for every ton of trash. The use of mercury in batteries is declining sharply, from 778 tons in 1984 to under 62 tons in 1990. Fluorescents, whose use has increased as an energy-conservation measure, require annually perhaps 50 tons of mercury to manufacture, and when the old tubes are routinely broken, much of it escapes into the atmosphere. Mercury occurs naturally, of course, in the earth's crust, including Everglades peat, which, when left exposed by low water levels (as have been common in recent years in the Everglades) likely liberates substantial quantities of mercury. Lead also enters the municipal waste stream through batteries and to a lesser degree consumer electronics. Stack emissions of lead are often nondetectable; the lead contained in incinerator ash, when properly landfilled, poses no threat to groundwater. Other unpleasant things alleged to be poisoning us—hydrocarbons, organics, and dioxins—are efficiently destroyed in the high-temperature combustion process.

These things exist, and they come to Wheelabrator's Broward County plants because ordinary citizens have tossed them into the trash. Waste Management did not create them; it just ends up with them, and when it makes available a recyclng technology like trash-to-energy, it is accused of making more pollution. Is there "smoke" coming out of the stack today? If so, it is not smoke but water vapor. Is there nothing visible from the stack today? Then the "pollution" must be invisible. What are they hiding? It is a hard argument to win.

Wheelabrator's pollution-control devices probably remove more than 95 percent of gaseous pollutants and flyash. But then, "poison is poison," and any amount is too much. Or is it? If not present in quantities of 5 percent, would they not, uncombusted, be present someplace else in quantities much higher? It is a point as simple as the process of trash-to-energy recyclng itself. We are speaking here of matter: stubborn stuff that, unless it is converted to energy, will not be wished, or even recycled, away. For much higher levels of toxic emissions, one could look with profit at more garden-variety sources that cumulatively pollute much more, and, because the perpetrators (ourselves) are infinitely more numerous, are much harder to tame: cars, trucks, wood stoves.

The notion that we can recycle all or most of our garbage is false. The complex of Waste Management facilities in Broward County (which will also soon include a major composting operation of International Process Systems, a Wheelabrator subsidiary) conjoins simpler, more practical ways of managing it, ways in which recycling plays a part. But it is still early in recycling's day, particularly in America, and it would be wise if expectations attached to it were tempered and the politically-correct definition of it were broadened to include trash-to-energy, a recycling technique that works (like few others) at every stage. A Wheelabrator plant takes something that nobody wants (garbage) and produces something that everybody wants (electrical energy). There is no paucity of buyers for its end product. The same can be said for few other "recycled" products returned to their original use.

Wheelabrator supports recycling, as conventionally defined, wholeheartedly. Communities that presort their garbage for recycling and composting create a better form of trash for burning in trash-to-energy plants. Bottles and cans that do not burn and end up in the ash are a good example of what should be pulled out. Presorting also can remove materials like batteries, which should be handled differently to begin with. Wheelabrator supports a "Recycle First" program to assist community efforts by providing incentives, such as credits for removing recyclables from the waste stream. Waste Management itself is the world's largest recycler— on the consumer end of the process, where, thus far, the cultural mandate for recycling has had its most profound impact. Citizens fill their "blue boxes," sort their bottles, and stack their newspapers with an earnestness worthy of the civil rights movement thirty years ago. "Movement" captures the mood: surely, this is something that all good citizens must support.

So it would seem. Yet the consumer end is the easy part. National goals for the amount of trash to be recycled are being established in this country (the EPA has established a goal of 25 percent; the reality is now 13 percent), but it will likely take years to reach that level. Other countries have been working hard to recycle for much longer than the United States. Japan manages to recycle or somehow reuse about half of all its refuse, but this has taken years of careful planning, public eduction, and the purposeful development of markets for recycled materials. Moreover, it has occurred within a culture historically and geographically conditioned to the urgencies of crowded living and scarce resources.

In America, perceptions and realities have been understandably different, and it is not surprising that we are "behind." Complex issues involving protection of the public health (recycled plastics cannot be used to package food products) and the volatility of commodity markets (virgin paper is both higher quality and cheaper than recycled stock) make the economic equation of recycling unstable. The economic infrastructure of the recycling industry is still new. Markets are undeveloped, and there is no assurance that, once developed, they can be sustained over the long run. While it may seem, to many, just a matter of good will and diligence in organizing recyclable materials into useful categories, the materials still have to be collected, packaged, sold, processed, remanufactured, and finally sold again as a recycled product.

Of all the ways historically that men have chosen to manage their wastes, recycling entails by far the most complex chain of events. It is also, therefore, expensive. It is like the wonderfully clean exhaust going up a Wheelabrator stack: the pollution control technology that makes it clean represents, typically, one-third of the cost of the entire trash-to-energy plant. Recycling can also be undertaken as a matter of cultural and legislative mandate, the costs being laid to our environmental consciences. It will work best when it makes economic sense as well. Nor is recycling always as pristinely green as it pretends: a truckload of recyclable, ever-so-diligently sorted brown, green, and white glass bottles weighs a great deal and consumes gallons of air-polluting fossil fuel to transport; old newspapers can be recycled only after de-inking with potent solvents and chlorinated bleaches, which themselves pose other waste management challenges and are no friends of the environment.

System

Today's public mandate to recycle could not be stronger. Waste Management's Recycle America and Recycle Canada programs grow every year and presently serve six hundred communities and 4 million households. The company operates eighty sorting plants (material recovery facilities or "MRFS," as they are known in the industry) that process something close to 2 million tons of reusable material every year. The supply of newsprint and paper fiber, aluminum and other metals, plastic and glass is endless (and usually, except for aluminum, far in excess of the demand). The company is engaged in two significant recycling joint ventures, which are designed to maximize access to end markets for recycled materials. With Stone Container Corporation, it operates Paper Recycling International, which has become one of the world's largest recovered-paper brokers. In 1991, it marketed 2 million tons of the stuff. With American National Can Company, a multinational container manufacturer, Waste Management operates the Container Recycling Alliance, which processes metal cans as well as clear and mix-color glass containers. With Wal-Mart, it operates drop-off recycling centers at seven hundred stores in thirty-five states.

It is what the customer wants. The challenge of providing it, however, must increasingly be met through integrated systems of total waste management. Recycling is not a panacea. Many localities object to the presence of incinerators, no matter how clean the emissions or how much costly oil they conserve. Few localities want a dump nearby, even if it is the most modern landfill. As yet, public policy encourages only feeble understanding among the citizenry of the true cost of these things, and that ultimately it is waste producers—that is, all of us—who must pay for them.

A vision of what our waste management future (and the future of Waste Management) may hold can be seen today in the far West. It affords a glimpse of a way out of the "garbage crisis," which is in truth less a crisis of too much waste than a crisis of too little political will. Consider the fact that the population density of the United States, outside our coastal corridors and perhaps two dozen inland metropolitan areas, remains by world standards remarkably thin. Air travelers, used to the dense chaos of O'Hare or LAX and a diminutive view of the world from 40,000 feet, forget this. But take a train ride from Chicago to the West Coast (time: two nights and two days; altitude: twelve feet) and become reacquainted with this geographical fact—much of the place is empty.

One must of course be careful. "Wasteland" is not a fashionable word these days. "Empty" will do. It is not pejorative, and it requires us to ask, "Empty of what?" The techniques of intensive modern agriculture being what they are, more of these vast spaces can be rendered economically productive than ever before. Even so, vast expanses of the West remain as they have been since the land last rose up out of an ancient sea: a desert decidedly uncongenial to the plow and to water-consuming human settlements in general. Emptiness has always been part of the West's allure to visitors from greener, more crowded places. And nothing is ever completely void. Numerous species of plants and animals make the desert their home, a fragile ecosystem (as the nature magazines put it) easily undone by the careless hand of man. Anyone who has taken that train ride—or seen a John Ford Western, or thumbed through an issue of *ARIZONA HIGHWAYS*—at least can agree that the Great American Desert (as Americans once called it) is a place of surpassing natural beauty and, like all of nature, a gift and a trust.

The perfect place to site a landfill? Actually, yes, when one considers two other facts: the waste-intensive manner in which we choose to live, and our acute anxiety about waste once we generate it. These two facts have sparked, in the state of California, perhaps the nation's most draconian response to the waste problem. Some of its particulars will no doubt remain unique to California, but in general it is a fair foreshadowing of a broad national tendency. "Assembly Bill 939," California's Integrated Waste Management Act of 1989, calls for a reduction by half, of the state's municipal waste stream by the end of the century. It requires a reduction by a quarter by 1995. It sets the stage for a more formidable task of source-reduction and recycling than was ever attempted in this country. It raises a challenge for integrated waste management that can only be met if there is a successful conjunction of political will, financial resources, and technical know-how, all on a vast regional scale.

In southern California, which has the world's fifth largest economy and whose population is estimated to reach 21 million over the next thirty years, the challenge is especially acute. It produces 80,000 tons of garbage a day. A public sensitized by years of the "smog" problem has rejected widespread incineration. Most of the region's existing, close-in landfills are nearing capacity or will be closed under Subtitle D regulations. In 1991, the city of Los Angeles Solid Waste Plan predicted that by 1993 there would be a 22,000 ton per day shortfall in close-in landfill capacity. Reduce or recycle even half of that, and much of it will still be looking for a home. It is a situation in which long-haul by rail outside the Los Angeles Basin makes common sense.

This large opportunity has prompted from Waste Management a large response, regional in scope and conceived with a long future in mind. "Rail-Cycle," as it is called, is a 50-50 limited partnership between Waste Management of North America and the Atchison Topeka and Santa Fe Railway. It will provide communities throughout southern California with a comprehensive waste management system, the key of which will combine integrated source reduction and recycling with environmentally friendly rail transport of residual wastes to a modern sanitary landfill far from populated areas. The schedule calls for a start-up early in 1994, after five years of planning.

It is an entirely private enterprise; the investment between the two partners will exceed $100 million, a level of commitment that has compelled executives to embrace a long planning horizon. To respond to community needs as massive as those facing the Los Angeles Basin, with solutions of commensurate scale, requires thinking decades down the line. This is not easy in big corporations that find it hard to look very far ahead if no revenue is coming in. It entails an educated bet, with a great deal of shareholders' money, that decades hence it will prove to have been more than worth the considerable risk. The top level operating executives at Waste Management in Oak Brook—Bill Hulligan, Jerry Girsch, Phil Rooney—have backed the idea since the start and are close to seeing it happen. Hal Cahill and Stu Clark, who live with it daily in Los Angeles, are the men who will see that it does happen.

The core of the plan are the Materials Recovery Facilities, the MRFS, which will be located adjacent to existing Santa Fe tracks throughout the Los Angeles area. Each site is designed with a capacity of approximately three thousand tons per day and will be capable of sorting the full range of nonhazardous recyclables. They will accept separated recyclables (paper, glass, plastic, aluminum and other metals, yard and green waste) from residential curbside and commercial programs, recover recyclables from loads of mixed waste, and screen out hazardous materials which the system is not permitted to handle. Recyclables will be marketed immediately, while nonrecoverable residual waste will be compacted into sealed steel containers, loaded aboard unit-trains, and shipped by night to the system's landfill planned in the high desert of San Bernadino County 80 miles east of Barstow and 225 miles east of Los Angeles. That site, near Amboy, California, is on land that belonged to the Santa Fe and covers, with substantial buffer areas, 7 square miles. In the more crowded East and Midwest, three or four years of "airspace" in a landfill permit are much coveted. Here in the West, possibilities are still larger, and so too the risks required to realize them. The Rail Cycle landfill is designed with a capacity of 200 million tons and should last over one hundred years.

Figures like that pack a decided emotional kick, whether one is for, or against. Rail Cycle has done a highly effective job of educating its desert neighbors on the benign characteristics of modern landfills and on the economic and environmental benefits that this one will bring the residents of San Bernadino County. Only a few voices have been raised against—the stock Not-In-My-Backyard complaint that "we don't want to become the dumping ground for the nation." But the truth is that no one has ever seen 200 million tons of garbage, and no one ever will, certainly not here. As at all Waste Management landfills, this one will be worked one small cell at a time. The waste will be covered over at the end of the day, every day. Were the proverbial visitor from outer space to arrive at night, he would not have much of a clue, other than reading the signs, of what was there. A hundred years from now (and much sooner, as the first cells are filled and revegetated) it will all, safe to say, have gone back to desert, with the trick that everything hidden in it will be permanently isolated from the desert. The area is seismically stable. It is extremely arid (the drier a landfill the less likely anything will ever leak out). The site is not near any area preserved under the California Desert Protection Act. The nearest residence is five miles away.

Does this amount to responsible stewardship of the desert environment? Consider the whole problem, and it does. Consider less a figure like "200 million tons of garbage" than the fact that not a single ton will go in that could be managed in some other way. No want *wants* to bury the stuff. Everyone shares responsibility for what *must* be buried. Rail Cycle offers the realistic chance simply to bury less—and bury it better.

People at both ends—out in the desert and back in the city, voters and officials—need to understand that promise and the system that will implement it. In Commerce, California, the heavily industrial suburb of Los Angeles where Rail Cycle will build the first of what it hopes will be seven MRFS, Waste Management and Santa Fe officials host a pancake breakfast for the neighborhood to get the word out. The neighbors, some still out of work from when the adjacent galvanized wire plant closed down three years before, are friendly, curious—and largely ignorant of what this is all about.

"Are you going to build a landfill *here?*" (It will be 225 miles away.)

Pointing to a spit-and-polish Waste Management truck on display next to the breakfast tent: "They're going to haul the garbage out in *those?*" (It will be hauled out on hundreds of Santa Fe intermodal container carriers like the one prominently spotted on a nearby siding.)

"But won't there be *rats?*" (Many a rat has slunk away hungry and disappointed from a Waste Management MRF or landfill.)

A fancy architect's model shows what the Commerce MRF will look like with renderings of how it all will work. Cahill, Clark, and Santa Fe's Del Miller work the crowd, inviting conversation, being friendly, helping people get it straight. The sleeves of their Rail Cycle polo shirts carry the message: "We're The Solution."

No Birds

The challenge and the promise of Rail Cycle lie in putting all the parts together. Each of the parts, on its own, has been tried and proven somewhere else in Waste Management. The company operates more than eighty MRFS nationwide. It runs 130 sanitary landfills. And in Washington and Oregon, it already works with another railroad (the Union Pacific) in the long-haul business.

Every Monday, Wednesday, and Friday nights around six o'clock, the solid waste generated by the city of Seattle, waste that is not recyclable, begins a 320 mile journey in sealed containers on a unit-train toward Portland, the Columbia River Gorge, and a new landfill in Gilliam Country, Oregon. The thirty-eight year contract with the city was negotiated in 1990, service began in April 1991, and it has proceeded uninterrupted ever since. Long distance rail-haul of solid waste had not been done before; it was triggered by the heightened public sensitivity to the dangers of close-in disposal and its changing economics. Today, it is cheaper by a third to ship Seattle's waste to Oregon than to bury it locally.

The work was meticulously planned by people like special project manager Norm Wietting, special waste expert Pam Badger, and environmental engineer Doug Coenen. Mountain Region

Vice President Art Dudzinski then hired ex–Marine Corps logistician Skip Wray to work the plan, which he does with precision. At each of four transfer stations, an Amfab 500 compactor forms the residual waste into 7×7×27 foot bales weighing 27½ tons and fitting neatly into specially designed (vents, steel floors, watertight seals) intermodal containers. The containers then move by truck to the Union Pacific rail yard for loading on the unit-train. It is quick: the trash that moves out in the evening was picked up at the curb that same day or perhaps the day before. The railroad covers the distance to Arlington, Oregon in eight or nine hours (the garbage train has top priority, second only to passenger trains) and by sunset the second day Seattle's trash is tucked away tidily beneath its daily cover of Oregon topsoil.

Waste Management's 2,000 acre Columbia Ridge Landfill site in Gilliam County, Oregon, which opened in 1990, is the largest in the Northwest, with a capacity of 60 million tons of solid waste. It hints at what will soon appear in the Mojave Desert to handle the much greater waste stream from the Los Angeles Basin. (Seattle generates three trains per week. Rail Cycle anticipates seven per day.) It is extremely remote. The setting is strikingly beautiful. The landfill, worked into the natural contours, hardly intrudes. As a piece of nifty environmental engineering, it features all the bells and whistles that Waste Management engineers can give it. It is in the right place: little rain, ground water a comfortable 500 feet down, urban population centers far removed. The residents of Gillian County are happy as they can be with the new jobs, free waste and recycling services, host fees, and the general psychological boost that the facility has given to the area. It is a regional facility: Portland's waste comes here (by truck), as does Seattle's, as does Condon's (county seat of Gilliam County), and there is room for others' trash as well. There is also room for other such large-scale, long-life regional facilities. Butterfield Station Landfill, forty miles from Phoenix's Sky Harbor Airport, in rural Maricopa County, Arizona (named for the historic Butterfield State route that once passed nearby), opened a few months after

Columbia Ridge, and while not served by rail-haul, shares all of the fundamental characteristics of a big place built to last.

Wherever the trash comes from and however it gets there, once it arrives at a Waste Management facility no detail will be spared to render these leftovers of modern life as safe and unobtrusive as possible. The effort is summarized in striking fashion at Columbia Ridge by something that you don't see: a canopy of birds.

"No, there are no seagulls, and believe me, that's not a coincidence." The authority on the matter is Doug Coenen, who before joining Waste Management worked for the Wisconsin Department of Natural Resources and is now general manager of the site: "It takes a lot of work; we're not that far from the Columbia River; it's a big challenge."

He points to a small device by the roadside—a propane cannon set on a timer. Every day at dawn, when the gulls and ravens send out their "scouts" to spy out forage for the day, the gun, which spins on a swivel, goes off, scattering the birds who can't tell from which direction the feared noise is coming. It does the creatures no harm, but confuses them mightily. Coenen does it largely for the aesthetics. This is a business where the smallest appearances are subject to wild misinterpretation. ("Look at those birds! I told you that dump was dirty—rats too!") Besides, these high plains are a region where there are a lot of aesthetics to protect.

Leaving LA

If you return east from Los Angeles, also by train, chances are you will travel over the double-track mainline of the Santa Fe, fabled route of "The Super Chief," Death Valley Scotty, the Harvey Girls, and, before long, Waste Management's Rail Cycle. Today's "Southwest Chief" leaves gracious mission-style Los Angeles Union Passenger Terminal at 8:20 in the evening. Dinner in the diner starts off the 41 hour run to the shores of Lake Michigan. At ten, the train pauses at San Bernadino before heading up Cajon

Pass for the 4,000 foot summit. Barstow comes close to midnight. The next stop isn't reached until Needles, at the Colorado River where the train crosses into Arizona. In between, if you keep the curtains in your compartment open and the lights out, you can catch a glimpse of Amboy (pop. 27; estb. 1858) just about midway between the long-forgotten stations of Bagdad and Siam, California, in the shadow of the Bullion Mountains to the south and the Marble Mountains to the north. The "Chief" does not slow down, but if the air is clear, as it almost always is, the stark desert landscape reveals itself. It is empty—but not without intelligent use.

It was the railway that brought the ancestors of many present-day Californians to this immense and immensely beautiful land. It is fitting that it should help with the daunting job of cleaning up after them. That job and thousands like it elsewhere, without end, are the basic business of the waste management industry and of Waste Management, Inc., the company that leads it today. Of Waste Management—this do-the-right-thing, get-the-job-done, hard-working company—it is commonly said that they do exactly what their straightforward no-nonsense name says. And they are good at it, whether "it" happens to be the simplest hauling contract or a Rail Cycle, a waste-to-energy plant in Gloucester County, New Jersey, a waste-water treatment system in Fulton County, Georgia, a hazardous waste treatment facility in Port Arthur, Texas—or one in Hong Kong. The name—"Waste Management"—is the core, and it is also the beginning.

"Ship and Travel Santa Fe All the Way," the old timetables used to say. "All the Way" will still today carry you 2,227 miles from Los Angeles (through Amboy) to Chicago. This too is fitting. In the Waste Management story, to get to the beginning you have to get to Chicago.

2

Family Business

DEAN BUNTROCK came to work in Chicago in 1956. He was twenty-five, newly wed, and he had never tried the big city before. What he found in this particular big city, and what he built from it, while related, turned out to be vastly different things. The distance between those Chicago origins and today's worldwide results marks off the stage on which a striking drama of enterprise has been played out. Dean Buntrock was never far from its center.

Chicago in the 1950s was a fine place to get started. Carl Sandburg, its poet, lived nearby on the Indiana dunes. The city he had written about years before still resounded to the cadences he captured. Tourists found it a destination in itself. Other travelers, en route to somewhere else, never failed to marvel at the astounding place they were passing through. No one "flew over" then. Everyone changed trains (or for that matter, planes) in Chicago.

When they did, as they trundled between depots on the Parmalee Transfer or peeked up through the great colonnade of Union

Station on Canal Street, their eyes filled with the full panoply of *the* great American city at midcentury: great buildings of steel and limestone, massive department stores, countless shops and restaurants, streetcars, taxicabs, policemen on horseback, sidewalks packed with people. Its attractions were already legendary: Palmer House or Sherman House if you needed to sleep; Stockyards Inn, Como Inn, College Inn, Cafe Bohemia or Fritzel's if you needed to eat (or drink); Marshall Field & Co., Carson Pirie Scott or the Fair Store if you needed anything at all. If you came from older, more cramped cities in the East, Chicago seemed fresh and open, bidding genuine welcome. If you came from the vast open spaces of the West, Chicago seemed dense with possibility—and Lake Michigan the sea itself.

If it looked that way to tourists, natives liked it too. One of them was the new mayor Richard J. Daley, an Irish Catholic from Bridgeport, who liked to speak fondly of "this Great City of Chi*caw*go." Daley was not an articulate man; his sentences ran like train wrecks. But the thousands who thought and lived like he did never doubted what he meant. Chicago was a good place to raise a family and make a living: a good place to live.

But Daley's "great city" reached far beyond the Loop. Its heart, or hearts, lay in scores of neighborhoods divided and subdivided by railway and roadway and waterway—by history itself. This was the "flat city" of three-flats and bungalows, of parish churches and schools, of corner grocers and taverns, that reached for miles out from the lake. Successive waves of immigrants filled these enclaves, and then emptied them. For awhile, they made them small tight versions of "home." Then, as immigrants to America have always done, they took up the new habits called forth by new circumstances. Nearly all of them became "American" because nearly all of them wanted to. The ethnic tangle that made for wars and endless sadness on other continents had a happier outcome in an America roomy with freedom and opportunity. As some groups moved faster than others, so too with individuals: some soared ahead while others dawdled.

42

For people coming into them from the outside, Back of the Yards, Brighton Park, Canaryville, and hundreds of other neighborhoods were the great city's equivalent of the small towns and villages left behind. For those born in them, they defined a community where one could, with work and patience, get on with life and perhaps improve it. By midcentury, Daley's great city of Chicago extended in spirit well beyond its extensive formal boundaries to the scores of jealously autonomous towns and villages of the suburbs. They too went into the ever-rising total: "Chicagoland," as Col. Robert R. McCormick famously put it.

In the 1950s, this Chicago was in remarkable possession of itself, the plausible product of an understandable past and with little yet to shake its confidence that the future could be worked out along more or less the same lines. A homey, even a homely city, Chicago had few pretensions, but lots of substance. It was as Sandburg had imagined it: straightforward, heavy duty, hard working, a place where a man could get things done. It was a good town for business.

Out there in the neighborhoods—up and down the Western Avenues, the Milwaukees, the Lawrences, the Broadways, the Ciceros—the business of Chicago was palpable. In countless small enterprises and many large ones, men with quick minds, skilled hands, and strong backs made and traded and carried away everything under the sun. Times were good, America's economic preeminence unquestioned in the world. What Americans made, the world wanted; the way Americans lived, the world envied.

Many a working man and his family then grew used to the happy feel of folding money. The cost of living was still low, and a working man (especially in a well-paying union town like Mayor Daley's Chicago) could support a wife and children with his check alone. Thousands, of every race and ethnic persuasion, did just that: men who bore the mark of much harder times, whose fathers had raised their families during the Depression; men who were determined to secure something better themselves, but who understood all about the hard work it required.

Thousands of ordinary men fit comfortably into this world of work. They held their jobs, worked hard, took home an honest wage. It was a world where the modest horizons of ordinary men, and the opportunities to attain them, nicely matched up.

Luther and the Store

Circumstances in which some men see only the chance of a comfortable life, reveal something more to others. Besides, comfortable times have a way of not staying that way. The 1950s certainly did not, in Chicago or anywhere else, because they were too latent with change.

Dean Buntrock arrived in midcentury Chicago, as did a lot of other aspirants, drawn by whatever it is that brings people from province to metropolis, from the edges to the center. That pull has been one of Chicago's historic traits: a substantial literature records it. But in Buntrock's case, he took what he found and changed it almost beyond measure. Nor was Buntrock exactly "drawn." For it was the accident of marriage that brought him to Chicago, not the lure of any particular bright lights or big opportunity. But it probably is fair to say that if it hadn't been Chicago, it would have been some other place whose scope and scale matched his own potential.

Not by a long reach had the settings of his youth inspired big horizons. Dean Buntrock is, literally, a son of the Middle Border that Hamlin Garland had depicted with such appalling bleakness fifty years earlier. (Garland himself fled East to Boston and Chicago. To his credit, in his best writing he never "left home," and he was at his best when sympathy leavened realism.) If bleakness broke the spirit of some people, it bred staunchness in others. In the more cheerful imagination of Laura Ingalls Wilder, the very same landscape fairly rang with staunchness and courage, as several generations of readers of the *Little House* stories (the boy Dean Buntrock included) will attest.

An awesome gulf, however, can stretch between reading about

life in a place, and actually living there. But for Buntrock, growing up in Columbia, South Dakota, on the Jim River in the 1930s and 1940s, this was not so. Its patterns confirmed the ordinariness that the novelists, at their best, also captured. And as with the characters in those books, long after he had left his home behind for more bracing venues, the place implanted in the heart of this particular native son a deep and lasting affection.

Dean Buntrock was raised a Lutheran, bred in the bone by two powerful strains, Norwegian and German. His mother was Norse from Minnesota; his father belonged to the German Missouri Synod—together about as orthodox, *sola Scriptura*, Lutheran as a child could get. He lived with his parents, brother, and sister at different times in three houses, the last just across the street from St. John's Lutheran School, where he was a pupil from fifth to eighth grade. In this, culture and convenience conspired. It was not because St. John's was any better than the public school (he remembers that it wasn't as good), but because it was, well, right across the street, and "if you were Lutheran, that's where you went." At school, he was a steady student, an unaccomplished athlete, a stumbling trombonist. When school was out and when work permitted, he headed outdoors to fish and hunt in the Jim River bottom.

In Lutheran homes of that older order, religion and daily life were never far separated. Depending on a child's temperament, a pervasive piety can prompt later rejection of religion altogether or lay the groundwork for a mature faith. Neither fierce nor mild, the faith of the Buntrock's suited their son, Dean, fairly well. He recalls two pastors in his youth, the first a starchy sort who frowned on high school dances, the second a Southerner from North Carolina who smiled and loosened things up.

For two years, he studied his religion at school, where from *Luther's Small Catechism* (translated, but otherwise unchanged since 1529) he learned Christian doctrine—the Ten Commandments, Apostles' Creed, Lord's Prayer, Sacrament of Holy Baptism, Office of the Keys and Confession, Sacrament of the Altar—and memorized the hundreds of Bible verses that proved it all was so. On Palm Sunday, 1942, he was confirmed and took his first communion. On a shy boy, this sort of orthodox, "Remember the Sabbath day to keep it holy"/"What does this mean?" training was bound to leave a mark. He might, when he was older, conclude that some of it was silly. He might also find that much of it had become part of his character. For a boy, and later a man, drawn to neither extremes of skepticism nor devotion, this plain upright Lutheranism with its fine balance of Law and Gospel "seemed to fit."

The faith was a gift, the rock a man stood upon. Everything else he had to build for himself with hard work, and maybe some luck. So it was with Dean's father, Rudy, who was prosperous as well as pious. Rudy was a small businessman in a small Western town that lived by agriculture. He was the town's mayor for twenty-five years and owned and operated the combination farm implement/hardware store (the only one in town, and the Standard Oil distributorship besides): everything from tractors and combines to the nuts and bolts and bailing wire that sometimes held them together. He was good at it, managing a fair living through the ups and downs of good harvests and bad. In a time and place where money was sometimes scarce, Rudy Buntrock's family always had enough to eat in restaurants and take shopping trips to Aberdeen.

He used his business, however, for something else than making a living. He applied it to the training of his son Dean (and Clayton, his brother), an experience that probably left a deeper mark on the boy than any of his youthful formal schooling, and provided a worldly complement to all that Missouri Synod religion.

Dean worked in the store usually after school, sometimes sweeping up Saturday mornings, in the summer, into the evenings, for stores stayed open late in small towns then. The image could hardly be more prosaic. The experience—serving customers who were strangers and neighbors alike, selling parts and hardware, setting up new machinery, pumping gas, fixing tires, taking inventory—could hardly have been more valuable. His father saw to it that their relationship in the store was kept on a very business-like footing. He "employed" his son. No doubt the change in his pocket at the end of the day made it easier for Dean to look fondly on his job, not that it amounted to much or that there was much to spend it on in Columbia. But the mere fact of "earning" enabled him, as with most young people, to see himself in a fresh relationship with the world about him. The literal connection between wage and work is obvious to the simplest soul. It takes other sensibilities (and the proper prompting) to see beyond the money to the value it represents, and the process—"trade"—that creates it.

Not that a teenaged Dean Buntrock, working in and about the seed drills and tractor parts, pondered the abstract economics of it. But, in addition to his pay, he was taking notes about doing business, about profit and loss, and was filing them away for future reference. This was as his father surely intended. It was the greatest legacy he could leave. Among many memories of a happy youth, this is the one the son holds with special intensity.

What neither his father nor mother nor pastor nor anyone else from that happy time bequeathed him was the sort of towering ambition associated with the builders of great, as opposed to small, businesses. One of the nice things about nice little families and nice little towns is their self-contained quality, their comfortable coziness. It is also one of their limitations. From that vantage, other horizons are sometimes hard to perceive. A boy might be well raised, well tutored in home, school, and even the family business, and still not have much of an idea of where to look next. It is one thing to have learned the virtues of working hard. It is another to be able to focus and drive that effort toward some lofty goal. Dean Buntrock, as he prepared to leave home for the first time in the late 1940s, had some good training and instincts, but not a great deal else.

St. Olaf College in Northfield, Minnesota, was familiar and not far. It was his family's choice. It offered good teachers, a solid liberal arts curriculum based on an intact canon, and fellow students who looked and sounded a good deal like he did. At that time, a bachelor's degree at St. Olaf cost $7,000. Rudy wrote the checks (Dean started his own checking account in the fourth grade), but he kept a record, and his son understood the sum was to be repaid. But at his graduation in 1955, his father tore up the note—a surprise gift.

Dean Buntrock left St. Olaf still without clear direction, but with his eyes fixed at least on his future bride, Betty Joanne ("B.J.") Huizenga. After a stint in the army in Ft. Leonard Wood, Kansas, he married B.J. two days after their graduation from St. Olaf. They went west, and through his father's influence, he toyed with the idea of working for International Harvester in Denver. Instead, he decided to sell life insurance in Boulder, Colorado, and he turned out to have the touch. In his first and only year at it, he earned $25,000. Where that might have led is anyone's guess. But his new in-laws led him elsewhere. Elsewhere was Chicago.

Calvin and Trash

The Huizenga family bears on the history of Waste Management in two distinct respects. One of its members (H. Wayne) was to become, alongside Dean Buntrock, in the 1970s and early 1980s, the driving force behind the growth of Waste Management into today's industry giant. Another (Peter, a lawyer) still sits on its board of directors. Their story belongs in later chapters. Many stories of the other members of the Huizenga family belong to the 1950s and earlier. In their center, their themes are not unlike some of the themes of Buntrock's family story. They represent the stories of other immigrant families who made their way in America along similar paths.

Their story defines a beginning; it speaks of immigrant America, of the migration of other nationalities to other towns, and cities. The world the Huizengas and their fellow-Dutchmen had made for themselves in Chicago was the world that Dean Buntrock moved into in the 1950s. He found life there—amid the Hovings, Hoekstras, Huiners, Ottenhoffs, Evenhouses, Vandermolens, Mulders, Groots, and Boers—at once familiar, and fraught with new possibilities. Several characteristics stand out.

It was first of all a world of work. Calvinism shaped the culture of the Dutch with special fervor, and prepared them well to make their way in strange settings far from home. Strong paternalistic families were built and sustained in times of rapid change on straightforward pieties. They formed themselves into communities where they worshipped God, schooled the young, entertained themselves, and made their living. Calvin was a stern master. Christ's admonition to make this world into something that God could once again be proud of, interpreted through Calvin, was a fearsome responsibility. In his wisdom, God gave men but one tool to meet it: work.

The possible connection between success at work in this world and the likelihood of salvation in the next—that prosperity was a sign of "election"—had goaded generations of Calvinists to prodigious labors, starting in America with the founders of the Massachusetts Bay Colony in the seventeenth century. "By their works ye shall know them." The images of hell fire grew dimmer as the world grew modern; they certainly had faded in the minds of the Dutch-American Calvinists living three hundred years later in Chicago. But something remained, a residual memory of why "work" somehow meant more than just "making a living." In time, as theology thinned further and Christianity mingled with the civic religion of "the American way of life," the idea reduced to a phrase acceptable to all: "work ethic." To work hard—to arrive early, stay late, apply oneself diligently in between—falls short of capturing the meaning as it came down through the Calvinist culture. Not just how one worked, but what one was working for, measured the man.

As men matured, where they proved out most fully was in the world of work. Harm Huizenga, a Dutch emigrant who arrived in Chicago during the World's Fair of 1893, started hauling garbage at $1.25 a wagonload. At the time, the job called more for strong backs than quick wits, though he and the sons who later joined him had some of both. If there was any "skill" involved, it was handling a horse and wagon, which came easily enough to the

Dutch smithy from Groningen Province. Many Dutch had settled in southwestern Michigan and southwest of Chicago, where they prospered as truck farmers. Their wagons (and later their trucks) were familiar sights at Chicago's wholesale markets, their vegetables prized by the best hotels and houses in the city.

Edna Ferber's portrait of this world in the novel *So Big*, set at the turn of the century, captures a scene not much changed until World War II (except that wagons had given way to trucks): "They turned into the Haymarket. It was a tangle of horses, carts, men. The wagons were streaming in from the German truck farms that lay to the north of Chicago as well as from the Dutch farms that lay to the southwest, whence Selina came. Fruits and vegetables—tons of it—acres of it—piled in the wagons that blocked the historic square. An unarmed army bringing food to feed a great city. Through this little section, and South Water Street that lay to the east, passed all the verdant growing things that fed Chicago's millions. Something of this came to Selina as she maneuvred her way through the throng. She felt a little thrill of significance, of achievement."

People eat. They also throw things away, and the Haymarket in the hours after the truck farmers trundled home was a hodgepodge of trash. Businesses that serve such constant human needs (feeding a society, or picking up after it) have a certain simple attractiveness. Moving materials around, whether prime asparagus and strawberries, or vegetable crates and furnace ash, was good straightforward work. For a newly arrived immigrant in a big city, and one with no capital, removing other people's refuse was easy work to get into. Demand was self-evident to anyone with eyes in his head and a decent sense of smell. And a man could work for himself. Compared to the regimentation of employment in a factory or other large commercial concerns, to be his own boss appealed to independent-minded people like the Dutch. The chance for sons to work shoulder-to-shoulder with fathers appealed to people with strong family ties. The obvious, backbreaking nature of the work—shoveling, lifting, hauling, dumping—fit the culture of people who, without belaboring it, saw a connection between sweat and salvation. With the help of aching muscles and a hearty appetite, a man knew at the end of the day that he had gone the distance, had done his share. And if he were the sort who needed to feel that basic "little thrill of significance, of achievement," well, the garbage business could supply that too.

Eager as they were for a better life, immigrants might nevertheless hesitate, attempt to insulate themselves from their new culture even as they learned its tricks and advanced themselves according to its regime. The Dutch in Chicago certainly did, and in this the garbage business must have seemed God-sent. Hauling garbage was not highly favored among many people, but for those who didn't mind, it became something of an ethnic preserve in which they could become American and stay Dutch at the same time. They worked for no one else, they didn't work on Sunday, and they kept their business interests largely among themselves. Hauling garbage, moreover, required little communication, a plus for people faced by a strange and difficult language. Most important, perhaps, a growing city meant there was lots of trash to go around. The normal ups and downs of the business cycle did not affect them unduly. Work was steady, and if they stayed healthy and worked hard they could live well. Others might disdain garbage, but in that very distance the Dutch took comfort and found strength.

Harm Huizenga started with a single team and wagon. He was good at what he did, and his business grew. In time, his wagons and then his trucks were proudly emblazoned "Huizenga & *Son*, Private Scavengers." The "son" was his second, Tom, who when the family came from Holland in 1916 was fifteen and did not return to school. He worked downtown at the Boston Store, Marshall Field's, and Carson Pirie Scott, waiting for his father to let him into the family business. Harm told him that if he could sell three new accounts, he could go on the road full time. Shortly thereafter, he began buying into his father's business and stayed in garbage the rest of his life.

Late in the 1920s, Tom began a business of his own to cover

different routes and called it Ace Scavenger Service. In the 1930s, he went into partnership with other Dutchmen (Dick Evenhouse, Charlie Groot, Charlie Boersma, George DeBoer) and formed Chicago and Suburban (C&S) Disposal to consolidate routes in the western suburbs of Cicero and Berwyn, hiring his older brother Siert as bookkeeper. Younger brother Pete got to manage Tom's Ace routes. Then, during World War II, Pete set out on his own, buying Tom's Ace routes north of Madison Street and changing the name to Arrow Disposal Service. He too began with one truck but within a few years ran half a dozen.

In 1943, Tom expanded, buying Citizens Service Bureau with six trucks and three flushers from John T. Morris and Earl Huge for $25,000. In 1946, a year after Tom's death, his widow Jennie sold two Ace routes to brother-in-law Siert and Jake Bilthuis, who formed Metro Scavenger Service. In the early 1950s, an expanded partnership brought together Ace, Arrow, Metro, C&S, and C. Groot & Sons. Office and garage were centralized at 4730 W. Harrison Street. From there, the Dutchmen's trucks lumbered out to haul Chicago's trash.

The artifacts of those old businesses suggest something of their close ethnic solidarity. A list of C&S shareholders contains four Huizengas, four Evenhouses, a Boersma, a Bos, a Groot, a Grypstra, a Jaarda, a Tholen, a Teune. And the next generation carried on in the business. Siert's son Clarence followed his father as manager of C&S, then with his brother Harry, and finally, on his own, started Busy Bee Scavenger Service, Industrial Disposal Corporation in Grand Rapids, and Dispos-O-Waste in Kalamazoo. Frank Post, who married Siert's daughter Ruth, bought OK Scavenger Company in Chicago. Brother Harry formed a company called Disposal Systems. Tom's son Harry was part owner of Dump All and Nickles Sanitation in Florida. Tom's son-in-law Henry Evenhouse bought Merchants Disposal and Best Waste Systems in Texas. Son-in-law Tom Huiner built up Acorn Disposal in Geneva, Illinois. Pete's son-in-law Herman Kanis managed Wheeling Disposal. Son-in-law Dean Buntrock managed Arrow Disposal and Ace.

For these Dutch-Americans of Chicago's West Side, the garbage business made for good livings and, it seems, good lives: steady work, respectable incomes, provisions for a man's retirement, or (as was common with the Huizengas) for his widow. A fellow could work hard, do well, and still be home for dinner with the family. Pete Huizenga liked to finish up by four. "Comfortable" describes them. So do "inbred" and "parochial." They had worked their way solidly into America's middle class without special favor, fancy education, or exceptional intelligence. Bookkeepers, not accountants, kept their books; everything they borrowed from the bank they signed for themselves. They learned to be good citizens and neighbors. They lived in big bungalows and had few pretensions. They fit well into Chicago.

It takes nothing away from them to say that theirs was an ordinary achievement. Tens of thousands of other families did, and do, the same thing in other lines of work all over America. The Huizengas, the Evenhouses, the Vandermolens, the Mulders, and the other families that made their way in the garbage business, were proud just to be counted in that company.

Business or Industry?

From the time they went into the business (and indeed long before) until midtwentieth century, the Huizengas' particular line of work had some strikingly constant characteristics. It was labor-intensive. Men and not machines, literally, lifted most of the load. In a country rich with willing hands, therefore, entry was an easy thing. It was a service-based business. The trashman removed the discards, and the same trashman came back the next week to the same customer and did the same thing. At that time, the business's chief challenge was collection, not disposal. The business was also on the eve of enormous change.

Harm Huizenga started out in the horse-drawn era, when horses themselves—their manure and carcasses—constituted a substantial segment of America's municipal waste. In 1912, ten thousand horses dropped dead in the streets of Chicago alone. Harm is said to have told son Tom, with exasperation, "When I can't do it with a wagon anymore, then I'll quit!" That was in the 1920s, but with persistent urging from the younger generation, Huizenga & Son soon had a truck, a "Reliable" manufactured by Reliable Trucks, Inc. at 3927 S. Michigan Avenue in Chicago. It looked every inch the motorized wagon it was: box cab all at right angles, lantern-like headlamps, runningboard, spoked wheels with hard rubber rims. The "box" tilted back hydraulically (an innovation) but it still had to be filled by hand. A shovel was provided (and is today on WMI trucks) for what spilled. A somewhat later chain-drive "Mack" boasted a racier streamlined nose, but otherwise still had about it that World War I tank-like quality. On the sides was emblazoned: "Huizenga & Sons, Private Scavengers, 1348 S. Ashland Ave., phone Canal, 5930."

But trucks were expensive and at first poorly adapted to certain uses. They could not, for example, negotiate all the narrow alleys and sharp turns. In many cities, including Chicago, municipal waste services employed a combination of trucks and wagons until techniques improved. Side-tilt horse-drawn carts made their way through the alleys and, when full, were hitched in tandem and connected train-like to a tractor truck for the trip to the disposal site.

Residential trash collection in many American cities had fallen to the public sector: a "city service" like police and fire protection, in keeping with the "gas and water socialism" that came out of the Progressive era. In patronage-ridden cities like Chicago, it was an open question whether the most important service of the city sanitation department was in picking up the trash, or providing jobs to party faithful who ended up, in abundance, on the trucks.

For the "private scavengers" like the Huizengas, who built their businesses on commercial and industrial (and some residential) hauling, the motives differed. Theirs was a constant quest not to make jobs, but to reduce costs and increase profits: to stay competitive. Improved collection techniques helped them; the business itself made many of them instinctly inventive. Inventiveness cost, however, and technical innovation, in time, cost more than they could afford.

The hardware told the story. From wagons, the haulers moved to trucks. Gadgets and attachments abounded. In San Francisco, trucks featured a spiral staircase between the driver and the dump body, from the top of which the crewman dumped his can. The body then was raised to half-mast to distribute the load. Dustless "refuse-getters" carried trash forward on tracks to the front of the truck body where they would tilt into the bin. Side-loaders appeared in endless variation, some rectangular, some tubular with various mechanical handling devices. Rear-loaders with load-compacting blades and ejectors multiplied.

The "Dempster Dumpster"—the one word from the waste business that became a generic like Kleenex and Coke—was introduced in 1934. Though also limited, it foreshadowed things to come. With a large steel container fully enclosed with a curved steel top, entry doors, and dump release bottom, it was designed to be hoisted mechanically onto a truck for transport to the dump site. In the 1940s and 1950s, equipment manufacturers like Garwood, Leach, Heil, Packmore, E-Z Pack, and Lodal plied private haulers with ever newer models. Leach introduced the famous one-yard container in 1954. The VanderMolen family, another prominent Dutch hauler in Chicago, developed a container that could be dumped into the hopper by the hydraulic action of the forward-moving compaction blade. The Leach company first marketed this famous one-yard container in 1954. Front-loaders, capable of use only with containers, also made their appearance. Stationary compactors, roll-off trucks, and bulk transfer trailers all changed the industry vocabulary.

Yet "industry," in the sense of business that employs large personnel and requires substantial capital, did not truly describe the garbage business in the era when the Huizengas and their Dutch brethren held sway in Chicago. Partly, this was a matter of self-perception. The very potency of the bonds—family, religious, and ethnic—that helped make them successful made it difficult for them to conceive and embrace, on their own, broader forms of association. They had experienced modest growth, and had made innovations, as needed. But, as a body, they had done these things without prescience, "as they went." Horizons were close; ambitions modest; goals visibly attainable. The garbage business—nondiscretionary, not highly cyclical, for many years requiring sweat not capital—suited such temperaments.

It was wonderful proof of the immigrants' vision of America as a place where a man with simple skills could prosper mightily, of how successful unsophisticated folk could be. None of them was an "expert": not in finance, management, technology, and certainly not in the "environment," a word still unknown in the popular tongue.

How these men viewed themselves shaped their day-to-day behavior and, quite as powerfully, their reaction to change. As change came, businesses that had been a family blessing could become, strangely, a burden. What had been a nice little family business wasn't necessarily a nice big family business even if it made more money. The capacities required for growth could change the nature of the business itself, not just its scale. A threshold was reached in the garbage business in the 1950s, beyond which arose the waste industry to take its place. The stage was thus set for the appearance of another sort of character, with another breed of talent, indeed, with many more kinds of talent. Dean Buntrock was chief among them.

3

Widows and Working Men

THE OLD Chicago mosaic of proud ethnics and old neighbor-hoods, all different yet all ambitiously American, was the way America used to be, and not just in the polyglot big cities. Dean Buntrock of Columbia, South Dakota, recognized it when he arrived in Chicago in the midfifties. He found two things at once. The first was yet another version of the world he already knew, only multiplied many fold: "a whole lot of Columbias all piled up next to one another" was how the sprawling flat city of endless neighborhoods impressed him. The second thing he discovered in Mayor Daley's "great city of Chicago" was a scale and amplitude of human activity that bowled a man over. Everybody, he observed, seemed busy; there were lots of jobs and lots of money moving about.

The context in which he made these observations was the Huizenga family and the Huizenga family business. Pete Huizenga knew a good thing when he saw one, whether a new route for hauling trash, or a prospective son-in-law. When his oldest daughter, B.J., brought Dean home from St. Olaf to Berwyn, Pete took a fast liking to the young Dakotan and was quick to show him around.

Pete was not well and knew it; he had a heart condition and had slowed down considerably. His oldest son, Peter, was still in high school, and nobody else seemed ready to take over. Understanding that the garbage business might not be the first choice of work to strike a young college-educated man's fancy, Pete described to the twenty-four-year-old Buntrock the dreams that he himself lacked the drive and ability to realize. Pete knew the opportunities were there however; he sensed the potential for growth.

Whatever Buntrock knew about business he had learned growing up in his father's store in their small agricultural town where one year the customers might have money in their pockets from a bumper crop, and the next none at all. By comparison, the year-in, year-out solidity of the garbage trade was striking. If the business did not literally run itself, at least as the Dutchmen had developed it, it didn't require a lot of fancy management in order to make money. On the other hand, it also seemed evident that if a man wanted to put in the effort, much more might be gotten out of it. Buntrock also was able to meet the people in the business, most with Dutch names, constituting a nice group of upstanding, prosperous fellows. These were Pete's competitors and his friends. Chicago itself was building and growing, and there was not the slightest shortage of trash.

Meat and Potatoes

There is a story, perhaps apocryphal, about the Swedes and Danes and the Dutch in the Chicago refuse business. The Danes, on the North Side and the South Side, concentrated on hauling ashes. They had little interest in garbage, which was nasty stuff better left to the Dutch. But the Danes did sometimes hire Dutch helpers, who they knew to be stout fellows and hard workers. Shoveling ashes out of sub-basements required a good deal of stoutness. To see they got their money's worth, the Danes fed the Hollanders high-energy food: sandwiches of thickly sliced bread, thickly spread with lard: "Feed 'em that lard, and watch those Dutchmen go." What today seems horrific, fifty years ago was sound enough nutrition, especially for men who worked outdoors in a cold climate and did lots of heavy lifting. Without doubt, it helped the Dutchmen get through their strenuous days. And when they went home at night, likely as not they piled plates high with sausages, potatoes, more bread and butter. It may also, as we now know, have helped shorten their lives.

No Huizengas ever worked for Danish ashmen, but their diet probably wasn't a lot different: heavy food for heavy work. All three of Harm's sons by his first wife Altje died young: Siert at fifty-five, Tom at forty-four, Pete at forty-eight. All died of heart disease. Whether it was too many pork chops and Dutch "ollie-ballen" or just bad genetic luck, the consequences for the businesses they had built were the same. By the mid-1950s, partnerships were saddled with widows, partnerships that were already a tangle of family connections.

It was fortunate that Pete Huizenga talked to Buntrock when he did. For not much more than a year after Dean and B.J.'s wedding in June 1955, Pete was dead of a heart attack. During that year, the young couple lived in Colorado, far from the family trash business. But Pete kept closely in touch. A generous and affectionate man, he followed Dean's early success selling insurance, cheered on B.J. in her teaching job and new domestic responsibilities, and welcomed them home at Christmas.

Shortly after Pete's death on Labor Day 1956, his widow Betty and his children gathered to close up the family cottage in Michigan. Dean and B.J. (who had come east for a few days) and B.J.'s brother Peter were there. Peter was only a freshman at college, but it was Peter whom Dean took aside to ask a grown man's question. Dean had a decision to make. For close on the heels of Pete's death, Betty and Larry Groot (his partner in Ace Scavenger) had approached Dean about coming back to Chicago to manage the business. Dean judged it was the right thing for him to do, but before he said yes, he wanted to discuss it with Peter.

Peter already admired his new brother-in-law, but this—asking his advice—left him flabbergasted because it was no mere courtesy. It was an early example of Buntrock's inclination to weigh his own ambition in light of the consequences it could have on those around him. In this case, young Peter Huizenga heartily acclaimed the idea that Dean take charge. Had Peter disapproved, Dean Buntrock, without much fuss, might well have gone back to selling insurance. He was the shy one, and he was after all (marriage or not) the outsider.

As it was, Dean took his "yes" back to Betty Huizenga and Larry Groot and signed onto (but not into) the family business. He started his new line of work in October 1956, strictly as an employee without a stake. And he took home a lot less money than he had made the previous year in the insurance business.

Old-Fashioned Fellas

The comfort of the Huizenga and the other ethnics' garbage businesses was in proportion to its creakiness. It is not unfair to the operators who had brought it to that point to say that they were not likely to have taken it a great deal further. It was not that the business in Chicago lacked talent—men who knew how to collect trash, get rid of it, and keep their customers happy. But it did lack leadership—not surprisingly, given its history. Organized largely as family partnerships, Chicago's private refuse haulers had built businesses suited to an earlier era of immigrant solidarity, and when "out of sight, out of mind" still captured the essence of society's attitude toward its own wastes. They were not businesses best structured for change. They were not individuals temperamentally attuned to the future.

And the future that was soon upon them beheld the rise of a world that these old-fashioned businesses could not have hoped to deal with. Theirs was a workingman's world where physical labor lifted heavy loads, and before they knew it capital was king. Theirs was a familiar local world with plenty of business for everybody, and before they knew it the need to compete was compelling. Theirs was a business conducted for years in almost total obscurity, and before they knew it this same business was subject to stringent federal regulation and scrutiny by the general public.

Just ask any manager of garbagemen, or better yet ask a garbageman himself. As he gets tired toward the end of a day of heavy hauling, he is more prone to making mistakes, and is easier prey to accidents. His thoughts run to the hot shower and supper ahead, and less to the job still in front of him. His efficiency declines. The garbage business as a whole in the 1950s had some of the same end-of-the-day quality. The operators could look with pride on a job well done, and be happy in the confidence that the same job would be there tomorrow, the next day, the next year. They could look forward to rewards well earned: the nice car in the driveway, perhaps a cottage at the lake, vacations to places warmer than Chicago. They could retire more than comfortably, provide for their widows, pass something on to their children. Trash had treated them well, and they were not unmindful. In the circumstances, resting on their laurels was not an unnatural inclination.

But it did forestall cultivation of that very different human drive to grapple with tomorrow ahead of time. This was especially unfortunate because "tomorrow," as it was taking shape, looked to be more radically different from "today" than the garbage business had ever imagined.

If the old haulers largely failed to become the moving agents of change, they were far from oblivious to it. They could perceive things happening and to a degree react to them. To the limited degree that they thought of themselves as an "industry," it was as part of the sanitation industry. Since the middle of the nineteenth century at least, sanitation and improved public health had been seen as two sides of the same coin, first by reform-minded elites and then by the broader public: eliminate the pigs, privies, rats, and refuse and wipe away the scourge of all manner of pestilence. Actually doing the job, and not just talking about it, was nasty but necessary work. If a man needed the added self-esteem, it even had the nobility of being not-so-nice work that needed doing but that nobody else wanted to do.

By the 1950s, the business was also getting complicated— largely because of general social changes and resulting pressures in the local marketplace, not yet because of federal government regulation: the rage to regulate still awaited the anxieties of environmentalism. A burgeoning population and the advancing technology of hauling, however, were enough to push private refuse haulers into searching for greater operating efficiencies.

More people, and especially more people in the suburbs, created the need to find cheaper ways to cover longer collection routes, and as machines began to do more of the actual work, the old labor-intensive business of trash-hauling began to be transformed into a capital-intensive one. Community ordinances prohibited open trucks, and the advent of packer vans doubled the weight-to-volume ratios of older equipment. A key measure of the efficiency of new equipment was that it required fewer men; four-man crews gave way to three, and two, and eventually to trucks that could be run by the driver alone. For commercial work, closed containers designed to be picked up by trucks equipped with cab-operated hydraulic lifts began to supplant old-fashioned drums and barrels.

Distance affected disposal too. As suburbs filled in, old close-in disposal sites with finite capacity filled up and shut down. And as the public grew more fastidious, finding sites for new disposal areas not impossibly far away posed an alarming challenge. New sites almost inevitably meant longer hauls to get rid of trash. The longer hauls made contractors look for ways to reduce expensive to-ing and fro-ing, resulting in costlier trucks packing bigger payloads.

Public health anxieties about disease-spreading vermin and bad smells marked the beginning of the end of "the dump" itself. As toleration diminished for open, frequently burning heaps of garbage, a change in technology and vocabulary ensued. Sanitary landfills, in which the garbage got a blanket of protective soil every night, were first adopted widely as an emergency measure around crowded army camps during World War II. They were destined to become very fancy pieces of civil engineering. About all they shared with their dump predecessors was that both required real estate.

The new technique greatly improved aesthetic and sanitary conditions in countless cities and towns, but it also increased disposal costs for the haulers and raised the general cost of doing business. Some haulers consequently experimented with other means of disposal. Incinerators, though hardly new, had high capital costs, which restricted their operation to public, usually municipal entities. In the 1950s, two private Chicago groups broke that tradition to open their own commercial facilities for reducing trash to ash, and to salvage metals and steam. A firm near Pittsburgh, Organic Corporation of America, even tried composting.

E Pluribus, Pluribus

But the context in which all this was happening was highly fragmented. Probably some ten thousand private entities engaged in the refuse business in America in the 1950s. Their sophistication varied with their numbers, from the most casual here-today-gone-tomorrow "fly-dumpers" to responsible family concerns like the Huizengas, Groots, and Vandermolens with reputations built over several generations. These were the sort of people who talked to each other over the back fence, in meetings of their local associations, and in a young trade press (*Refuse Removal Journal*, their first journal, began publication in 1958) about the daily problems and future prospects of their business, and the urgency of changes overtaking it. It was hard not to know that things were going on.

Sharing information about meeting local challenges, and taking comfort in the knowledge that the next fellow had some of the same problems you did, was one thing. Tackling the questions that lay at the root of many of those challenges was something else. The solutions offered by the garbage "industry," as then constituted, to meet the challenges of change fell into two types. The first was simply technical: all the snappy new hardware pouring forth from the manufacturers—Moto-Loaders, Roto-Hoppers, Load Luggers, Beaver Brush Chippers—designed to help a man do an old job even better. Tom Huizenga had convinced his father Harm to trade in the horse-and-wagon for a Mack truck and, well, there would always be a better model truck.

The second sort of response was simpler yet: bluster. The garbagemen were not unique in this, and the attribution is not unkind. For these companies were blessed with the unflagging self-confidence, the prideful independence common to the best small businesses everywhere. To read today what they wrote about each other then, is to be almost convinced that there was no difficulty, no new condition, no awkward fact, that the owner-(often as not, family-) operated refuse contractor could not overcome when he put his mind and his back to it.

Almost. There was just one awkward problem. They were small, in an industry that was rapidly becoming enormous.

Men on the Truck

If it seemed "small" to Dean Buntrock when he decided to try the garbage business in 1956, it was, on the surface at least, a good enough initial fit. He was used to small things: towns, businesses, schools, outfits that operated close to their roots among folk of their own kind. His decision may not even have been, at that moment, such a bold move. Compared with selling insurance, running garbage trucks was not a terribly difficult business. As Pete Huizenga well knew, they almost ran themselves, if you let them. But that was where Buntrock was different. He wouldn't let them "run themselves." What was small did not necessarily stay small, and garbage, he quickly determined, almost certainly would not.

What followed his arrival at Ace and Arrow was years of work. Though he was a German-Norse Lutheran and not a Dutch Calvinist, work suited his temperament and the habits learned in youth. Sooner than expected, moreover, he was saddled with a great amount of responsibility. Larry Groot, who with Pete's widow Betty, had asked him to come to Chicago and manage the business and was his great admirer, also died four months later of a heart attack, still in his forties. With Pete and Larry gone, and the other partners and widows unprepared for leadership, the task fell to Buntrock.

The Ace Partnership then operated some fifteen routes, each with revenues of about $4,000 per month. It also had a large interest in Incinerator, Inc. Arrow disposal, Pete Huizenga's company exclusively, operated two trucks. Buntrock, just an employee, was paid less than some of the drivers ($200 a week). The money was tough for the young couple to live on, and it gave him every reason to learn fast. While he knew it was a business with nicely sustainable cash flow, he soon discovered that after the partners drew their share, not a lot was left over. He needed to make the business grow.

After Clarence Huizenga moved to Michigan, Buntrock was more or less on his own. He caught on quickly, with the other employees and with his competitors. Where leadership was weak, people soon learned to look to Buntrock for direction. This was remarkable, for he was an ethnic outsider among notoriously clannish people fond of expressions like: "If you're not Dutch, you're not much." It may also have been lucky timing, given the state of the business at that moment.

By the 1950s, the old power of ethnic allegiance was waning;

the business the Dutchmen had husbanded and profited from so nicely had reached a plateau. When sons had followed fathers, they had shared attitudes grown from a common heritage. The garbage business was therefore probably more than ready for a healthy kick from someone who had not grown up inside of it, someone who did not have, as the Dutchmen liked to say, "garbage in his blood." The Dutch had habitually hired other Dutch. The first people Buntrock hired at Ace were a Greek bookkeeper (George Tertoipis), and two salesmen, one an Italian and the other a Jew (Vito Stella and Peter Abels).

But to achieve his ambitions, Buntrock understood that he first had to master the basic business as it was, and that meant with the men on the trucks. The work they did—driving the routes, lifting the drums, stomping the trash—required some fortitude. And it left Buntrock with renewed respect for the fundamentals, which he never forgot. Some of these men, whom Buntrock led and who in their turn taught him in those early years, continued to work the same way for many years more and would never think of working for anyone else.

Leroy Elmore, a black man, came to work at Ace Scavenger in 1952, when Pete Huizenga was still alive, Conrad Douma was managing, and Herman Bosman, yet another Dutchman, was foreman. Elmore, right out of high school, was looking for a job, when Ace driver Cleo Freeman brought him into the garage at 4730 West Harrison. Elmore was hefty—one of the requirements for a good helper on the trucks—and they put him to work the very next day. Within three or four years, he had worked his way up to driver. "You're the youngest guy I've ever seen who would actually show up for work every day," said Conrad Douma, the manager who promoted him. "Well," Elmore replied frankly, "I don't have anything, and the only way I know to get something is work."

John Bakker, a white man, came to Ace in 1958. His father had also hauled garbage, but by the time the young man was ready for work, the old man was selling out. His cousin, Clarence Dagma who already worked at Ace, told Bakker to "give Dean a call." He came in on a Saturday and on Monday was out on the truck with Elmore. "The first day, I'll never forget it. All they said was, 'You follow us.' Ashes, and ashes, and ashes; I think we hauled eight or nine loads of ashes that day."

Julius Newsom, a black man, came to Ace in 1966 after losing his job with a tire company. Bosman, ever with his ear to the ground for good men, heard about it and asked him to come and work for Ace. Newsom started out fixing flat tires in the shop. After a year, he was on a truck picking up ashes with the rest.

Rich Drolenga, a white man, came to Ace in 1957. He did load work, which was mostly called in and could be anything from street light poles at a commercial light company, to cleaning up after a tuckpointer.

Infusing all their experiences was a "you name it, and we do it" air. There was no such thing as " 'We can't' or 'You can't.' If you had to do a little at a time, you did a little at a time, but you got the job done." Their days began (it was before the strict antinoise ordinances) about midnight on the downtown routes, where business had to be finished before the morning rush hour. They punched in, stowed their gear upstairs in the locker room, checked the trucks, and were on their way. The Gold Coast route ran from Chicago Avenue south to the river, from Halsted west to Michigan Avenue. On any given day they might make sixty or seventy stops. On lucky days, they found the trash set out for them in the alleys. Usually, though, they hauled it up themselves from basements and sub-basements in fifty-five-gallon "carry-cans." Chicago has some very deep basements.

Meals were eaten on the route—not just "en route," but courtesy of happy customers whose trash these big men hauled away. The Ace truck hit the Como Inn on Milwaukee Avenue around 7:30 A.M. "They opened the door, and anything you wanted to eat, you ate. After you ate, you cleared up everything they had, and you were off and running." By lunchtime they might find themselves at the Kungsholm on Ontario or the Cafe Bohemia kitty-corner from Union Station on Clinton: solid heavy duty eateries where large lunches awaited men who paid with the coin of hard work and reliable service. At the Cafe Bohemia their timing was crucial, for an expletive-laden dressing-down awaited any garbageman who disturbed the chef while he was removing the restaurant's famous roast ducks from the oven (the trash, of course, was in the basement, reached only through the kitchen).

If a man was good, the customers took care of him. The protocol was less rigid in those days. A man might pick up some sewer grease and make a dollar or two extra. Such then was the custom of the trade. Buntrock, who appreciated the little traditions and understood their value, was known to say with good humor that "you're not a garbageman if you can't hustle your own breakfast."

They earned every bit of what they made and ate, and then some. Hart, Schaffner and Marks, at 719 Quincy just off the expressway, was famous for its men's suits. For the men of Ace Scavenger, it was famous for its soot and cinders. They remember it with special awe—as does Buntrock. The cinders, as usual, were in the cellar, and though a conveyor belt lifted them to street level and the waiting truck, getting them on the conveyor meant hours of work with big Number Eight coal shovels. If the pile completely filled the cellar (as it frequently did), every shovelful took the shoveler farther and farther back from his target; and as a man tired, the work got tougher. Besides, it felt like the hottest place in Chicago: "It must have been 110 degrees down there, and if you went in weighing 200 pounds, you didn't weigh 190 when you came out."

Then there were the times when Chicago felt like the coldest place on earth: "Those trucks! You know, today we're pretty comfortable, but then, well, the heaters weren't hardly worth a damn. We built fires right there in the cabs to keep warm—a shovelful of hot coals lasted a long time."

At 1608 Ashland Avenue (the old American Theater Building at Ashland and Madison), the basement was deep but with no conveyor to help with the lift. The Ace men first had to build an intermediate platform from wood, heave the ashes onto it, take careful aim at the manhole opening to the street, and then .heft them one last time from the sidewalk into the truck.

In other basements, the ceilings were so low that the men had to crawl in on hands and knees with the cans on their backs. The Fair Store on State Street (later, Montgomery Ward) was equipped with an elevator from the alley off Dearborn that would carry the Ace men, truck and all, from floor to floor. The trash itself usually waited in the basement: cardboard and packaging materials, and drums of fly ash (incinerators were still widely used by individual businesses). The men's eagerness to maximize each load, and the tendency to overdo, went hand in hand. When the elevator balked, they had to take something off and later lift it all over again. It took strong backs, and sometimes strong stomachs too. At an old medical school on the near West Side, the men removed ashes that sometimes contained incompletely incinerated human remains, the final end of teaching cadavers.

They also hauled from the Stewart-Warner Manufacturing Company on Diversy, the Lawson YWCA on Chicago Avenue, the Pick-Congress Hotel on Michigan, the main Post Office on Canal, the Chicago Sun-Times on Wabash, and the Monadnock Building on Dearborn, which had a hand-crank chain-dip conveyor from the basement to the sidewalk as venerable as the building itself.

Whatever it was they lifted in those day, they lifted largely by hand. New equipment was expensive and came slowly even to the best companies. Carry cans, not containers, symbolized the era. Powerfully built men still climbed ladders with cans on their backs, or rode tailgates and side-loading platforms to dump their loads into the hopper of a truck. To pack more into each load (the garbageman's perennial challenge), they smashed glass bottles, broke down boxes and crates (to stack on the side of the truck), and discarded as much wood and cardboard as they could. They compacted what they carried with their boots, without mechanical assist. "Walking it in" was the name they gave to the ritual of filling the load evenly and tightly. A fellow's fitness was measured by two things: how much he could carry, and how hard he could stomp.

Driving a garbage truck, however, required mental dexterity as well. The routine encouraged a certain disciplined independence in a man who, after all, had to maneuver an expensive piece of company equipment in crowded alleys and busy streets. Whether he met customers face-to-face or never saw them at all, the driver was the "front-man" of the business. On the reliability of his service everything else depended. Getting the job done, in an old-fashioned city like Chicago in those days, required both diligence and street-smarts. Everyone had his hand out in those days—that's the way the world was—and every driver knew it was wise to have some money in his pocket. "Stuff was always flying off those trucks, and they [the police] were always hauling us over, looking for a couple of bucks."

Buntrock was everywhere, looking after business and looking after men. When he rode the trucks it was with an eye for efficiency. He wanted to see how distance might be shortened. He noted how comfortable a man seemed with the job. He observed what kind of waste and how much of it different stops produced. Material like corrugated cardboard was something to watch out for because it took up a lot of room.

As much as their hard work, he valued his men's loyalty. He bought it with fair wages (set by the union) and fatherly attention to their lives. "Dean always took care of us; you always knew that if you had a problem you could go right to Dean and he'd tell you the best thing to do." He helped out more than once with financial and family problems, and encouraged them to save and invest some of what they earned. In slow times, he spread the work around to keep from laying people off. "You've got some people down South, don't you, Leroy? Why don't you take some vacation and this [the 1958 recession] will all blow over." It usually did, and when the men came back the work was there at Ace.

To define a good man to work for, ask the men who did the

work: "He understood what we did and always tried to make it easier and better. He always made clear what he expected, so we always knew where we stood. He was fair and didn't care about where you came from, just how hard you worked for Ace. He would listen."

Buntrock was the man who made decisions. If he could give a man more responsibility, he would. And he knew their tastes—small things like the barrel full of cold beer waiting back at West Harrison Street late on a hot summer afternoon.

Learning from the Locals

Personalizing a business is a matter of endless detail. Making each employee, from the bottom up, feel like he "works for the boss" requires time and a special gift for human relations.

When Buntrock came to Ace in 1956, he inherited some good men and added others as the business and his confidence grew. The experience stood him in good stead later on when he found himself managing many different sorts of men who, like those first stout drivers, worked for money, but also "to please Dean."

For an observant newcomer, eager to get involved, there was an education in watching how these men worked together and in learning what moved them—and how far. What moved them most was the desire to stay in business, which, simple as it sounds, was not quite so simple for them as it had been in their father and grandfather's day. Where to dump the trucks was a rising anxiety among Chicago's private haulers even back in the 1950s. Their response shows how economic pressures alone can drive business-men to progressive solutions.

While environmentalism was years away from decreeing every dump undesirable, the simple geography of growth in the post-war years was putting a premium on reliable waste disposal sites. Two things that kept changing made the haulers' life more diffi-cult, and planning nearly impossible: dump sites kept shifting, usually moving farther away, and the price of disposal kept escalating arbitrarily. The haulers also wanted to do something better with the waste. The challenge was enough to move forty-five Chicago companies to band together and develop the nation's first commercial waste-to-energy incinerator.

Back in 1953, Pete Huizenga was a leader of the movement to take action, and by the time Incinerator, Inc. burned its first load of garbage in 1958 two years after Pete's death, the Ace Partnership held the biggest interest of all. Part of Buntrock's job was to look after it. At first, incineration had not seemed to hold the answer because of its well-known high capital costs, and in their early explorations the Chicago haulers concentrated on alternative sites for landfill or open dumping, even investigating the feasibility of commercial composting. When all failed, they looked carefully at exactly what a privately built and operated incinerator would cost, and a group traveled the country to see what the big operations were like. All of them of any size were municipally run, and the Chicagoans understood that to build one privately carried all the uncertainties of something never before done.

But they persisted, and a plan was prepared under the auspices of their local trade association to present to members, who would also be the investors. Each of the forty-five companies committed to shares in proportion to their prospective use of the completed plant, which varied greatly. Among themselves, they raised enough to begin life as a corporate entity, but for the balance of the $1.7 million construction cost they had to knock on doors outside their own business.

This was a new experience and for a time a disheartening one. No Chicago bank or other lender would come close: "Where does a garbageman get the nerve to ask for that kind of money?" So successful in their own eyes, it must have been chastening to discover in what low financial esteem others held them. After much rattling of the cup, financing was finally secured through two Massachusetts insurance companies, and under the leadership of Conrad Douma (who was a partner in Ace), construction of the massive plant began in the village of Stickney. With a capacity of five hundred tons per day, it was the largest commercial waste incinerator in the world, and it burned trash beautifully.

But it was both ahead of and behind its time. For even as it was being constructed, a major new landfill was opened at 31st Street and the Tri-State Expressway in Oak Brook. What seemed a long way out then turned out not to be; the site lasted for twenty years and it made the economics of incineration a tough battle from the start. Burning waste is more complicated than burying it, but the incinerator's operators spared no effort to make it work, squeezing revenue from every byproduct they could possibly find a market for. Steam went just across the street to Koppers Coke. Tin can residue went to copper smelters in Montana. Ash was reprocessed into a patented product called ChemPack. They worked for years trying to make it successful—and they failed. Air pollution regulations made the technology obsolete, and as the market for the byproducts slipped away, they decided to close down.

Failed or not, it gave Buntrock an early insight into the problems and the promise of incineration, and the potentially enormous value that inhered in disposal resources, whether they were holes in the ground or fancy furnaces. Those insights were soon to become useful.

The episode also revealed something more immediate about the character of the companies that had joined hands to attempt it. By the standards of forty years ago, they had accomplished something quite remarkable. Incinerator, Inc. needed to reach beyond the neighborhood as never before. It entailed serious risk. And it called for leadership and organization and a great deal of perseverance.

But it was also an ad hoc, one-time shot, and as such it tested the limits of association among staunchly independent, owner-operated companies. That they had come together for this one effort signaled no change in their fundamental, go-it-alone, nature. As events overtook them, they were neither equipped nor inclined to carry on for the long haul. When the incinerator closed down, that, more or less, was that. The group that had built it built nothing else. Other challenges that change was thrusting their way triggered no comparably bold response.

Learning Farther Afield

Association of another ilk—one that did not involve being in business together or encroach on old identities—came easier. Companies like the Huizengas' commonly were organized into local trade associations. In Chicago, when Dean Buntrock arrived, the group was the Chicago and Suburban Ash and Scavenger Association (later the Chicago and Suburban Refuse Disposal Association). The hauler members used it for several purposes, among them, as a voice for their collective interests when dealing with city and suburban governments. Such organizations also served modest educational functions, as members convened and exchanged information about new lines of equipment and commiserated about labor problems, dumping regulations, and other matters of daily business life. They also enjoyed one another's company. A small group of more progressive contractors and equipment manufacturers gathered to form the Detachable Container Association, a symptom of the growth of containerization in the waste business.

The industry was obviously ripe for a national association. As the population grew with the baby boom of the 1950s, the quantity of America's wastes grew with it. And as volume rose, so too the opportunities in the business and the difficulties of conducting it. Such developments were easy enough to discern. While few haulers wished to diminish the influence of their local groups, many acknowledged the advantage that a larger organization could have when they needed to make a point with municipal authorities or state legislatures. As equipment grew more sophisticated technically, and therefore more expensive, they sought to establish minimum standards as a sign of their own reliability and as a tool to discourage cut-rate competitors whose equipment did not bear the association's seal of approval.

Disposal problems pressed the issue further. Every contractor felt the need for more, and more dependable, disposal locations (the anxiety that had given birth to Incinerator, Inc.). But trying to educate public authorities about the differences between modern sanitary landfills and old-fashioned open dumps, and about the necessity of keeping hauling distances within reason, caused constant frustration. Only a national organization, it seemed, could mount the kind of educational campaign needed to get these messages across. It might also serve as a clearing house for information on all phases of the refuse business—available to members, but also to government officials, the general public, and the press. Framing everything was the haulers' staunch conviction that the role of the private sector in the waste business should expand, that the country's growing needs for waste disposal services could be met most efficiently and most economically by the forces of private enterprise.

All of these evidenced a broadening of the world in which the refuse collection business was operating. Some operators were more comfortable with the prospect than others. Dean Buntrock was among the most comfortable of all. He took the lead in the movement to form a national association, which finally came about in 1962.

At the outset, the National Council of Refuse Disposal Trade Associations (NCRDTA) included three already existing groups: the Chicago Ash and Scavenger Association, the Coordinating Council of Waste Collection and Disposal Associations of California, and the Detachable Container Association. Half of the first board of directors hailed from Chicago. Two, Henry Hoekstra (of the Hyde Park Scavenger Company) and Harold Vandermolen (whose family company had built Chicago's other incinerator), were Dutch; the third was Buntrock. Buntrock, Vandermolen, and Marshall Rabins (from California) each put up $5,000 to hire a lawyer to incorporate the group, which elected Buntrock its first

and founding president. The Chicago association contributed office space at its headquarters at 330 South Wells Street, along with
the administrative time of Harold Jensen, its president (and a
Dane).

Some of the subjects of NCRDTA's early deliberations sound
familiar today, others seem remote. At their very first meeting,
they focused on the position of the refuse industry under the Fair
Labor Standards Act of 1938 (the Wages and Hours Law). After
hiring special counsel, they began a campaign for exemption, on
the grounds that the refuse business was not in control of its own
economies, that it was subject to ordinances and laws stipulating
the time and method of operations, that the service was vital to the
public health and welfare, and that its sales were intrastate and its
activities thus not subject to regulation by Congress. (Exemption
was never achieved.)

And they did much else besides. They laid plans for a member-
ship drive to recruit every local association in the country. They
looked to the creation of a library of ordinances and statutes
regulating disposal activities, and the codification of minimum
standards. They sought to begin an analysis of different types and
methods of disposal. They moved to establish relations with the
Business and Defense Services Administration of the Commerce
Department, the Interagency Health Advisory Board of the Office of Defense Mobilization, and other government agencies with
an interest in their work. They considered the broad subject of
public relations (something few local haulers on their own had
ever thought much about, except to provide superior service to
their customers and let reputation take care of itself). And they
anticipated their need for publications, for educational meetings,
and for trade shows.

Their concerns are significant: labor law, public health, trade
practice, public image. Although no whisper was yet bruited
about "the environment," the garbagemen unquestionably sensed
their increasing engagement in worlds beyond the can, the truck,
the dump. Elements of society other than their immediate cus-

tomers were interested in what they did and how they did it. Responding to that interest would henceforth occupy much time and attention. As the 1960s moved ahead, much of that time and attention focused on activities in Washington, D.C.

Buntrock and other leaders were soon testifying at hearings on Capitol Hill on behalf of the NCRDTA—from passage of the first National Solid Wastes Disposal Act in 1965 and the U.S. Tax Court Ruling that same year approving tax write-offs for spent landfills followed the endless train of legislation and regulation that continues to this day. A voice in shaping it became vital to the private waste industry, and through their newly formed national association, they sought out permanent professional representation in the nation's capital. The job went to a small public relations and association management firm, Larry Hogan Associates.

The original inquiry to the associates came in the summer of 1966 in a letter from "Dean Buntrock of Ace Scavenger Service of Cicero, Illinois." When the two young Washington partners learned that there was now even a national association for garbagemen, they laughed. Neither Larry Hogan nor Harold Gershowitz leaped at the new account. But since Buntrock was offering to pay expenses to Chicago for an interview, they drew straws. Gershowitz got the short one and with it the honor of meeting the Windy City garbagemen.

They surprised him. Some seemed reasonably sophisticated; some did not. But just about all of them struck Gershowitz as men practiced in business, who knew their way around at least their part of it. Buntrock and his colleagues liked what they saw too, though it took them a couple of months to say so.

In October 1966, Hogan and Gershowitz (chiefly Gershowitz, who functioned as NCRDTA executive secretary) went to work on the account. It started as their smallest, but quickly became their largest. The name soon changed to the National Solid Wastes Management Association, and when Hogan decided to run for Congress, Gershowitz was invited to become executive director of a full-time Washington office. He orchestrated the first industry trade show in Chicago in the summer of 1968 amid 100-degree heat and a telephone workers strike. And he shepherded the organization through its early years, when the industry it represented began to grapple with escalating capital and operating costs and an increasingly rugged regulatory climate. He did so with Buntrock always close at hand.

Gershowitz had grown up the son of a grocer in Washington, D.C., in the 1940s and 1950s, a hard-working atmosphere that taught many of the same lessons about life that Buntrock had learned in a small South Dakota town a few years earlier. He was also, like Buntrock, an outsider to the trash business. The difference between him, and the Dutchmen and their ilk, is instructive. It is the difference between interior and exterior perspectives.

The Dutchmen knew their own neighborhoods and, as the saying went, "had garbage in their blood." Gershowitz was a studious man whose neighborhood was the nation's capital and who dealt in a world of words. Back when the business pretty much drove itself, the old ethnics' perspective had been enough to assure success. But as time passed and regulations increasingly drove the business from the outside, Gershowitz's perspective grew in value. Henceforth, success depended on preserving one perspective while enhancing the other. Articulating the business to the outside depended on seeing it from the outside. Buntrock, not himself a voluble man, recognized articulateness in others. Perhaps not surprisingly, the two men took to each other, and when Buntrock moved on to larger things he saw to it that Gershowitz came along.

4

Business Beyond Chicago

MAJOR SHIFTS in the way cultures behave, in the way people within them order their lives and conduct their business, have long intrigued historians and futurists alike. Between the way people in the developed Western countries thought about the issue of waste thirty years ago, and the way they think about it today, yawns a gap so wide that only a major shift could account for it.

To have been successful in the waste business during that time means to have engaged in two distinct, though related, types of activity. It means to have been acted upon—"swept up" is not too strong a phrase—by society's shifting sensibilities and marketplace forces. It also means to have exerted oneself upon those forces, with the aim of controlling their consequences. This dynamic of challenge and response, of reacting to change and in the process actively shaping it, is observable in many realms of experience during such major shifts.

It could certainly be seen in the waste business from the 1960s onward, which happened to be when Dean Buntrock was in it. The unfolding of his story in the business, and the story of the businesses he built, illustrate the operation of this dynamic. Several events in those early years afford pertinent hints.

Leaving the Old Neighborhood

Buntrock was a great one for talking to people from other parts of the country. He liked to attend trade association meetings actually in order to work, to listen and learn things. What he learned from bright operators elsewhere, coupled with his own needs and ideas, led him outward, beyond the comfortable world that the Dutchmen had made for themselves. His challenges were different. After Larry Groot died, he found himself in charge of a business saddled with the support of a group of widows and passive partners. He himself was not earning much money, and he had been able to buy into the business only modestly. When all was said and done, not much remained to invest in growth. Yet growth was where the future had to lie. The provincialism of the business in Chicago was a discouragement, but it had a positive consequence. It pushed Buntrock to reach out beyond the neighborhood.

Beyond did not have to be far, just different. Milwaukee, thought Buntrock, would be fine. It was his first move outward, and it was all his own. Had it required actually buying a business there, it never would have happened because Ace had little money for such things. So Buntrock characteristically found another way.

Harold Vandermolen, a friendly Chicago competitor (who happened to have grown up across the street from the Pete Huizengas in Berwyn), had several Milwaukee routes that were giving him trouble. The two men talked. Buntrock borrowed $250,000 to buy some city routes in Chicago from Herman Mulder and traded them for Vandermolen's Milwaukee operation plus a small suburban Chicago hauler, Wheeling Disposal, on behalf of Pete's widow Betty (in whose name he had borrowed the money). The new business in Milwaukee was named (for originality, quite the equal of "Ace" and "Arrow") Acme Disposal. It presented Buntrock, however, with a new challenge. He had never before run a company through somebody else. He had never managed a manager.

The manager whom he hired to do the job in November 1959 (and who remains at Waste Management over thirty years later) was Stan Ruminski. Buntrock paid him more than he himself was earning. He didn't care much for rank and stuck to the simple principle that, if that was what it took to get the job done, then it was all right with him.

Ruminski had worked for several years as a salesman and sales manager for a company called Dispos-O-Waste, which was a pioneer in containerization systems for waste hauling, and then for the Chicago Floor Maintenance Company, a growing janitorial services firm. He met Buntrock in the course of servicing commercial buildings in downtown Chicago. When Buntrock needed somebody good "on site" Ruminski headed north. Both the time and the place were fortunate. Milwaukee, at the time, was probably five or ten years behind the postwar growth that had burst upon Chicago in the early 1950s. The Marine Bank Building, begun in 1961, was the first new downtown construction project since 1938. Acme prospered on the wave of growth's waste.

It serviced mills and factories, gas stations and grocery stores. Heavy industry still thrived in Milwaukee, and Acme captured opportunities with big companies like A. O. Smith, which manufactured car frames and water heaters, with International Harvester, and with the Milwaukee Road Railroad. They began with just a few trucks and rented garage space from Gimbel's department store, which they shared with several other haulers. There were no office facilities, and Ruminski (who lived at the YMCA until he could relocate his family) carried around the company typewriter, all the billing and payroll information, and the checkbook, in the trunk of his car.

After six months, they moved to the Quality Biscuit Garage at

Pierce and Sixteenth streets, where garage, maintenance, and office space were all brought together. Buntrock drove up from Chicago once a week. He and Ruminski discussed new equipment, containers, customers, billing, all the basic matters relevant to running a refuse company. And they discussed growth, which was why Acme was there. The previous owner, Gus Magestro, stayed on as foreman. There was also one mechanic, the drivers, and their helpers—plus Ruminski. Ruminski was no office-bound manager. You could find him, when you could find him, on the trucks or on the street selling new business. It was his nature, but it also came from Buntrock, himself typically "in the field," observing how the business ran and how it might be made to run faster and better.

Acme, when the Ace Partnership acquired it, was a business that needed some work, and on the trucks was where the work got done. Ruminski rode them long hours, learning the routes, observing the quantity and quality of the waste picked up at different stops, noting how the men handled their jobs and how the equipment performed. The examination was unrelenting, the purpose single-minded: "Is this route operating at peak efficiency? Is it making as much money as it might?" Each truck, Buntrock believed from his first days in the business, had to be understood as a rolling profit center. If the route along which it rolled was poorly drawn or carelessly operated, profitability would suffer and growth would prove elusive.

The two men figured it meticulously, and began to develop guidelines for operating good routes. They looked at the cost of running each truck—labor, fuel, equipment, plus disposal—and then asked if, at the end of the day, they had 30 to 35 percent coming off the operating line. If so, it was a decent route. If not, they had to find a way for the truck to haul more trash and generate more revenue, or increase efficiency by tuning up the driver's routing and shortening the distances he had to travel. Milwaukee's competitive marketplace disciplined them in this. Big price increases to cover for inefficient operations were risky when customers had many other haulers to turn to.

The Quality Biscuit location happened to have the local Teamsters hall just down the street. After several false starts the union successfully organized Acme's hourly employees in 1963 (all the drivers, helpers, and mechanics). This made Acme the only unionized private waste hauler in Milwaukee (a situation that lasted until 1971), and it required of its managers yet another discipline. They paid higher wages than the nonunion shops, and unlike all but a very few of them, also provided medical and retirement benefits.

Unions, if they are doing what they should, bring predictability and stability to a business through the collective bargaining process, even as they look after the welfare of the workers. The garbage business, at that time especially, could be physically grueling, and the union presence provided added incentive for owners and managers to behave responsibly in meting out tasks and setting expectations.

Buntrock's men back at Ace were Teamsters too, something he had learned to get along with just fine, partly by being a better father to his men than the union was a brother. Whatever, the union also worked out for him in Milwaukee. It made him and Ruminski even more attentive to learning how to manage their people at just the right levels. When a man works when tired, he becomes not only inefficient but, in lines of work like trash hauling, dangerous to himself and others. Accidents at the ends of long hard days are probably preventable accidents. It was important that a man go home not utterly beat, because it was even more important that the same man come back the next day and do it all over again.

Because labor costs per man were higher for a unionized operation, Acme's incentive to scrutinize other costs increased. When Ruminksi arrived, all Acme trucks had two-man crews: a driver and his helper. After the union came in, he and Buntrock decided to try it with one. Ruminski laid the groundwork carefully, anticipating a fight. Again, he got onto a truck and tried it himself with one of the routes. He told the driver just to drive and stand by; for a week, he did all the lifting and hauling alone. If he (whose physical prowess was not out of the ordinary) could handle it, he felt the drivers could too. At first, there was lots of hard feelings, lots of resentment that too much was being asked. But the change took hold, gradually, from one route to another, the men accepted it and learned newer, more productive ways of work.

The company tried to make it easier. Containers helped immensely. Ruminski also went back and did his homework, visiting customers and explaining that because of rising labor costs some of the old "valet service" they were used to would have to be eliminated. From now on, the trashmen would far less often trundle down into the basements and wrestle drums of waste from elevator to dock to truck. He encouraged customers to understand the company's position and to help simplify the system by having waste material on the dock or in the alley, ready to go. It helped the company keep price increases modest, and it helped keep customers loyal when those increases inevitably came along.

Disposal was the other challenge that Buntrock and Ruminski sought to address, both because it represented an immediate operating cost that had to be controlled, and because it was one of the key factors that determined the long-range prospects for growth. In the early years, Acme tipped its refuse at two dumps (neither anything close to a modern landfill): one operated by the county at Loomis Road and 76th Street on the South Side, and the other a private operation on Goodhope Road on the North Side. Trucks went to one or the other depending on where they were when the load got full. At neither were the tipping fees exorbitant, but, then again, Acme had little to say about what those fees might someday become. The municipality ran hot and cold about being in the dump business at all, and if either site were ever suddenly to close down or be restricted by price, the impact on a hauler like Acme could be disastrous.

"Everybody loves the garbageman when he picks it up, but hates him when he puts it down" is an old saw that has become even truer with the passage of time and the rise of environmentalism. In Milwaukee in the 1960s, the problems associated with "putting it down" seemed to Dean Buntrock even then to crystallize the single largest challenge facing the industry and to be the key to its growth. Business hates uncertainty. While Acme was learning to control costs and fine-tune its management of the collection, or front-end, of the business, it was utterly dependent on disposal, the back-end. As long as this was so, growth could not be planned; it might not happen at all.

It helped, of course, to have a nose for where growth was likely to occur, and if possible to lay oneself across its path. As Acme prospered, Ruminski moved the headquarters west to Brookfield, Wisconsin, intent on capturing the hauling business associated with Milwaukee's suburbanization. And they did more than that, for, at Brookfield, the opportunity arose to develop their own landfill site. It was an old quarry, whose owner had died leaving a widow not much interested in rock. Buntrock and Ruminski convinced her that if the hole were no longer going to be gouged out for gravel, they would like to pay her for the opportunity to fill it in with garbage. She agreed. They signed a ten-year lease, and Acme was in the disposal business.

This was in 1967, and though environmental regulations were still in their infancy, Acme operated with a careful eye on the sensitivities of the neighbors. There was no burning, and they laid on a dirt cover each evening. They promised the city of Brookfield, moreover, that they would deposit only commercial and industrial waste hauled by Acme. They also provided special roll-off containers open by special pass to the citizens of Brookfield for the deposit of bulky items.

But more than local politics was at work here. It was becoming apparent—certainly to Dean Buntrock—that disposal capacity was the key to controlling one's fate in the waste business. Every landfill he acquired, from this, the very first, had therefore to serve a dual purpose. It had to serve both as a place to put the trash today, and as a tool for building reputation. One landfill that was well run—that met or exceeded the expectations of the neighbors and numerous other onlookers—helped when it came time to open the next one.

In Milwaukee, the rising premium on disposal space was brought home by the difficulties the city was then experiencing in retro-fitting its municipal waste incinerators to meet increasingly stringent air pollution requirements. When the city finally threw in the towel and quit burning garbage in 1969 rather than build entirely new incinerators, Acme bid on and won the contract to convert the old plants into transfer stations.

One Last Huizenga

Wisconsin turned out to be a good place to have gone. Acme grew to thirty trucks, and, in fact, got bigger than the Ace operation back in Chicago. They started up a small operation (City Disposal) in Madison and took on work in Kenosha. In addition to the one in Brookfield, they operated landfills in Muskego and Slinger. Reaching outward, Buntrock showed he could compete where the competition was real, and that he had a grasp of the one element most essential to survival in the waste business of the future: development of disposal capacity.

All this would have been hard to do in Chicago alone. Yet it was to Chicago, specifically to the Huizenga family connection that had brought him there to begin with, that Buntrock owed the relationship that became most central to his effort to reach outward and implement a vision of the industry.

Harm Huizenga had had a fourth son, the only child by Aaltje, his second wife. He was Gerrit Harry ("Harry"), born in Groningen Province in The Netherlands in 1916, at the end of Harm's temporary sojourn back in the old country. When the other boys, Siert, Tom, and Pete, were moving into the waste business with their father, Harry was still in school. He became a house builder, not a garbageman, working largely on the South Side of Chicago. He lived in the suburb of Evergreen Park with his wife, Jean

Riddering, and their son Harry Wayne ("Wayne") and daughter Bonnie. Wayne was born in 1937. A typical Sunday in his childhood would find them all, after church, in good Dutch fashion, visiting at the house of one of Harry's half-brothers in Berwyn or Cicero, with lots of cousins to go around.

In 1953, when Wayne was still a freshman in high school, Harry moved the family to Florida, where the building business looked deceptively attractive. But the Floridians gave him a bad time, and although he stayed on, he found another line of work. The same forces of growth that fuel construction work also make for waste, and waste was what he turned to. Wayne, meanwhile, finished school but then went North and operated a bulldozer for two years before entering Calvin College in Michigan. Bored with student life, he stayed just a year, joined the army reserves, and thought he might finish up his education later at the University of Miami. He liked Florida, but he never went back to school.

Shortly after he got out of the service, Wayne, along with Harry, had a chance meeting at a restaurant with Harry's old high school pal from Chicago, Herman Mulder. Mulder hauled garbage with the other Dutchmen, but he had interests in Florida too—not many, but enough to give him problems, which was what had brought him to Ft. Lauderdale. In response to the Huizengas' "Well, what are you doing in town, Herman," Mulder told them, directly, that the manager of his little three-truck operation up in Pompano Beach was stealing from him, and he needed to find a local replacement, fast. Wayne was two days out of the army and planning to go to work with Harry, again building houses in Ft. Lauderdale. But before lunch was over, Mulder had his new manager. The older man dismissed the young man's protest that he didn't know the first thing about the trash business with a brusque, "You don't need to." Whatever he did need to know, he learned in the time-honored workingman's way: on the job. Wayne Huizenga never lost the knack.

First off, he learned that Mulder hadn't exactly given him a "manager's" job. Garbage from the vast unincorporated areas of

Broward County was being hauled by a loose association of small operators, called Associated Independent, working under a master contract, each outfit taking an assigned part of the territory. They owned their own trucks and looked after their own payrolls, but Mulder handled all the customer billing and paid all the bills out of his office in Chicago.

What was left for the local "manager" was seeing to the business at the most basic level: getting (and keeping) men on the trucks, seeing that they did a good job, keeping the trucks repaired and rolling. The young Huizenga's office was his pickup. He took phone calls at a desk he had at the gas station where the trucks parked at night. All day, every day, he rode the trucks, made sure the work got done, and never shied from doing some of it himself.

After working two years for Mulder, Wayne answered an ad in the paper and became an owner himself—not much of an owner, but enough to get started. From a man named Wilbur Porter, he bought an old beat-up open truck and hauling business worth maybe $500 per month. He left Mulder, returned to Ft. Lauderdale, and went to work. At first, there was one truck, one helper, a few containers. When the truck got full and the helper drove off to the dump at Deerfield Beach to unload, Huizenga used the hour and-a-half to knock on doors, hoping to have a couple more customers by the time the truck got back. Often as not, he did—enough to make the business grow, adding a second, third, and fourth truck.

In 1962, Wayne bought out Mulder's three Pompano Beach routes, then being managed by his father Harry, who had gone to work for Mulder when the construction business slumped. They renamed Mulder's old portion, which were residential routes, Southern Disposal. Huizenga's own commercial routes in Ft. Lauderdale were called Southern Sanitation.

Even in bad times, a hard worker can prosper in the garbage business; some Dutchmen lived better than most even during the Depression. In good times (if he picks the right place), he can prosper very well indeed. Not since the 1920s had south Florida seen growth such as it experienced in the 1960s. Wayne Huizenga happily was there, and he grew right along with it. He bid on city contracts, he bought out other companies, his trucks hauled trash in Ft. Lauderdale, Tampa, Miami, and Key West.

Growth required reach, however, and all those trucks belonged to him—and to the bank. The garbage business might generate wonderfully reliable cash-flows and give its owner a fine living, but a family-owned, partnership-dominated business was not poised for rapid growth. Huizenga experienced this drawback, first hand, every day. His trucks were making money, but he never had any cash—and never enough credit to get the jump on change.

Many years later, Dean Buntrock would say of Wayne Huizenga that "his skills require a business ready for change." He spoke in reference to Huizenga's ventures that were not the waste business, but the observation fit the waste business in the 1960s precisely. Huizenga knew about growth, but while he may have had the skills, he hadn't the resources to take full advantage of them. Buntrock, by contrast (though far from a financier), ran a business with cash in excess of the local opportunities to use it.

These two men did not, at the time, know each other well, and their business relationship, as it developed, did so largely external to the Huizenga family. Huizenga knew that Buntrock had married his cousin B.J., that he ran the old companies in Chicago, Ace and Arrow, and that he had expanded into Milwaukee with Acme. Buntrock, for his part, on his occasional vacations to Florida, visited with his wife's cousin, who like himself hauled trash. What was striking were the different growth rates of their two concerns—and the different demands thus placed upon them. The Chicago operation, solid and healthy and located in a prosperous big city, enjoyed stable high-quality business. Growth was measured and orderly, adding perhaps one truck a year to Ace. Huizenga's Florida companies had to fight with tougher competition, but they were growing very quickly (perhaps faster than their financing was growing), adding three or four trucks a year.

Standing at a distance, the complementary quality of the two is evident. Huizenga, busy charging around his growing company, adding routes and keeping trucks on the road, was hardly able to step back. Buntrock, from his more secure perch, was. His discovery in faraway Florida of this other Huizenga, already astride the tiger of growth, fit in with his own desire to reach outside the old family business. Many years later, Huizenga would still credit Buntrock with seeing in such early bits and pieces the vision of a nationwide waste management company. The coming together of Wayne Huizenga's southern company, and the companies that Dean Buntrock ran up North was the next step toward making that vision real.

Wayne Huizenga built his first business on two things: high energy and abundant debt. He had no money himself, and when growth dictated a new route and another truck, or purchase of a piece of someone else's business, he tried to buy with nothing down and payments strung out as long as possible. To stand up to the competition, which threatened constantly to invade Broward County from Miami, he had to buy more containers and constantly keep after the new business.

Though the energy and much of the sweat were Wayne Huizenga's, his business was actually a three-way partnership: himself, his father, and father-in-law. When Huizenga's first marriage, to Joyce VanderWagon, ended in divorce in 1965, his former father-in-law, John VanderWagon, felt awkward and asked to be bought out. He, and his wife especially, were uncomfortable with an arrangement that not only was no longer in the family, but that had become risky from cosigning Huizenga's many notes. How to buy him out, however, was something of problem for the stretched-out Huizenga who had no money.

Huizenga and Buntrock's friendship had become warm over the years, but this problem was what triggered their business relationship. Peter Huizenga, now a young lawyer (Pete's son, Wayne's cousin, Buntrock's brother-in-law), proposed an imaginative solution that accomplished several things at once. They would buy out VanderWagon's interest in the Florida business and relieve his obligations under the notes, by exchanging them for the Arrow Disposal business plus notes and a small sum of cash. At the same time, Peter Huizenga and Buntrock negotiated with Wayne Huizenga for him (Buntrock) to acquire for a nominal amount a 16²/₃ interest in the southern companies (8¹/₃ came from Wayne; 8¹/₃ from Wayne's father, Harry). The family trust also bought a small interest.

It gave Buntrock an interest in the southern companies, and set Buntrock and Huizenga soundly down the road together. Henceforth, they would sit on the same side of the table, making deals with others.

Pick It Up and Put It Down Too

The two enterprises together still only dimly foreshadowed the larger things to follow. At that point, it might have turned into just a larger hauling company, half in family business-dominated Chicago, half in growth-crazy south Florida. But hauling, as everybody in the garbage business knew, was only half the equation. The difference between those who knew that, and those who were able to do something about it, was the difference between resting comfortably with the business accomplishments of others, and seizing control of a new sort of business opportunity altogether.

"Vision" is a quality commonly ascribed to the builders of large, successful companies. And that quality, with good reason, is widely ascribed to Dean Buntrock twenty years after having built one. To mean something historically, however—to be more than an easy encomium to an acknowledged leader—the word must be connected with something concrete. In the case of Dean Buntrock, that something had two components: disposal and consolidation.

Here caution dictates that others not be slighted. Garbagemen from time to time have worried intensely about what they were going to do with the trash, and sometimes this worry led to common action, which was how Chicago got two large incinerators in the 1950s before Buntrock ever came to town. The distinction was that Buntrock put disposal—whatever changing meanings the word might come to have—at the center of his thinking about the industry. He understood it as more than just a pressing immediate problem that demanded practical solution.

Disposal also suggested the broader social and cultural problem (beyond just the operating needs of those in the business), awareness of which lay in the not so distant future. The problem was the planet's finite capacity to absorb the waste of the human society it sustains. How could that limit, which is partly natural and partly man-made, best be managed?

The changing demands that sprang from a new public sensibility about the issue of disposal were partly what dictated the second component: consolidation. Disposal soon became the toughest, riskiest, most costly part of the trash business. If you couldn't provide a place to set it down, it mattered less and less how good you were at picking it up. Assuring disposal capacity meant investment in real estate and, as regulations multiplied, technology. That in turn required capital beyond what many small (even though very successful) hauling businesses could command.

Shortly before Christmas 1955, Pete Huizenga wrote to his daughter, B.J., and new son-in-law, Dean Buntrock, about a new aspect of the family business on seventy-eight acres of property at 138th Street and Calumet Drive. They were in the process of excavating it and transporting the sand to the new Calumet harbor development nearby. "They are digging about 1,200 to 1,500 yards a day with a single shovel. This is expected to double when they put in a second scoop." It was the beginning of what would become Waste Management's immense CID (Calumet Industrial Development) Landfill.

The Ace partners began hauling trash there and also profiting from tipping fees collected from other haulers. By the standards of the time, they ran a good operation, which would probably have met their own disposal needs for a good many years to come. But in the middle 1960s, Buntrock put his own mark on this, another part of the Huizenga legacy. In doing so, he changed it into something fit for a very different sort of future.

Adjacent to the original eighty-acre Ace property that was located inside the Chicago city limits, was a larger 150-acre parcel of land, just across the boundary in Calumet City. Buntrock's inquiries led him to the St. Louis owners who were willing to sell, and (something that didn't hurt at all) were good Missouri Synod Lutherans like he was. But since it was a bigger piece of land than Ace could afford, additional partners were required, people whom Buntrock knew in the Chicago business and had confidence in: Tom Tibstra and Larry Beck, a Dutchmen and a Dane.

Larry Beck, the Dane, along with Buntrock and Wayne Huizenga, became a founder of Waste Management, Inc. Like Huizenga, he had grown up around the refuse business. His father came from Denmark in steerage at age fifteen and started hauling ashes in Chicago's South Side. The son started out in 1953 hauling trash in the southern suburb of Harvey. He had a single, open truck with a seven-step ladder at the back, and he wore a thick leather pad for protection when carrying cans on his shoulders. His first year he did $16,000 of business and was proud of it.

Tom Tibstra, ten years older, had been in the business since the early 1940s; Beck joined him as a partner in the late 1950s and together they worked the southwest suburban towns. Beck met Buntrock ("the bashful young fellow from Ace") at meetings of the Chicago Ash and Scavenger Association. Buntrock got to know Beck as a progressive young man (he had taken the lead in persuading the local association to abandon the old appellation "scavenger" in favor of "Chicago and Suburban Refuse Disposal Association") with a reputation for knowing the basic business and more about driving trucks and running bulldozers than most of the men who operated them.

When the opportunity arose to expand dramatically, Buntrock characteristically looked for the means to make something happen that was beyond his reach alone. How it was divided up mattered less to him than not missing a big chance. He himself did not, in fact, get a share in what became the CID Landfill, although without him there would have been no such place. On first approach, Beck and Tibstra hesitated. Buntrock gently persisted: "Why don't you come over and see what you're saying no to?"

Finally they did, and the result was a 225-acre parcel of property, permitted for use as a sanitary landfill, which would figure prominently in the future history of Waste Management. They began work there in 1967. (The eighty acres in Chicago were on relatively low land and in the 1920s had been subdivided; the Calumet City section was on higher ground.) Larry Beck, sensibly enough, was on site and in charge.

Larry Beck was a workingman's manager, the sort who saw the refuse business as a type of materials handling. He never hesitated to remind people, even as things grew more and more complex, that if they really wanted to know what was going on they had to put down their briefcases and get their shoes muddy. Since that time twenty-five years ago, the primary importance to the waste business of the men who "picked it up and put it down" has not diminished. In this sense, the nature of the basic business is immutable. The garbageman provided and provides a service essential to human survival. Someone, at some point, has had to see to society's leavings, and removing other people's trash has always been a respectable business.

Buntrock liked to say, in tribute to the men who did this basic work, that "nothing happens until somebody dumps the can." That was certainly correct—but it was also just the beginning. The bigger future challenge, he knew, lay with what was going to happen after somebody dumped it. A major shift was underway, and he was in the midst of it. The value that society placed upon this ancient service was about to undergo a radical inflation, and so too the expectations placed upon those who provided it. The challenge of those changed circumstances required other kinds of work, and they shortly called forth other kinds of workers.

5

Minds Over Matter

IN THE summer of 1972, Dean Buntrock observed that "the solid waste management industry is, by necessity, entering an age of professionalism." Only a year earlier, Waste Management, Inc. had become a public company, and Buntrock knew what he was talking about. He foresaw an accelerated search for solid waste management techniques that were both environmentally sound and economically sensible, and he predicted that increased responsibility for solving the nation's waste problems would fall on the private sector.

There were several reasons for this. The costs of municipal governments (which collected most residential waste and operated the lion's share of disposal sites) were rising rapidly. As costs rose, so did incentives to find more efficient (usually private) disposal alternatives. At the same time, more stringent pollution-control legislation at federal, state, and local levels was forcing expensive upgrading of equipment and procedures. Finally, the mountains of trash kept on growing. Even as public concern over the quality, particularly of the urban, environment reached a new high pitch, the per capita generation of solid wastes steadily increased. In such circumstances, it was possible either to read the prophecy of doom or to discern the outline of opportunity.

Whose Job Is This, Anyway?

History divided the waste business into public and private components. Hauling other people's trash had been perfectly respectable private business for centuries. Hauling residential trash in American cities, however, tended to fall under municipal government— a natural consequence of the way urban reformers had elaborated and then driven home the connection between sanitation and public health. But the balance between public and private sectors began to shift in the late 1960s and early 1970s as the volume and the velocity of the business increased. The tension between the two sides of the business was evident even in the early efforts to survey it and learn who actually did what, and what the size of the solid waste "problem" really was.

When in 1969 the Solid Wastes Program of the U. S. Public Health Service released its "Report on the National Survey of Solid Wastes," the private sector fairly roared in protest. The survey questionnaire, it seemed, had gone out only to municipal sanitation executives whose responses could hardly reflect detailed knowledge of private operations. In an industry that was, in the aggregate, one-half to two-thirds private, this was a startling skew. There were calls to begin again from scratch. The result, "The Private Sector in Solid Waste Management," produced by the NSWMA for the Environmental Protection Agency and published in 1973, painted a different picture that left little doubt about the growing role played by private enterprise.

Another government-sponsored report, this one produced for the Bureau of Solid Waste Management by the National Academy of Engineering-National Academy of Sciences ("Policies for Solid

Waste Management") was more sympathetic and predicted increased reliance on private sector initiatives and resources. Analyzing collection, transportation, and disposal, it found great potential in new technology and new operating and management methods. But it acknowledged the problem of getting people to pay the true cost of such services. It called for a federal program to carry out a variety of activities, including research and development on equipment and systems, and for funds for biological, ecological, and engineering studies relating to residue management. The authors estimated the yearly costs of the solid waste problem at $4.5 billion in 1969, and with utopian fervor twenty years ahead of its time, they looked forward to "the development of a closed system in which all residues are reprocessed or otherwise made suitable for return to the national resources."

In the early days of evolving federal policy on solid wastes, the line between constructive public policy, and what to the private sector was excessive central planning, was not always easy to draw. The NSWMA, with executive director Harold Gershowitz as its spokesman, strongly encouraged a developing partnership between private enterprise and public administration in the field of solid waste management, but with the caveat that economic viability be considered along with technological innovation. Every objective study pointed to the need for stimulating capital improvements in an industry long characterized by its labor-intensiveness. This was an issue fundamental to the future of the private sector (and to solving the "waste problem" generally), and it was a perilous one.

In 1970, Gershowitz testified to Congress about it. Federal "demonstration," money after the manner of the Federal National Mortgage Association or the Small Business Administration, might conceivably prove useful, providing it was ultimately treated as a loan and returned to the government with interest. But about the concept of direct federal construction grants to state and local waste authorities, NSWMA members were not in the slightest ambiguous. Gershowitz argued forcefully that there was no surer way to dry up the interest of private capital in the waste management field. Even public officials feared that such funding would always be too little, too late, and of no lasting help in getting on top of the problem.

To have had an impact on the solid waste problem through its own "direct investment," the federal government would have had to forego a couple of aircraft carriers at least. That did not happen, and the role Washington gradually crafted for itself was to regulate, not to subsidize. For private companies in the waste business, this had long-range economic consequences that would be hard to overstate. Few better examples existed of the way government regulation can create and drive a market, than the market for waste management services since the early 1970s. The expression in legislation of society's rising anxiety about the fate of the environment affected the private sector in two fundamental ways. It required private businesses to meet uniform operating standards, and to evolve in ways that were as much the product of political as of economic processes. This could sometimes be burdensome. It also ensured that the amount of business out there to do would be enormous. This proved an immeasurable blessing.

Together Now, Boys

To this day (perhaps even more so today than ever) nothing more infuriates militant Greens than the knowledge that big companies make money out of the environment. The rage, oddly, is greater even than that against those who pollute: it is bad enough to spill crude oil into the sea, worse somehow to make a profit from cleaning up the mess. The emotional intensity reminds one of the people whose knuckles go white at the knowledge that highly paid doctors and proprietary hospital chains profit from the services they provide to the sick. These subjects are highly charged and poisoned by ideology. In the former case, veiled in greenery, is the hard Left's old antibusiness agenda. Profits are dirtier than dirt or, in the latter case, deadlier than disease.

The nastiness of this attitude is in direct proportion to the size of its target. The big corporation, as America had known it ever since the nineteenth century, came late to the waste business. When it finally arrived, it arrived with a bang that shook up even the sleepiest old family proprietors. Dean Buntrock was not alone in understanding that the magnitude of new opportunities made a restructuring of the waste industry imperative, and he was not the first to act upon that understanding. But he acted with more lasting effect than anyone else who touched the business. Ironically, the company he created has become one of the greenest corporations on the planet, and the biggest-ever target for militant Greens.

It seemed self-evident to Buntrock that only private enterprise could harvest the vast new fields that new environmental standards were opening up in solid waste management. But for the private sector to prove that it could tackle the waste problem more effectively than government, required size. Size was dictated foremost by the need for more money. Since the waste industry was already large but highly fragmented, size meant putting little pieces together.

Buntrock saw the progression logically: "The pressures from environmental regulation, increasing costs of solid waste management techniques, and rising per capita generation of solid wastes are contributing to the centralization of the private sector. The costs of developing adequate large scale and environmentally preferable storage, collection, transfer or interim processing and disposal techniques within the strict confines of small business practice cannot easily be borne by the small, local solid waste contractor." The answer lay with publicly financed companies that could command the financial strength and management sophistication to get the bigger job done in a rapidly maturing industry.

Buntrock always had a weather eye on the big picture, but his big picture was always informed by the condition of the basic business at the local level. By the end of the 1960s, the experience of the Ace companies, of Acme in Wisconsin, and of Wayne Huizenga's southern operations, coupled with even a rudimentary appreciation of the potential for growth all around them, left no doubt about the urgent need for capital.

The problem was not unique to them. As trucks got fancier and demand went up for containers, local operators large and small found borrowing a growing problem. Hauling companies with perfectly respectable cash flows were finding that interest payments were a significant burden on their operating statements. Historically friendly bankers began looking at loan balances with new wariness. It was not an uncommon experience for the proprietor of a local company, on visiting his neighborhood bank for yet another loan to buy a new truck or a load of containers, to learn that his credit was already extended past the prudent limit, and that perhaps he should clear up some of his outstanding debt before shopping for more hardware. But if the reason the hauler was shopping was because he had just committed to a large new contract at the local Ford assembly plant, the banker's reluctance could have dire consequences. There was always, of course, another bank happy to get in on a good little business, but if the hauler was not well known, the first thing the banker did after the handshake was ask for three years of audited statements in order to begin a loan application. Sad to say, more than a few little companies kept their records on the back of an envelope in the pickup or, at best, on the checkbook stubs.

At Ace, Buntrock had a real accountant who kept a good ledger, but bookkeeping was not the real problem. The real problem was the escalating velocity of the business, particularly after forging the link with the Florida companies. Speaking of what led up to the decision to put the companies together and go public, Peter Huizenga, the young lawyer who did much of the putting-together, said, "It was money that brought us to the table. We didn't have enough money to take advantage of what was right on the platter in front of us."

For all their business instincts and the considerable experience that the then-young Buntrock and Wayne Huizenga already had under their belts, the Ace/Acme/Southern/CID gaggle of businesses still had about them a remarkably hand-to-mouth quality. The market beckoned with growth, but the means were lacking. Huizenga was perpetually out of cash, scrambling just to meet the payroll, with payables reaching higher than he cared to look. They went through every bank they could possibly think of getting signature loans. They signed stacks of notes. They leveraged Pete's widow, Betty, for they themselves had no collateral.

False Starts

Reaching out to new markets and finding ways to finance that reach were challenges felt all across the industry. In the early 1960s, another privately held company of Dutchmen, National Disposal Contractors owned by the Vanderveld family of Barrington, Illinois, had branched out, won contracts, and acquired hauling companies as far off as Pittsburgh, Omaha, and Seattle. These were big operations, and they were far from home base. It was a new pattern. In 1965, contractors in major metropolitan areas other than Chicago approached former Vanderveld employee Don McClenahan about forming a new company that could become a vehicle for industry amalgamation.

Sanitation Systems, Inc. (SSI), which resulted, was headquartered in rented offices at 15 Spinning Wheel Road in Hinsdale, Illinois, in Chicago's western suburbs, which was where McClenahan lived. Unlucky for him, McClenahan was just a bit ahead of the curve. SSI was a halting affair capitalized with the shareholders' own modest investments ($23,000 or less, per firm), and it reflected the one-foot-in-the-old-school, one-foot-in-the-new character of even progressive hauling companies at that time. Uncertainty held them back. They feared for their business should the Vanderveld's National Disposal Contractors come into their town, but they also liked things the way they were. McClenahan pumped hard about the advantages of a true pooling of their companies. He brought in securities brokers to explain the advantages of going public and even persuaded several companies to have three-year audits done by Arthur Andersen. But they would not make the big jump, and McClenahan was not the leader to impel them.

Oddly enough, McClenahan and his investors viewed the Chicago firms and their powerful association as distinctive and separate and likely uninterested in reaching out, and there was no Chicago representation in the SSI venture. But McClenahan (who earlier had worked for the Elgin-Leach Corporation on the hardware side of the business and had called frequently at Ace) knew Buntrock, and he turned to him when SSI finally stalled. He invited Buntrock and Ace on board, frankly declaring his need for both Ace's revenues and Buntrock's leadership. Buntrock, whose thinking was not yet firm, balked. Neither man had it quite right. McClenahan's group eventually sold off the two companies they had acquired, in Finley, Ohio, and Parkersburg, West Virginia, to Service Corporation of America (SCA), and liquidated itself. Buntrock continued to wrestle over how to transcend the limits of his own little group of family-held enterprises.

Bigger Thinking

Buntrock's determination to do something bigger with the old partnerships and scattered pieces took concrete form as the 1960s came to an end. He had served these firms well; Pete surely would have been pleased. And he recognized that opportunity was ripe to craft something new for himself. In 1968, he hired Ben Essenburg as general manager of the Ace operations to free himself for larger matters. The pressing need for financing, in the context of an industry bursting with growth and poised for consolidation, made a compelling case for going public. Consolidation was taking place in structurally similar industries (such as vending machines, which were the first business of SCA), and even within the waste industry itself (Browning Ferris Industries, "BFI," went public as a waste company in 1968). This pointed to the increased scale on which the business henceforth would need to operate. And scale redefined the terms for competing within it.

Waste Management, Inc., chartered in October 1968, was conceived as a vehicle whose first purpose was to bring together the numerous operating segments of the Huizenga patrimony and the additions that Buntrock had grafted onto it. It functioned as a holding company to achieve the critical mass (revenues of $10 million were thought to be the threshold) necessary for a public offering. Everything, up to then, still stood alone: the Ace subsidiaries were separate; Larry Beck and Tom Tibstra's Atlas was separate; Acme in Milwaukee was separate; CID Corporation was separate; Wayne Huizenga's Florida companies (in which Buntrock had a share) stood off by themselves. First, Ace Scavenger Service, still a partnership, was reorganized as a corporate entity. Some of the real estate assets were retained in order to make lease payments to the partners in the landfill. Ace, Acme, and City Disposal then became subsidiaries of the parent corporation, Waste Management. Reorganization of the northern companies (except for Beck and Tibstra's Atlas) was accomplished in January 1970. The southern companies were reorganized into Waste Management a year later, along with Atlas, in exchange for shares. When they figured it up, Buntrock, Huizenga, and Beck ended up with about the same number of shares in the new entity. They became its founders.

Names and Places

Together, Buntrock, Wayne, and Peter Huizenga planned how they wanted it to go. The name, "Waste Management," was Buntrock's alone. In all of American corporate history, there are few better examples of a name that both fits the times and describes what a company actually does. Each of the two words, "waste" and "management," signified the up-to-dateness of Buntrock's vision.

"Waste," since the 1950s, had progressively replaced "refuse," "garbage," and "rubbish," in professional parlance. It was also a marginally nicer word for what was widely regarded as a not-so-nice business. But unlike many other language changes undertaken to pump up somebody's esteem, this change sharpened meaning instead of muddling it. "Waste" was waste—things you throw away. They considered going with "solid waste" as had the national trade association NSWMA, but they pulled back: the simpler the better. "Management" was another stroke of concision. It flattered the garbagemen even as it anticipated the changing character of the work they did. From "scavenger" to "manager" was a linguistic leap that described a profound shift in cultural and economic realities.

In the eyes of both public officials and the private marketplace, the waste business henceforth would be judged on how well it "managed" the whole equation of waste, from beginning to end. As environmentalism ratcheted up the expectations, and as the political, legal, and economic risks of the business exploded, the choice of the word "management" turned out to be appropriate in more ways than even Buntrock probably guessed. As a phrase too, the words worked. "Coke" and "Kleenex" (new products when they appeared) took a while to catch on. "Waste Management" (an old service changing fast) was a generic right out of the gate. It became impossible to talk about the business without naming the company—a happy coup in a business more and more talked about every passing year.

Where they did business mattered, to a degree, in the same manner as what they called it. The old company letterhead had read: "Ace Scavenger Service: Garbage, Cinders and Rubbish Removal, 5245 West 38th Street, Cicero 50, Illinois." If they wanted to do something big, however, "Cicero, Illinois," was a problem. The comfortable old town of three-flats, bungalows, and bars on Chicago's western edge was simply not an appropriate address for the headquarters of the company they had in mind to build. So Buntrock went west. He rented shared-services office space in the

Oak Brook Towers at Route 83 and 22nd Street in Oak Brook, a modern postwar suburb set astride highways not railways, an open landscape of broad lawns, big shopping centers, and, in time, corporate headquarters. Downtown Chicago, in contrast, would not have suited them at all. Theirs was not a heavily clerical business that needed lots of office space, and they all lived in the western suburbs anyway. Oak Brook, with its highway interchanges and proximity to O'Hare Airport, made sense and was a nice-sounding address besides.

Enter an Irishman

Phil Rooney, who is today president and chief operating officer of Waste Management, Inc., chairman and chief executive officer of Wheelabrator Technologies, Inc., and the company's acknowledged captain after only Buntrock himself, grew up in the 1950s just 2 miles from the old Ace garage. The son of a Cicero police captain and fifteen years Buntrock's junior, Rooney was as Irish as the Huizengas were Dutch. His father knew Jim DeBoer, a Dutch hauler who had a contract to dispose of Cicero's municipal waste at Incinerator, Inc., and in 1962 he inquired about summer work for his teenage son. DeBoer passed him off to his partner, John Groot. Groot (an investor in the incinerator and future partner in CID) put him on and was glad he did. Rooney came early to work, stayed late, did everything they asked of him, including all the grunt jobs, and did them well. He always asked if there was more work to be done, and never asked to be paid more money. The next summer, Groot didn't have anything for Rooney but passed him along to Buntrock at Ace, with an endorsement that the kid was an incredible worker.

Buntrock measured men by work and loyalty, and the day he hired Rooney he got both almost beyond measure. After graduating from St. Bernard College, a small Catholic school in Birmingham, Alabama, in 1966, Rooney shipped off with the

105

Marines to Viet Nam as a second lieutenant. Two years later, he mustered out, a captain and a decorated combat-veteran, and promptly wrote Buntrock to see about possibilities. Soon they talked. Buntrock still needed an all-purpose assistant, a prospect that appealed to Rooney more than law school, and he signed up on March 1, 1969.

Rooney was twenty-four years old, and about all that was clear to him was that it was clear to Buntrock that they were going to put together a national company. Inexperienced in business, he moved along with Buntrock and the part-time secretary into the little office in Oak Brook Towers. There Buntrock set him to work on everything from buying the stationery and the typewriter and reading back issues of *Refuse Removal Journal*, to tackling a major rail-haul project in Milwaukee, and the CID landfill that was also just getting started. From the beginning, Rooney learned fast and earned a reputation as a young man blessed with bountiful energy and intelligence, who could get things done. Though not then an owner, he became in every other sense a founder, and was equally considered when the company came together and went public. No one, over the next two decades, labored harder for the company or more effectively applied that labor to leading others.

Counting v. Hauling

Two orders of work needed doing. The basic businesses had to be run and pushed to grow toward the $10 million of revenue necessary before attempting a public offering. And the business they already had, had to be sorted out and properly accounted. The garbage business was not a business famous for accounting sophistication. The Huizengas' was probably better run than many family firms, but the accountant who had done the company's statements for Pete Huizenga back in the early 1950s, Ed Egan, was still doing the work in 1969, with the help of his Irish bookkeeper, Morrie Mahoney. For what they had in mind, however, Buntrock and the two Huizengas needed the services and credibility of a Big Eight accounting firm. They turned to someone they knew, Fred Stegerta, a Dutchman and a friend who was a partner of Arthur Andersen and head of its small business division. From that decision much good fortune flowed.

Arthur Andersen was not totally unfamiliar with the business. Several of the shareholding companies involved with Don McClenahan in SSI had had Arthur Andersen's three-year audits, and another company involved in the consolidation of the waste industry, Service Corporation of America, was also an Arthur Andersen client. When Buntrock and Peter Huizenga appeared there, late in 1968, they carried with them Buntrock's concept for taking their group of small garbage companies public, of achieving more broadly based financing, and of consolidating the industry through the process of acquisition. Amid all of Arthur Andersen's expertise, one man in particular stood out and would soon become the chief financial architect for Buntrock's vision.

A CPA trained at Marquette University in Milwaukee, Don Flynn had worked at Arthur Andersen for five years and was on the track to becoming a partner. When Stegerta called him in to meet Buntrock and Huizenga, Flynn was senior manager in the small business division. After they retained Arthur Andersen, in mid-1969, it fell to Flynn to begin sorting out the companies that were to compose the nascent Waste Management, Inc. It was quite a tangle: books that wouldn't balance, numbers that were incomplete, year-ends that didn't match, all the maddening idiosyncrasies of little companies with different histories. Flynn worked out of Chicago and traveled to Florida, where he met Wayne Huizenga. He and his staff worked long and hard— probably four or five man-years—to reach two years back, and then prepare for the 1970 audit.

The financial picture Flynn assembled became the cornerstone for the Securities and Exchange Commission registration statement required for the initial public offering. It documented an attractive, profitable business poised for growth, if it could harness the power of the capital markets. Flynn mastered every little twist and turn of the financial performance of the twenty-or-so companies. He also learned enough about Buntrock and Wayne Huizenga to convince him that not only were the numbers promising, but that these men understood the value they represented. It was still very early. The judgments they all made of each other were inevitably subjective—hunches yet to be proven. But what Flynn discerned in the columns of figures was the inherent profitability of a business whose service was nondiscretionary and largely nonpostponable. He concluded that the businesses could sustain an annual growth rate of perhaps 15 percent from internally generated cash. Anything in addition would require external resources.

While Flynn was busy doing his sums on the outside, Buntrock bolstered financial talent on the inside by hiring Bob Paul, another CPA and veteran of Arthur Andersen. Paul became the fledgling company's first chief financial officer in April 1970 and began to figure out who in all the little partnerships owned what, and how the financial reporting systems in what was then still primarily a cash-flow, not a financial-statement business, should work. Some of the same things struck him as they had Flynn, including the sense of great possibility and the confidence that Buntrock's vision of a vastly changed waste industry and a vast role in it for this young company was the correct one. Paul joined the Waste Management corporate staff that then numbered a total of six, at the company's second address, 15 Spinning Wheel Road in Hinsdale.

That unpretentious address already had associations with the waste business. SCA happened to have offices on the second floor, and Don McClenahan's abortive SSI occupied 600 square feet of space in the basement. Early in 1969, in need of a bit more room, Buntrock subleased the three "lower level" offices from Mc-Clenahan who was closing up shop. He paid what McClenahan was paying: $4.32 per square foot. The space was strictly off-the-shelf and nothing fancy: low ceilings, bright fluorescents, cheap partitions. Buntrock took the furniture, too. It was indicative less of taste than of practical requirements. For Buntrock, Rooney, Dorothy Kuhlman and Rosemarie Nuzzo (their bookkeeper and office manager), Paul (who came a year later) and McClenahan (who worked for a time as a consultant), it was all they needed to do their jobs. It set a pattern. Rosemarie Nuzzo ("Ro" as she soon became known) was hired by Rooney, and ran the office from day one. She hired all the other secretaries, put in hours as long as anyone's, and set a certain tone of formalism around the office. Thanks to her, even in the free-spirited 1970s, no secretaries at Waste Management wore pants or jeans on the job. (The men wore suits—except an unsuspecting Phil Rooney who when he came to talk to Buntrock probably didn't have one and showed up in a sports outfit; he never did it again.) "Ro" worked terribly hard, helping to establish the Waste Management habit of coming early and staying late. In her own way, she established an important presence at the growing young company, and her attentiveness in managing the office and in general seeing that things were done properly, figured immeasurably in its early success. At the company's third address, 900 Jorie Boulevard back in Oak Brook (a rental building operated by the same developer who owned Spinning Wheel Road) everyone again had "Ro" to thank for a comfortable and tasteful place to work. Her influence has persisted, as several years after Buntrock's divorce from his first wife, she became the second Mrs. Buntrock in 1984.

When the company moved finally into its own home on Butterfield Road in Oak Brook in 1981, the work setting improved markedly again and reflected their by-then substantial success. But by the standards of late twentieth-century corporate opulence, no one could say it was ostentatious. Comfortable, functional, adorned with good art, the headquarters of Waste Management, Inc. in 1991 still somehow fit the character and the priorities of its founders: a place for working people with a job to do.

To Market

If Waste Management, Inc. in 1970 and 1971 was not quite a "start-up" proposition, it faced risks that nevertheless demanded some fortitude. The particular cast of characters involved had never done this before: neither Buntrock nor Rooney nor the Huizengas was seasoned in corporate finance. They knew about little companies that they hoped to transpose into a larger and much different company. To use a musical metaphor, they were used to a bunch of talented soloists, but no one had ever conducted a choir. None of them had been to business school, and so they learned on their feet, as they went. As in music, they learned that the ear is as important as the voice. How well you perform depends first on the accurate reception of sounds in the world around you. Buntrock and company had, and continued to develop, a very fine ear.

To convince the capital markets that what they heard was true—that this was the moment to launch their company and start to build an industry—they needed first to convince an investment banker. As it turned out, one came to them. Don McClenahan's experience again played a role. During his efforts with SSI, McClenahan had worked with an owner of the Chicago Corporation, Don Whales. Whales was one of the figures who had put together Automatic Retailers of America (ARA), an agglomerate of vending machine companies, and when McClenahan approached him about his ideas for the solid waste industry, Whales was struck by the parallels: both industries were fragmented into many little firms and ripe for consolidation, and both industries were capital intensive and, in the case of the waste business, becoming more so. With ARA, it was the cost of the vending machines; with the waste business it was the cost of the real estate (for the landfills) and the rolling stock (the trucks and containers). When SSI came to naught, Whales backed away from trying it again with a new set of players and passed it off on one of his partners, Neil Emmons.

Emmons made his first call on Buntrock in January 1970 and through the springtime developed his thoughts on what Buntrock needed to do in order to go public. Discovering that the northern partners, who were Ace Scavenger, had been providing the money that Wayne Huizenga's southern companies needed to grow, he said the two halves must be put together. It wouldn't do to have an investment over here on one side (like the southern operation), and a public company on the other (Waste Management née Ace), and then find oneself with acquisition opportunities in yet other markets. He also emphasized the burden of financing costs as the companies were then experiencing them. They were borrowing, in effect, individually. A historical look at the financials revealed how they had started out with a bank in Cicero, outgrown it and gone to Avenue Bank in Oak Park, outgrown it and found their way to LaSalle National in downtown Chicago. Evaluating the situation from the outside, Emmons said they needed a $4 million revolving line of credit.

When LaSalle would not go over its per customer lending limit of $2.5 million, Emmons suggested talking to Continental where he had old contacts with their transportation group. Familiar with lending on the basis of a pool of equipment (basically trucks), Continental set up a credit line of $6 million. This was in the spring of 1971 when the net worth of the combined companies was a little short of $3 million. Because the bank would not advance funds in excess of a 2-to-1 ratio over net worth, the extra money to trigger it depended on the public offering. When that occurred the effective cost of borrowing fell by half in one fell swoop. Much of the money went down to Florida where it had the effect of a long-awaited transfusion. These needs were not news to Buntrock, but the Chicago Corporation's help in positioning the companies to deal with them was certainly welcome. Emmons went on the board of Waste Management in 1971 and remains a close counselor to this day.

In going to the market, they were not a moment too soon. Others had gotten there first, and while Waste Management was in the throes of preparing its initial public offering, one of them, Browning Ferris Industries (BFI), knocked on the front door. BFI had gone public in 1968 and although its founders had little lineage in the waste business, they looked ahead to goals similar to Buntrock and the Huizengas': to build a nationwide waste services company through internal growth and acquisitions. They had made a substantial splash, and when they approached the not- yet-public Waste Management first in the fall of 1970 and then again in the spring of 1971, they had been busy on the acquisitions path for more than a year. They wanted for their stable the companies that the Huizengas and Buntrock had built and reorganized as Waste Management, Inc. It was an intelligent wish, and had it worked, it might have saved them many competitive headaches in the future. They thought they had a deal worked out, and Buntrock (who would have become an executive vice chairman of BFI) was almost convinced.

But Wayne Huizenga, who had also been interested, now demurred, arguing that Waste Management could do just the same thing, perhaps better. So why do it for somebody else? Peter Huizenga and Wayne got the razzle-dazzle day at BFI headquarters on the top floor of the Fannin Bank Building in Houston (which the BFI brass shared, via a convenient connecting door, with a fancy private dining club). They looked down on the lineup of the officers' brand new Lincoln Continentals, and were later ferried by helicopter to the airport. The style was a little different from Spinning Wheel Road. But style wasn't substance, and Buntrock, who saw it as probably the right business decision, also hated the thought of losing the chance to do it alone.

The next morning, with Wayne increasingly negative, Buntrock took responsibility for calling it off. He also got Wayne's commitment to do it themselves. It was not easy for Buntrock, who was seeing increasingly clearly the sort of company Waste Management would have to become if it did not go with BFI. In the course of the courtship he had learned greatly from Lou Waters at BFI, and BFI's perception of the opportunities did much to raise his own sights. Buntrock had had in mind building perhaps a $100 million company. BFI was talking about $1 billion. Could he lead such a company?

About the dubious advantages of joining up with anybody else, their instincts proved as correct as Buntrock's doubts about himself proved incorrect. They were better off by themselves, and

Buntrock was the man to lead them. Emmons had seen lots of promising deals, based on bringing companies together, fall apart because it was never quite clear who was in charge. When he met Buntrock, he never had any doubts. Neither did the Huizengas, or anyone else. For his part, Buntrock understood that being in charge meant being responsible for the future of the business and the people who depended upon it. At the moment when BFI came knocking, it meant keeping the team playing together toward the same goal. Most especially, it meant keeping Dean and Wayne together. The public offering went forward.

On June 17, 1971, the Chicago Corporation served as managing underwriter of an offering of 320,000 shares of Waste Management, Inc. The price was $16 per share. Timing was important, and in this case they got it just right. The market had been high in the late 1960s; it tightened down in 1970 and then opened up again in 1971. Had they not been ready, or had they for any reason hesitated, by 1973 the door would have slammed shut again. The offering raised approximately $4 million, which seemed a great deal of money at the time. The proceeds went principally toward retiring equipment debt and buying yet more hardware.

They certainly needed the cash, but even more they needed the credibility that only a publicly traded stock could give them. With it, they firmed up their bank lines of credit, and themselves set out on the acquisitions trail with shares of measurable value in their pocket. It would be hard to overestimate the importance of this asset to the early growth of Waste Management. As the company doubled, tripled, and quadrupled on an annual basis, there were a lot of shares moving around.

At the end of 1971, Waste Management, Inc. had annual revenues of just under $17 million and a net income of $1.3 million. The numbers represented service to some fourteen thousand industrial and commercial customers, and forty thousand private households, in six states. During 1972, the company grew internally and through acquisitions to revenues of $82 million and net income of $5.7 million, and their reach extended to sixty thousand commercial and industrial accounts and 600,000 households in nineteen states and the province of Ontario. In the first nine months of 1972, 133 other firms were gathered into the fold. Those companies brought revenues over $38 million, and for them Waste Management issued 1,888,011 shares of common stock.

By the end of the year several other acquisitions called forth another 448,501 shares. The company put candidates for acquisition to a rigorous financial and operations analysis, and while the list looks long, it is important to remember that with some ten thousand private entities in the business, they had a long list to choose from (granted even that BFI had sometimes gotten there first). Within many desirable market areas, some excellent solid waste companies were ripe for acquisition. They could afford to be selective and considered only firms of above-average profitability and growth potential. Larger operations generally continued under the management of the former owners assuming they demonstrated a capacity of running expanded operations within a larger geographic territory. Smaller firms might remain under the original owner or be folded into a larger Waste Management company in their area.

With very few exceptions, the company's acquisitions were made on a stock for stock basis and were accounted as poolings of interest. Pooling, in which an acquired company is accounted as if it had always been part of the parent firm, had eluded McClenahan's SSI effort (indeed not many knew about it then), and it was key to the success of Waste Management's early acquisitions campaign. Pooling worked best, was most attractive to both sides of the transaction, when the stock market gave the shares premium value.

In 1971 and 1972, that was just what it did. All the shares issued for acquisitions were registered with the Securities and Exchange Commission and could be sold by their holders in the market, although the company generally secured an agreement that those who received Waste Management shares not sell publicly more than 20 percent of their holdings on a cumulative basis during any year following their acquisition. Such was their precaution against driving the price down. A second major stock offering of 1.25 million shares in June 1972 raised additional equity capital of $25 million, but as with the initial public offering, the proceeds went to retire debt and finance equipment and disposal sites, and not for acquisitions. There, the token of value were pieces of paper designated "Common Shares in Waste Management, Inc."

That the company succeeded so strikingly in using its stock to spur its growth was due to the stock's high multiple, to the young company's dramatic financial performance and the persuasiveness of its acquisitions team, and to the financial needs of many independent, often family held, waste companies. To join forces with a corporation financed in the public markets and with the resources to grow was an opportunity to participate in the national expansion of the industry. It meant the ability at last to get out from under years of personal financial guarantees and to increase estate liquidity. With pleasant surprise, they discovered the worth, to someone else, of the businesses they had spent lifetimes building. Personal standards of living rose nicely overnight.

Accepting stock in a new company was, of course, risky. But behind the risk lay an entirely other order of value. Share appreciation was the key. With a stock trading at a multiple of up to forty times its earnings, the attractions to the seller of an independent garbage company were enormous. Not everyone understood it right away, or was prepared to believe it, so different was the prospect from what they were used to: owning a private company with no traded stock, where the chance for growth was limited to the growth in the net worth of the operation.

By the early 1970s, Buntrock had spent fifteen years in the business, and he understood the anxieties of the people involved. He liked these independent-minded men, and he understood the straightforward work they did. Nor did he need just their companies. He needed them, if Waste Management were not to manage its sprawling operations with some centralized bureaucracy that he knew would never work.

When the company acquired a garbage company, it was not just buying trucks and holes in the ground. It was investing in people. As much as that sounds the cliché, attentiveness toward these former owners turned owner-managers revealed the truth behind it. Buntrock and the others took great care both in what they were doing, and in how they described it. "Buying-out" and "selling-out" were not their idiom. Rather, they thought and spoke, and urged those on the other side of a transaction to think and speak, in terms of "merging," "joining," "becoming a part of," "putting your company in with ours." It set a tone, and it had results. Probably 80 percent of the men whose companies they acquired successfully "stayed on" and learned, along with Buntrock, the Huizengas, and the rest, new ways of work.

The fourth company to "come into" Waste Management in 1972 was Tom Tibstra's Southwest Towns Refuse Disposal Service, Inc. Tibstra was partners with Larry Beck in Atlas Disposal and already involved through the CID landfill, but this transaction (all stock) confirmed him as a comfortably well-off man. Tibstra was typical of much of the industry: he had a high school education, had started life humbly (as a laundryman), and had built his trash business on suburban growth after the war. He knew the basic business as few others did, and he carried it all around in his head and most of his company's money in a checkbook (to the despair of Don Flynn, who believed that money uninvested was money wasted). He stayed on and managed operations in Illinois and Indiana for three years until retirement. Larry Beck himself had never owned any sort of stock before he got his Waste Management shares. Perhaps because of this, he never lost a certain closeness for the characters whose companies were the building blocks of a young Waste Management. The owners whom they needed to persuade demanded two types of credibility. They had to be made to understand, objectively, the opportunity inherent in the stock. They also had to be made to believe, subjectively, that the people offering it were worthy folk, solid characters, good men, who would carry on a "legacy."

Beck and Buntrock once sat at a kitchen table telling their story to an anxious widow in a housedress. The job was more one for gentle men than investment bankers: "My grandfather had this, and my father and my husband. What will they think if I sell?" It was like letting go the family farm. One night during the summer of 1972, Beck and Carl Hansen sat up into the wee hours under a catalpa tree in Hansen's backyard in suburban Skokie, Illinois. Hansen, like Beck a Dane, had a refuse company that his father had had before him. There were tears in his eyes. He wanted to "come in"—and he didn't want to.

Four days after Christmas, Carl Hansen Disposal Services, Inc. became part of Waste Management, Inc., the 107th company to join up that year.

6

Critical Mass

IN 1965, Congress passed and President Lyndon Johnson signed the Solid Waste Disposal Act, the first federal solid waste management law. It authorized the Department of Health, Education and Welfare (HEW) and the Department of the Interior to administer grant funding to public and private agencies for the purposes of research, training projects, surveys, and demonstrations including construction of facilities in the field of solid waste management. (There was a limitation that the government would pay no more than two-thirds of the cost of any construction under the act.) The appropriations were not huge, but not niggardly, either. Over the initial four-year life of the law, the HEW appropriation ran up from $7 million to $20 million per year, the Interior portion from $3 million to $12.5 million.

The act has been amended and renewed many times. From it has flowed a torrent of other legislation and regulation, reflecting our society's anxieties about pollution and the finite capacity of the earth to absorb waste. It foreshadowed the new world of regulation that changed the waste business beyond measure, and that goes far to account for the growth and prosperity of the industry today.

Watch the Words

Yet the vocabulary of the law has about it an unmistakably archaic feel. In the early 1960s, cleaning up the "waste problem" was as yet not an emotion-packed "cause," as civil rights then was a cause. Rather it was simply something that made good sense, and the lawmakers addressed it in an idiom that was well established and solidly mainstream. The logic went like this. America is rich and populous and growing more so. A vigorous industrial economy had brought about living standards that were the envy of the world. In the process, urban and metropolitan areas were filling up and spilling over. New construction boomed. Highways stretched in every direction. A consequence of this "off with the old, on with the new" quality of American life was (in the words of the act) "a rising tide of scrap, discarded and waste materials." This was only natural and, it then seemed, easily within the competence of the nation's know-how to handle. "Crisis" did not yet stir the air.

The problem as posed in 1965 would have been equally familiar to advocates of improved urban sanitation in the middle of the nineteenth century, and to promoters of national parks in the era of Teddy Roosevelt: "Inefficient and improper methods of disposal of solids wastes result in scenic blights, create serious hazards to the public health, including pollution of air and water resources, accident hazards, and increase in rodent and insect vectors of disease, have an adverse effect on land values, create public nuisances, [and] otherwise interfere with community life and development."

None of this came as a surprise. This was what happened when urban-industrial societies grew rich. But that very same wealth gave societies confidence that answers were within ready reach. That growth and (as we would call it today) greenery were not quite compatible had as yet few gainsayers. Waste was viewed as a serious problem because, if left unattended, it would threaten growth. The antigrowth agenda of some segments of the modern environmental movement had yet to be written. Indeed, not once in the National Solid Waste Act of 1965 does the word "environment" appear.

Obviously, our culture has traversed some considerable ground since. One of the keys to understanding the success of Waste Management, Inc. is that Dean Buntrock sensed ahead of time how great would be the extent of that journey. In the first annual report of the public company Waste Management, Inc., for the year 1971, the word "environment" *does* appear. The "movement" that surged out of the 1960s to save the environment, Buntrock told his shareholders, was both the context for the company's birth and (if he managed it right) the engine for its growth. What once had been understood as the means to an end—garbage-free streets, safe water supplies, improved public health—was becoming an end in itself. "Cleanliness" was no longer enough. "Environmental protection," the idea that supplanted it, assumed another order of value altogether—and it imposed vastly more complex demands on those who made the environment their business. Anticipating and meeting those demands was the goal that Buntrock set for himself and his company.

Just a year before Waste Management's initial public offering, environmentalists orchestrated the first "Earth Day" on April 22, 1970. The date became a kind of calendar totem whose observance quickly extended well beyond the counterculture. Waste Management employees have observed the occasion ever since. The environment also quickly became a good cause for politicians, as the legislation that year alone bears witness. The Resource Recovery Act amended the Solid Waste Disposal Act and required the federal government to issue waste disposal guidelines. The Clean Air

Act established federal authority to fight urban smog and airborne toxins; new regulations led many incinerators (including Incinerator, Inc.) to shut down. In 1970, Congress also created the United State Environmental Protection Agency, whose initials, "EPA" (and those of many state-based imitators), quickly entered the national vernacular. With passage a year later in Oregon ("the chlorophyll commonwealth") of the nation's first bottle bill, the green revolution could fairly be said to be off and running.

Fad or Forever?

What was to some a cause or, much in the spirit of those days, a "movement," was to others a necessary and respectable business. The Dean Buntrock and Wayne Huizenga who peered out from that first annual report were down-to-earth businessmen who knew much about the basics. They were also just making their debut into the world of publicly held companies. They stepped out with remarkable confidence, best attributed to clear vision and hard work. They told a story of a great beginning and left no room for doubt that it was just that—a beginning.

In those earliest years, the company stuck close to the basic business as the predecessor companies had known it, only now on a much grander scale. The scale in turn called for changes in operating techniques that themselves made the business different. In the first year after going public, they extended operations from the parent group to include twenty subsidiaries and operating companies serving markets in Illinois, Florida, Indiana, Ohio, Minnesota, and Wisconsin. Several smaller companies were folded into existing entities. This was a great deal by past standards, but in a market as enormous as the United States, it also measured how far they had to go to become a truly national presence. Within three or four years, they had gone remarkably far.

As they grew, their conception of operating the solid waste business remained anchored in a few functional categories. These stages of service defined the company to its customers. How well it provided them determined its success in the marketplace.

Storage came first and was perhaps the most visible phase of the process. To assure proper waste storage prior to collection for its then-14,000 commercial and industrial accounts, the company in 1971 provided and maintained 13,000 containers ranging in capacity from 1 to 44 cubic yards. (For a time, they manufactured their own containers at a Wisconsin subsidiary, Steel Systems and Service.) They provided specially designed stationary compactors (large steel bins equipped with powerful hydraulic rams) to increase the payload of collection trucks. Some of the Florida companies experimented and had some success with converting storage of residential wastes from the traditional garbage cans to special plastic bags, whose cost to the customer included the cost of collection. This had the signal advantage of directly tying collection costs to the volume of trash a household chose to set out and was an early example of how the "polluter pays" principle could be put into action.

For the next stage, collection, the young company then operated two hundred trucks—from 16-cubic yard rear-loading compactors, to 30-cubic yard front-loaders, to 44-cubic yard roll-off containerized units. Collection occupied men as much as machines: the major portion of the company's workforce was engaged in picking up the trash, even as managers streamlined routes without reducing service. Search for similar efficiencies marked the stage they then called "interim processing"—then the fastest-growing part of the business and the one in which waste, to one degree or another, changed form before final disposal. Transfer stations provided the bulk of interim processing. Two in Milwaukee were converted from abandoned municipal incinerators. In Hallendale and Delray Beach, Florida, waste was compacted before being loaded onto larger vehicles for economical transport to distant landfills. At its waste reduction center in Pompano Beach, Florida, the company pulverized waste to a shredded, odor-free material that made for easier compacting at the landfill.

The same facility was also equipped for experimental recovery of uncontaminated paper and cardboard, ferrous metals, and aluminum for recycling.

The final operations phase was disposal, represented that first year by the company's seventeen sanitary landfills, located in Illinois, Florida, Minnesota, Ohio, and Wisconsin. From the very beginning, "dump" was a banned word at Waste Management— banned for the intelligent reason that the distinction between a dump and a landfill was real and growing. Whereas "the dump" conjured up the old "out of sight, out of mind" attitudes toward waste removal, a sanitary landfill was the creation of more complex considerations. Over the years, many of these would be spelled out explicitly in the regulations, but even as they were described twenty years ago, the contrast with "the dump" was striking. To be considered a sanitary landfill, a disposal site had to have certain geological and hydrological characteristics to minimize the prospect of water pollution, directly or through leaching. Excavation could not be haphazard. "Dumping" had to be governed by a continuous process of spreading, compacting, and covering at intervals of a day or less. The site always had to be operated in preparation for its ultimate use for other purposes.

Gone Shopping

The company, Waste Management, which these operations defined, was both one company and many: one parent and, by the end of 1974, several score subsidiaries. This growth had happened fast, but hardly haphazardly. It was guided by Buntrock and Huizenga and a small circle they knew and trusted. John Melk was a year older than Huizenga and five years younger than Buntrock and had gotten to know them while selling heavy truck equipment to the solid waste industry for the Heil Company during the 1960s. They had rubbed shoulders often at meetings of the NSWMA and the Detachable Container Association, where Buntrock and Huizenga were, even then, building a reputation as leaders in the industry. Melk was impressed by their long-term, "Where do we go from here?" attitude that set them apart from most other operators, on the eve of the industry's consolidation.

As national and then international sales manager for Heil, Melk knew the business far and wide, and appreciated its limitations under the old regime. He also knew just how much all the fancy new hardware cost, and he sensed something of the potential of the business if it were soundly financed and vigorously led. When, shortly before the initial public offering in 1971, Buntrock and Huizenga approached him about doing market development and heading up an acquisitions campaign, Melk did not hesitate. That fall, he took up his position to search out new business opportunities and assist in developing maximum potential within existing markets. He had no acquisitions background beyond what he had learned getting an undergraduate business degree at Marquette University, but, like nearly everyone else in those days at Waste, he learned fast, on the job.

The very first acquisitions were companies Buntrock and Huizenga knew well from their personal experience in the business, the lion's share in Illinois: Dump-All Disposal Service; Elgin Disposal; Southwest Towns Refuse Disposal; Clearing Disposal. Others had to be identified more methodically. Determining what was out there to be bought and what companies were a good idea to buy became a team effort, and countless miles were put on chartered jets in the first two years by Huizenga, Melk, Flynn, Beck, Rooney, and a few others, as they combed the market. Equally hard to measure were the fatigue and the exhilaration of the effort that went into this first thrust toward building a national company. With the whole country to consider, they used everything—from their personal acquaintance with many owners and operators, to the local yellow pages—to identify good candidates for acquisition. Who should it be in Louisville, Kansas City, Los Angeles?

Beginning in earnest late in 1971, they analyzed perhaps 150 markets, with a few exceptions the big metropolitan ones first. They plugged in the names they already knew and rooted around for the ones they didn't, and they worked at it seven days a week. They perfected their pitch: "Here's what we're doing. We're going to take the restrictions off you for growth. This is a growth business. You've been running yours real well, and we'd like you to join our company. We need you as the management and together we're going to do something big. *And*, we're going to provide you with the vehicle to finance your growth."

Access to the public capital market was a significant inducement for capital-strapped small operators: "Well, gee, I could buy the landfill that I have always wanted but knew I could never afford, and I could buy hundreds of containers and thirty trucks. I could put in a new fleet. I could hire . . ." When that went through a man's mind, the team from Waste Management likely had a sale.

Buntrock's reputation alone established the operational bona fides of the young company and set it apart from its competitors, which was helpful in attracting only those people who cared about the business as much as they did. They learned how to sell themselves. At the same time, they learned to tread lightly on another man's pride, and to respect the relations that a man had built over the years doing business in his community. At first, no one from Oak Brook ever told a man to change the name of his company—or the color of his trucks. Or at least they were careful how they phrased it. "We went kind of slow," Larry Beck recalled. "We said, you don't have to change your name, you don't have to change the color of your trucks, but if you do want to change your name, then here's the name we'd like for you to use. And if you're going to change the color of your trucks, then here's the color we'd like to see."

It was Melk's job also to convince prospects that the Waste Management team was a sophisticated one that knew how to get an acquisition done. He brought in help—Dave Blomberg, Dave Quarterson—for the review process. If it looked promising, an operating group followed on the heels of Melk's team to examine routes, eyeball equipment and disposal sites, talk with the help, ride the trucks.

Larry Beck and Phil Rooney rode a lot of trucks that never even bore the Waste Management logo. In that frenzied atmosphere, with many little companies wakening to the possibility of being bought up for handsome sums, they had to be careful. Flynn and a few of his helpers combed through numbers that were not always models of the best accounting practice. Buntrock masterminded the big picture that everything was to fit into. They all met Monday nights to see what the week had wrought. They weighed the operations and financial reports, considered the characters of the men who might soon become one of them, and decided what to buy and what to pay for it. If a deal was to be made, they used Arthur Andersen to help with the audits, and outside attorneys from Bell, Boyd & Lloyd (who had become counsel for the company shortly after the first public offering in 1971) for the legal work. They rolled up their sleeves, ordered in Cokes with ham and cheese, and stayed late.

Buntrock's vision of what they were building combined superbly with Huizenga's instinct for what was and wasn't a good deal in the building of it. This was a crucial stage, when the company had to acquire the critical mass that would enable it to compete across many markets and prove that private enterprise was up to the job of tackling the country's solid waste problems. Huizenga's endless energy and deal-making nature assured that this would happen. Divorced and with two children living with him in Florida, Huizenga did not want to move to Chicago. So he commuted: Sunday nights north to Oak Brook, Friday nights south to Ft. Lauderdale for a little time with the kids. When he remarried in April 1972, he combined his family with his new wife's and came north for two years. But Florida had gotten to him, and soon he was a long-distance commuter again.

Tuesday, This Must Be Cleveland

Moving around suited Wayne Huizenga. At least, there was hardly ever a time during those years when he was still. Immediately after his wedding, Huizenga was on the road for thirty-five days without a break. (He sent his laundry home.) In 1972, when Waste Management brought over one hundred companies into the fold, he seldom saw home. It wasn't always easy to keep track of what was going on, either. He and Melk or Beck or Rooney, sometimes with Bell, Boyd & Lloyd lawyer Jack McCarthy or John Bitner in tow, would start early, fly to Cleveland for a meeting, then be off to Cincinnati to stroke anxious attorneys whose clients hadn't quite made up their minds, and end up that night in Boston. From Shane Disposal in Washington, D.C., to Benton Disposal in Toledo and Cleveland Maintenance in Cleveland—to Springfield, Massachusetts, Kokomo, Indiana, Detroit, Philadelphia, New Orleans, Atlanta, Toronto, Honolulu—on and on they trekked. They put a bench-like seat into the company Lear jet and caught a nap whenever they could. Almost never could they make the sale in one visit alone.

The figure of speech, lots of deals "were cooking" all at once, might well have been especially created for this situation. The words were Huizenga's, and as much as anybody he knew the difference between the merely "cooking" and the "done" dish. They might sign three or four letters of intent in a single day and still have to go around again, two weeks or three months later, tucking-up. Because the Waste Management stock that was the currency for nearly all of the acquisitions was on shelf registration with the Securities and Exchange Commission, and because the high volume and value of the acquisitions necessitated frequent restating of the acquirer's financials, they could not simply buy Viking Scavenger Service or Gerbitz Rubbish Removal on Monday, and then close the deal on Tuesday. Closings tended to be grouped, and during the interim lots of things could happen. A nervous owner of the family firm could get cold feet: the "Gee, Wayne, I'm just not sure anymore" routine. Or the competition (for Waste Management was not alone out there)—a Browning Ferris or a Service Corporation of America—could slip in behind them and try to sweeten the deal. These were exciting days, and it paid to keep alert.

Despite the feeding-frenzy atmosphere of those times, never could it be said of Waste Management that it was just doing deals to do deals. Those men knew too much about the operations end of the business not to be very respectful of fundamental questions of value. As much art as science, pricing an acquisition was critical to their success If they paid too much and an acquisition failed to perform to expectations, earnings and share value would slide. They developed formulas relating the value of the equipment, the real estate, and the good will, and (if they were in fact competing against a Browning Ferris) a premium might be added. But not always. Sometimes, the comforting knowledge that "these Waste guys are really just garbagemen like us, but BFI's an investment banker and some accountants" enabled Huizenga and Buntrock to snatch away a deal for the same, or even a lower, price: "Listen, Wayne, I've been talking to BFI, and they've made me one heck of an offer. But if you can match it, I'd sure rather go with you guys."

Heritage had value too: the company could trace its origins to the time when Harm Huizenga hitched up his first team on the West Side back in 1894. Buntrock referred to this longevity in his very first letter to shareholders in 1971, describing the initial public offering of that June as "the single most important event in the company's 78-year history." A bit of a stretch perhaps, since Waste Management, Inc. was in substance and in spirit very much his new creation, but the allusion had its uses. So did the fact that Waste Management, alone among the larger publicly traded solid waste companies, from the start had had as its sole business the collection and disposal of solid waste. It suggested a grasp of the fundamental business that struck a sympathetic chord across a range of observers, from other "garbagemen" hoping to be acquired to financial analysts judging new stocks for their clients.

Waste Management was new to the game, and it took them a while to learn how best to use the upside potential of their stock to full advantage. Browning Ferris was then the bigger company; it made even more acquisitions, and it was willing to pay more for them. Both companies' stocks were trading at extraordinary multiples. Both were buying other companies priced at ten- to twenty-times earnings, with their own stock priced at fifty- or sixty-times earnings. At Browning Ferris, Huizenga noted, this led to the attitude that "if some guy wants an extra million bucks, well who cares? It's sixty-times earnings, so what's the difference?" Among the more cautious Waste Management team, there was a clear difference. They looked at their fifty-multiple stock, and they looked at it as dollars. They believed they were worth fifty, and it made them hesitant always to belly-up and pay the price.

Inevitably, they lost some deals it would have been nice to have. The wisdom of their desire to get the best company possible in a new market, and not just another company, became apparent later in leaner times, in the ways they operated their acquisitions. Everybody was out there acquiring in 1972 and 1973 when the stock market so royally blessed everybody's shares. Not everybody settled down to the tough work of making those companies lean and efficient. When the young, publicly held waste firms emerged from the recession that humbled their stocks in 1973 and 1974, the consequences of this difference soon became apparent. From then on, Waste Management predictably outperformed the competition.

In the earliest days, Buntrock and Huizenga shared the thought (it was never much more explicit than that) that as the new company came together, Beck would look after the North, Rooney the South, and Huizenga Florida. Events, specifically the pace of acquisitions, soon rendered that notion obsolete. Shortly after Huizenga moved to Oak Brook in 1972, they were confronted with the possibility of extending their reach farther and faster than either had planned (had there been a plan, which there wasn't).

They talked with Marshall Rabins, who with Buntrock had helped establish the NSWMA in the early 1960s. His company, Universal By-Products, Inc. of Sun Valley, California, was no ordinary small family garbage business. It was the first publicly held waste company anywhere. It was not small, with revenues of $6.6 million (1971). It provided solid waste management services to customers in big growing cities: Phoenix, San Diego, and metropolitan Los Angeles. And it had a huge landfill. In addition, it had established a strong position in the recovery and brokerage of waste paper and corrugated stocks. More than once, Huizenga and Buntrock sat around Buntrock's kitchen table on Saturday mornings wrestling with the prospect of buying Rabins' company. Then, with a deal from Browning Ferris close in the offing, Rabins tried once more: these were men he knew and liked, men who knew his business like he did. Huizenga recalls Buntrock taking the phone call, turning to him, and saying: "Boy, we've got to have a look at this thing."

The value of the Universal By-Products acquisition reached beyond the numbers. Overnight, Waste Management found itself with a market presence in one of the fastest-growing regions in America. Overnight, plain for everyone to see, its scope was more national than regional. What remained to be seen was how fast they would occupy the spaces in between. In retrospect, it was a move with enormous long-term significance, the sort whose attainment might well have been the feature of a well-wrought, five-year strategic plan. But there was no five-year plan and wouldn't be for a number of years to come. It was just as well, and only added to the inside joke when Buntrock humored analysts by telling them that the company had completed its five-year plan— the first year!

But Could You Believe It?

The Lear jet was never on the ground for long. The stock market (Waste Management was listed on the New York Stock Exchange in the fall of 1973 under the symbol "WMX") propelled it. As long as the shares enjoyed a high multiple, they had to use them. Those shares made a lot of garbagemen wealthy. They also made

Waste Management, whose business was the not-so-nice-business of picking up what everyone else pitched out, into a somewhat glamorous company. It was not, of course, the first time that a young company had grown in this manner. Other businesses, like the big proprietary hospital chains that had appeared almost at the same time, performed similar prodigies of growth in markets ripe for change.

Depending on the hand at the throttle, such speed suggests either great skill or great foolhardiness. And the truth (in the case of Waste Management, it was great skill), when viewed from the outside at that time, was not necessarily easy to discern. It depended on one's perspective. If one were an analyst who took the position in 1972 that an overheated stock market was due for a tumble, and were consequently looking for sell ideas, the extremely high multiples of the solid waste stocks might well throw them into that (for the company) unenviable category. Nor did one have to be supercautious by nature to wonder generally about the way the industry was being formed, with a few young companies charging around the country making hundreds of acquisitions with unproven, high-multiple stock—or, as affectionately known in some quarters of the securities industry, "Chinese money." Was there real growth behind all the consolidation hoopla? Were there adequate internal controls being established within these young companies to enable them actually to manage all those acquisitions? Was there excessive debt tied to the prime, which, should it rise substantially, would cripple a key financing mechanism?

In 1972, one young analyst who had such doubts put them into a sell report and laid it before executives of each of the three largest publicly traded companies in the industry. The spirit of their responses revealed much about them. Service Corporation of America seethed with expletive-laced hostility. Browning Ferris never returned phone calls. Waste Management's Buntrock called back the very next day to deal with the problem.

"You know, Ms. Hahn [the analyst was Kay Hahn, then of A. G. Becker], we've never had to deal with a sell report on our company, and we don't know exactly how to deal with it now."

"Well, Mr. Buntrock, making investment decisions is what we do, and your business is running a waste company. We have found that, to a great extent, the way management deals with the bad news of a sell report is a good indication of the quality of that management."

How Buntrock dealt with it was characteristically straight on. He and Hahn sat down together and went over the fundamentals of the report, of the industry, and of the company. He did not change her mind right away, but he proved to her that Waste Management had something that the competition did not have. It understood fundamentals, and no matter how dizzying the multiple on its stock, he and its other managers kept those fundamentals squarely in front of them. Soon, in fact, the stock market did crash, the solid waste stocks along with it (Waste Management fell to below five), and the magic of the multiples for a time disappeared.

It could be a tricky business for other reasons, too. At the same time that the stock market went into a tailspin, the young company became the subject of a Securities and Exchange Commission investigation prompted by allegations by the disgruntled former owner of a firm acquired by Waste Management in Kansas City, of market manipulation. The regulators investigated the company's acquisitions agreements up and down for anything that was inherently manipulative: how were sellers who took Waste stock for their companies tied up? How weren't they tied up? How and when were they permitted to sell their shares? The investigation consumed fourteen months and untold SEC man-hours. They reviewed the company's records, interviewed and deposed many of the former owners of the then-approximately one hundred operating companies that made up Waste Management, and examined the company's accounting practices, particularly those involving poolings of interest in connection with acquisitions.

They uncovered no violation of the law, although they did ask the company to examine its political contributions. Two instances of impropriety came to light. The general manager of a division in Florida had made political contributions between 1972 and 1974, totalling less than $40,000, from an off-the-books cash fund. The company notified the SEC and established new controls on the handling of cash, plus a new corporate policy governing political contributions. (It prohibited cash contributions, established approval levels for contributions by check, and laid out procedures for the uniform accounting treatment of all contributions.) The SEC also alleged an improperly accounted political contribution of $35,000 by a Canadian subsidiary, to the Progressive Conservative Party of Ontario. No impropriety aside from accounting treatment was alleged, and the Royal Commission that investigated the donation for Canada absolved the company of any wrongdoing. To conclude the entire matter, the company voluntarily entered into a consent decree enjoining it from using corporate funds for unlawful political contributions, from violating the reporting requirements of the Securities and Exchange Act of 1934, and from maintaining off-the-books funds. The problem did not recur.

The SEC episode dovetailed with the decline of the stock market and the loss of the premium multiple that had fueled the first acquisition drive. For a time, acquisitions ceased, and analysts shied from the company as long as the federal regulators were busy burrowing. Access to the public capital markets dried up. Both conditions were temporary, and both helped make apparent, as much to the hard-nosed observer as to the insider, that the real magic was in the work.

Down to Business

It may have been a blessing. At least it was a breather. A crash, rather like a hanging, focuses the mind. With the crash, acquisition activity effectively ceased, and minds and hands turned to the business of setting in order everything that the past two years had brought under the tent. It was not that Buntrock, Huizenga, and company had not focused on these things from the very start, but their close attention to everyday operations enabled them to continue to grow despite the downturn. During the recession, they refined procedures and controls, so that when good times and new opportunities returned, they were better prepared than the competition to take full advantage of them.

After a company was acquired, a deal finally closed, the job of integration began. Because of the speed at which they were moving, it was absolutely essential to retain the local management. Making those managers comfortable with new arrangements, and gently educating and motivating them to new ways, entailed yet again endless cultivation out there in the field. More even than the deal itself, this took art, not science, and it wasn't something you did from a desk in Oak Brook. Much of it fell to Larry Beck, the experienced driver of trucks and bulldozers to whom being on-the-job meant being out-of-doors, to Phil Rooney who, still in his twenties, was a quick study about everything, and to Don Price who first had worked for Stan Ruminski at Acme in Milwaukee and then for Rooney as they barnstormed the country evaluating the operations of companies up for acquisition.

The acquisition process—the merging of companies, the pooling of interest—changed, for the companies acquired, the whole context of management. Understanding what this really meant, in terms of operations and expectations, was sometimes difficult for operators with strong habits of independence. Now there was a new boss with a certain meticulousness about results. Whereas some companies were used to looking at results quarterly, or annually with the tax statement, as part of Waste Management they looked monthly and at a new set of statements. The business quickly changed from a cash-flow business to a financial statement business with accrual accounting, depreciation, annual budgets. Some of the new men previously had managed their companies, quite simply, by "feel." "Feel" would no longer do. Without a process in place, a man loses track. In an industry growing as fast as this one, losing track could be fatal.

Rooney, on the road, showed these men how to look at their

numbers, and how to read what the numbers said about their operation. He helped them grow into the process. If the statements of a new company said a man wasn't making any money, he faced hard questions whose answers required hard work.

"How," Rooney asked, "are you going to make money? What is a reasonable expectation? When was the last time you raised prices? When did you do your route audits?"

"Route audit?"

"Yeh, a route audit: the only way you know if a truck is making money. You've got to ride the routes, take a stopwatch . . ."

Or: "Do you give the truck a brake job now, or don't you? You can't know the answer unless you see the whole picture, know where you're at, and the big picture is made up of lots of little pictures."

They looked at things with a microscope. A man might want to buy ten new containers, but a close look at how he used the ones he already had revealed that one hadn't been moved in six weeks. Calls were made to the customer to see if he really needed it anymore. (It wasn't uncommon, especially at construction sites, simply to forget about them and move on.) If he didn't, then the company needed nine not ten. If he hadn't increased his prices, they looked at that: raise the rates a few cents and a man might get the same revenue from eight containers that he once got from nine.

People adapted at different rates. Not everyone, with a fresh million or two in his pocket from the acquisition, was eager to get to work at 6:00 A.M.: "Now those guys on the trucks, well, they can work harder, but my brother-in-law and my brother aren't going to work harder; me, I'm not so sure . . ."

It wasn't easy work. Rooney and Beck and Huizenga gave people a lot of time, which was something else that distinguished Waste Management from its competition. They worked through the operations of each acquisition, one-by-one, again and again. They did not go away. It was an artful balancing act. For even as they imposed new disciplines, they looked on these men as new partners—men with stock in the same company that they themselves were banking on. That could of course lead to awkward moments. After the market crash of 1973–74, Rooney and company found themselves greeted with some long faces among the owner/managers who had sold their companies for big numbers, kept the stock, and suddenly found themselves holding a stack of badly depreciated paper that said "Waste Management, Inc." on it. It didn't help either that Rooney looked even younger than he actually was, which was a lot younger than many of the veterans he was sent to instruct.

"But, hey, wait a minute! The company's doing fine," the irascible Huizenga got used to saying. "Things'll come back; we're still making money."

And indeed they were. It was a credit to the character both of the individuals from Oak Brook, and of those who had been acquired and were learning to adjust, that there were very few defections even during that bad time. Gradually, comfort rose. But it was a comfort with each other, and is not to be confused with complacency with any one set of results. People got used to other people talking with them every month about where the progress was, or the lack of it. If they hadn't done it this month, they needed a good reason and a plan for doing it next month or next quarter or whenever. Rooney established the discipline of monthly and quarterly operating reviews ("MORs" and "QORs," as they quickly became known in company argot) and of annual budgets that defined the rules, but it also established a certain deliberative tone almost from the beginning. While financial results were the bedrock of the review format, the reviews provided a structured, formalized way to look at the business. What were the key decisions, the key acquisitions, the key market opportunities, the status of the landfill development, the status of the municipal hauling contract? Because of this discipline, there could be no lack of understanding about where a man stood and of how he was expected to get to where he needed to be. "Blocking and tackling," Rooney described it then, and it has not changed much since.

But no column of numbers or piece of paper told the complete story about anyone, and Rooney remained a staunch believer in the importance of making the visits and observing people in their own settings: the locker rooms, the maintenance garages, the truck yards, the managers' offices. He once discovered a manager who kept two pet rattlesnakes in a fish tank behind his desk; the idiosyncrasy had not shown up on the financials, and it did not continue. Far more often, he met men of remarkable responsibility and expertise; many became his friends.

New Know-How

As fast as companies came in, a framework and support structure took shape around them. Buntrock, his ear forever tuned to change within and without, oversaw it. If one simply stood back and counted the number of legal transactions entailed by all those acquisitions, it wouldn't take long to see the need for high-performance legal talent to match. In the first two years, this was supplied from the outside by Bell Boyd & Lloyd attorneys Jack McCarthy, John Bitner, Curt Everett, John Blew, and others, and the relations with that distinguished century-old Chicago firm has remained strong every since. In 1973, however, Buntrock hired a young lawyer from St. Paul to work on the inside. In Steve Bergerson, he found both youthful energy fit for the challenges of the moment, and a legal mind fit to master the challenges of a fast-changing business where the laws were still being written and opportunity for creativity abounded.

As general counsel, Bergerson came to oversee a daunting volume of legal work and assembled a team of high-performance attorneys equivalent to the talent found in the very best law firms in the country. He did so because the business demanded it. The swirl of legal activity surrounding the acquisition campaign alone, and the need to maintain constantly up-to-date shelf registration statements for the SEC, kept Bergerson and lawyers like Frank Krohn and Dick Houpt working (just like Buntrock, Huizenga, and everybody else) countless nights and weekends. An era of breathtaking change in regulatory law related to waste and the environment was then just beginning, which made "keeping-up" and keeping ahead tougher than in most other lines of work. And then there was the fact, increasingly apparent in the 1980s, that no business (unless perhaps health-care) was more litigious than waste management.

Good as most of the operating companies were at running trucks, hauling trash, and keeping customers happy, few had much technical expertise. Some didn't even know they needed it. These were largely men who had built successful businesses by doing what their fathers had done before them, in a field where training was something gained on the truck and where formal education was not a highly valued credential. Buntrock sensed that there was a hole here which, if left unfilled, was big enough for all the new national waste companies to disappear into. It had important consequences for his particular company.

He was joined in this insight by Harold Gershowitz, whom he had brought into the company as president in 1972 (snatched from off the doorstep of Browning Ferris who had wanted him for their man in Washington). No two men in the industry could have been better situated to foresee the increasing technical demands that rapid growth and intensifying regulation would soon place upon their business. From his perch as executive director of NSWMA in Washington, D.C., Gershowitz had watched the birth of the environmental movement as it manifested itself in public policy at the federal and state levels. Buntrock, who had envisioned a huge potential market for waste services, also understood that developing technologies would be key to dealing both with ever-larger volumes of waste and with ever-greater sensitivity about how it was handled.

With the many garbage companies that made up the early Waste Management, the company acquired many talented people and useful skills. Not many scientists and engineers, however, were among them. Buntrock's early attention to this lack illustrates that Waste Management from the beginning equaled much more than the sum of its acquisitions, and hinted at how different the company was destined to be in kind, not just in size, from the waste businesses of the past. Buntrock knew his new company's weakness as well as its strength and, in late 1972, with Gershowitz set out to redress the former.

They went directly to someone he and Gershowitz knew, a man who like themselves had spotted the trend but had taken advantage of it from a different angle. Peter Vardy was trained in geological engineering at the University of Nevada, and his early career had overlapped with the tail end of the uranium boom. By the 1960s, he had found something more lasting. He became involved with the below-ground design of the Mountain View Regional Park project near San Francisco, a then–path-breaking plan to situate golf courses and other recreational facilities entirely atop municipal waste from the city of San Francisco. It was one of the first large-scale efforts to use waste as foundation material for a sophisticated end-use purpose.

This experience led Vardy to establish the first, exclusively waste-engineering consulting firm in the country. He did so with the reasonable expectancy that it was a good field to be in, his homework having revealed that the money being spent then on waste collection and disposal was exceeded only by the sums going to defense, highways, and education. His firm, EMCON & Associates, opened its doors in San Jose in 1971 and over the next two years was involved in the design of some 120 landfills across the country, more by far than any other engineering group.

Waste Management was not alone in its search for technical know-how. All of the newly forming waste companies found their way to EMCON's doorstep, but it was Buntrock and Gershowitz who appealed to Vardy: "They were the ones I felt confident of, both of their understanding of the waste situation in America, and of their ability as businessmen."

Late in 1972, they flew to San Jose, where Buntrock bluntly asked what it would take to get Vardy to move to Chicago and work for Waste Management. He responded that what Buntrock really needed more than any one individual was a total capability such as Vardy's company represented. Talks then ensued about acquiring the company. Vardy was happy in the situation he already had and not especially eager to forsake Palo Alto for Oak Brook. But Buntrock's vision of an immense, largely untapped market, where technological innovation and profitability were destined to go hand in hand, and Gershowitz's persuasiveness, did it. The deal (again, for stock) that made EMCON & Associates another Waste Management subsidiary closed at the end of March 1973. It provided that EMCON would function as engineering consultant to the parent company, and that Vardy would indeed move east and take up the new post of vice president for Environmental Management and Technical Services.

The title was their collective invention, the phrase "environmental management" not yet the commonplace it would become. The job required some invention as well, and Vardy's role evolved as the company grew and grew more environmentally sophisticated. In the first years, when the laws and regulations were not yet a jungle, and when the company still was in the process of being fashioned, the new group of engineers, chemists, architects, and technicians learned their way into the operational heart of the company. There they had to win the confidence of the older-school, dig-and-bury garbagemen, while guiding them to higher levels of environmental consciousness and performance. In 1973, the company operated fifty-three sanitary landfills whose monitoring and upgrading were Environmental Management's responsibility. They helped the operating companies with permitting and in dealing with regulators. They learned to respond quickly to calls from the field, whatever the problem. Vardy became close to many of these men, so different by experience and temperament from himself, and on that trust grew a spirit of environmental responsibility that matched the company's growing environmental capability.

Environmental concerns also began to spur development of opportunity on the outside even as it reformed operations on the inside. Passage of the first Clean Water Act in 1972, which began to address the discharge of pollutants into the nation's waterways, moved the company to sign licensing agreements with Chem-Trol Pollution Services, Inc., a New York firm, and acquire patents and technologies for the design of liquid waste processing facilities. In the fall of 1972, the air pollution standards that took effect in the city of Chicago created the opportunity for the company to convert the city's Medill Avenue incinerator into a transfer station from which it would move 750 tons of garbage a day to sanitary landfills.

Vardy's technical group also developed a research and analytical laboratory at the CID landfill complex in southeast Chicago, where they explored processes for dealing with liquid wastes, and guided a pilot project to test the potential for generating pipeline-quality methane gas from decomposing solid waste. At the Greene Valley Forest Preserve in suburban DuPage County, Illinois, the company reprised Vardy's experience in California in turning a filled-up landfill to other uses, with plans to create, atop the county's solid waste, premium outdoor recreational space that included the highest ski hill in the Chicago area.

Nine hundred miles to the south, in New Orleans, a fresh-to-the-job Harold Gershowitz negotiated, and the company was awarded, a contract to build and operate a solid waste disposal system intended to demonstrate an environmentally and economically sound approach to the recovery, sale, and reuse of secondary materials from the municipal waste stream. Called "Recovery I," the project was the single largest undertaking of the company up to that time, and combined, for those days, advanced reclamation technology with prearranged markets for the recovered materials. A joint undertaking with the City of New Orleans and the National Center for Resource Recovery, it represented a bold, ahead-of-its-time experiment in recycling.

Getting Control

As the young company spread across the country (by 1973, it had operations in thirty-two states and the District of Columbia), Buntrock broke down its management into seven operating regions. These were to be the framework relating the company's ninety-five operating divisions to corporate management. Executive Vice President of Operations Phil Rooney and Senior Vice President Larry Beck kept all the operating pieces tucked in, and saw that the door of top management was always open—and seen to be open—to those on the front lines. To give support to the people in the field who, day-to-day, did the company's basic business, was a theme that Buntrock never ceased to drill into everyone at the corporate level. Financial management, legal services, corporate development, environmental engineering all existed to get that job done, and get it done better.

The new skills needed to meet that responsibility were reflected in the creation of a management services group, under the direction of Thomas R. Frank, a physicist by training and a risk manager by trade. Frank's experts in risk control and insurance, safety and maintenance, sales and pricing fanned out every week to far-flung operating companies, packing in their kit sophisticated new services. They might assist in preparing bids to municipal or industrial customers, help implement a preventive maintenance program, or negotiate insurance premiums previously paid by local divisions. Labor relations fell to David C. Coleman, a friend of Peter Huizenga from law school at the University of Illinois in the 1960s, with a specialty in labor law. John Melk's corporate development office targeted new acquisition opportunities, new municipal service contracts and franchises, and new landfill sites.

The initial rapid growth of the company through acquisitions depended on decentralized day-to-day operational responsibility. But the numbers that measured that growth were managed with stern centralized procedures. This was Don Flynn's doing, and it was applied from the early 1970s. Flynn's approach was unusual, and as the company boomed in subsequent years, it proved of incalculable value.

As Flynn set it up, the financial organization operated independently of the operating organization, in this sense. At the operating level, every general manager, or regional manager, or division manager worked with a financial counterpart—but one who reported to him only through a "dotted line" relationship. The financial person's "straight-line" relationship ran directly through to the central controller's office in Oak Brook. This organizational tool assured independence in the numbers and enhanced budgetary discipline. It also required a very special sort of financial person to make the marriage work: one who was half-operational and half-financial, both by skill and by temperament.

Early on (before it was common generally), Buntrock invested in mainframe computer capacity, far beyond the company's immediate needs, but that enabled it confidently to control the mountains of financial information its operations generated. With it, Flynn implemented a centralized financial information system in all operating divisions. By the fifteenth of each month, corporate management had available the detailed performance of each individual profit center, which compared monthly and year-to-date operating results with budgeted objectives and the numbers from the previous month. He pulled billing, payroll, and accounts payable into the central system, and also applied it in the area of cash management to improve the burgeoning flow of funds throughout the company.

By the middle of the 1970s, the financial performance of the young public company was a portrait of promising success and impressed even the coldest-eyed analysts. The achievement was the more notable, given the rugged economic climate of those years: record-high inflation, wage-and-price controls, a stock market crash and serious recession, the first energy crisis. Waste Management's revenues grew from $76 million in 1971 to $158 million by the end of 1974, its net income from $4.4 million to $9.3 million, its earnings per share of common stock from $.55 to $.93. It paid out no dividends, prudently retaining its earnings for use in the business.

The company's growth had been made possible by the surge of acquisitions, but not excessively, as analyst Hahn once had worried. Slightly less than half of the revenue growth between 1972 and 1973 (when the stock multiple was at its peak) represented the effect of the new companies brought into the fold, in consideration for which the parent had parceled out 4.8 million shares of common stock and $19 million in cash and notes. Slightly more than half of the revenue growth represented internal growth resulting from expanded service to existing customers, new customers, new projects such as landfill sites and transfer stations, and price increases. Operating margins steadily improved.

They stuck to the basic foundation of their business and kept the focus on operations. Waste collection and storage services accounted for approximately 80 percent of the company's total revenues, transfer and disposal services for approximately 20 percent. In 1973 and 1974, approximately 5 percent of the company's revenues came from reselling waste paper and fibrous materials and from the processing and disposal of liquid wastes. The company owned thirty-two sanitary landfills and leased twenty-one others in sixteen states and the province of Ontario. Four thousand employees did the company's work and depended upon it: 2,600 in collection and disposal activities, 1,100 in sales and clerical posts. Two hundred and sixty were managers.

A Matter of Value

All of those managers, and some of the others, were also owners—holders of Waste Management common stock (and sometimes of options to buy more). They were part of the approximately 3,475 stockholders of record early in 1975, some of whom had acquired their stock in the process of bringing their companies into Waste Management. The market, of course, treated them all alike, and in these first years it treated them all capriciously. By early 1973, shares had risen to thirty-two, and a sky-high price/earnings multiple convinced many a prospect for acquisition to trade their companies for speculative paper.

By the end of 1974 after the market crash, the stock hit bottom at 4³/₈, and more than a few disgruntled folk wondered just what it was they had done. Waste Management was not alone, of course, though that was cold comfort at the time; its two biggest agglomerate competitors, Browning-Ferris and SCA, suffered as much or more at the hands of Wall Street. But it is important to remember that the dramatic rise of 1971-72 occurred within the framework of a rising market generally, a circumstance that coincided with the waste industry's first great phase of expansion and consolidation, when out of necessity it handled increasing amounts of waste in more and more sophisticated ways. Later, as the economic environment in general deteriorated, pressure on earnings mounted. This occurred within the context of a falling stock market. Buntrock told his shareholders, simply, that "1974 was a difficult year" beset by "unusual pressures." Considering the national economic downturn—the highest inflation rate since 1946, all-time high commercial lending rates, and a soft equity market—he spoke with restraint.

He also spoke with quiet confidence that the business of waste management, and of Waste Management, Inc. especially, could not rest on sounder footing. The impressively consistent earnings sustained by Waste Management through the worst of the recession was witness to this. Projections pointing toward ever-larger quantities of waste to be disposed of, and budding regulations aiming to protect the quality of the environment from that waste—after air- and water-pollution, "the Third Pollution"—foretold rosy futures for well-run waste companies.

And Buntrock's Waste Management had gotten off to a well-run start if ever there was one. To sustain and build upon it in a future filled inevitably with surprise, was his next challenge. "The first third of this decade [the 1970s]," he wrote in 1974, "can be viewed as the dawning of a new national commitment to more sophisticated environmental management of our nation's wastes. The balance of this decade should, indeed, see this commitment crystallized into new and exciting levels of service by the solid waste management industry."

But to make something "crystallize" requires controlled conditions—in chemistry, a saturated solution and a catalyst. Even a dull observer could not fail to sense, as the 1970s rolled on, the country's rising anxiety over the issue of pollution and the beginning of its transformation into the global cause of environmentalism. It took a very sharp observer, however, to judge how to lay a young company across the path of this powerful cultural trend and there create an industry of enormous value.

Harold Gershowitz posed the big-picture question, retrospectively, to the company's shareholders in May 1975. "Is this company and this industry for real . . . ? Does it provide a service the demand for which will really endure into a long and uncertain future . . . ? How will it fare during difficult times as compared to the very large, tried, and true business institutions that have been on the scene for so much longer a period of time?" That question, he said, had been uppermost in many minds (especially in the investment community) four years before when Waste Management had stepped out as a publicly owned company. The final answer still lay years away, but in the tough times then passing, the company did not just tread water: "We have come through the stress of the past two years in an incredibly strong position," Gershowitz said, his desire to get on with the future almost palpable. He was then thirty-seven, like Wayne Huizenga. Don Flynn was thirty-five. Phil Rooney was thirty. Dean Buntrock was forty-three.

That future depended on their own exertions, but also on their ability to set in place others who could carry on as demands grew. Looking ahead, perhaps the most striking example of this would be with men like Bill Hulligan, Jerry Girsch, Jim Koenig, and Herb Getz, who in the 1980s reprised much of the 1970s' performance. Hulligan, whose family had built up a substantial hauling and disposal company in Cleveland and who knew the operating side of the solid waste business as few others anywhere in the country, came to Waste Management in 1979. He would become vice president of Waste Management of North America in 1984, president in 1988, and with the much-enlarged company's reorganization into four regional groups in 1992, president of Waste Management of North America-East. Girsch, who came in 1976, and Koenig, who came in 1977, were CPAs from Arthur Andersen in Chicago. Girsch became vice president and controller of Waste Management of North America in 1981, principal accounting officer in 1988, and with the 1992 reorganization, president of Waste Management of North America-Midwest. Koenig first served as Chief Financial Officer Don Flynn's assistant, became vice president and treasurer in 1986, and CFO himself in 1989. Getz, a young lawyer at Bell Boyd & Lloyd until 1983, became secretary in 1985, assistant general counsel in 1988, and vice president in 1990, and general counsel in 1992, following Steve Bergerson's move to senior vice president for law and compliance.

As the company grew and changed, it did so on the substantial talents of men such as these. The pace of acquisition in the 1980s, for example, was as great as in the early 1970s. But with Wayne Huizenga and John Melk gone off to other enterprises, it was Hulligan and Girsch who were ready and able to analyze opportunities and seize them, with an ever-greater sophistication learned from the company's previous experience. Hundreds of firms around the country were folded into the company's North American solid waste operations, along with those owner-operators who shared Waste Management's enterpreneurial, growth-oriented spirit. Some, as in the early seventies, were small family-owned and -named operations still typical of the garbage business: Hatter & Walker Trash Service (Indiana), Bushrod Disposal Service (Virginia), Rulo Hauling (Missouri), Bill's Sanitation (California). Some monikers still evoked the basic character of the business with descriptive precision: Rubbish Gobbler, Inc. (Florida), Pick-Up, Inc. (Illinois), Affordable Disposal Company (Texas), Dependable Rubbish Removal (New Hampshire). Others were themselves large companies whose acquisition was complex and which helped vault Waste Management boldly into new markets: the Warner Company (New Jersey and Pennsylvania), Empire Waste and Oakland Scavenger (California), Bayside Waste

Hauling and Transfer (Pacific Northwest), and largest of all, SCA Services (nationwide).

To enter new markets in non-major metropolitan areas, Buntrock would devise a strategy called Waste Management Partners, Inc. in 1983, which established joint-ventures with aggressive growth-oriented hauling companies. Partners, as it became known, was designed to appeal to entrepreneurial operators who might not wish to sell their companies outright (Waste Management acquired only the customer accounts from a local hauler who retained 100 percent ownership of his operating company for the ten-year term of the joint venture) but who liked the idea of an affiliation with a major national operation. The structure of the program provided another vehicle for Waste Management to participate in new markets through local entrepreneurs who would continue to build their businesses to the point where they could be effectively brought into Waste Management proper.

Melding such diversity into one organization—harnassing the talent of energetic entrepreneurs and focusing their efforts on corporate goals—fell over the years to a cadre of men who knew the operations side of the waste business from the ground up and who understood the imperatives of building growth, market by market, customer by customer. Jim DeBoer, Rich Evenhouse, Bill Katzmann, Bill Reichert, Joe Jack, Tom Blackman, Jerry Kruszka—while they all carried the large title of regional vice president, were all very much front-line sorts of fellows. Add in the complementary talents on the corporate staff of men like Dave Coleman, Tom Frank, John Slocum, Ron Jericho, Ed Bacom in human resources, risk management, finance and systems, plus the company's controller organization (by 1976 the company employed over seventy-five CPAs with one controller for every general manager) and the result was a managerial line-up distinguished beyond the young age of the company.

In the 1970s, all that experience was just beginning to build. What they then lacked in experience they made up for with energy. They thought of themselves, even then, with just a little time together, as a "can do" team. In 1974, they changed the company logo, from a heavy-set straight up-and-down affair to the one that endures today and that seemed more in step with the spirit of a progressive company going somewhere fast. One of the joys of their young business was that the opportunities to "do" were just beginning to be explored: they were present at the discovery, and everything lay before them. Well, almost. "Free Snow Removal" . . . "We Cater Weddings" was what the signs said on the shiny red garbage trucks belonging to Southern Sanitation Services in the City of Plantation, Florida, "A Waste Management Company." (The phrases came directly from Wayne Huizenga, who thought it a good way to lighten things up.)

Maybe not quite that. But soon, on the other side of the world, this young team surprised itself and a lot of others with something just about as unlikely, and that was no joke.

7

Cleaning the Kingdom

The King's Wish

Before he died, King Faisal, second son of Adbul Aziz Ibn Sa'ud, the founder of modern Saudi Arabia, wanted to pray in the al Aqsa Mosque in Jerusalem. The consequences of Faisal's wish created the conditions for Waste Management's first foreign adventure. Only slightly simplified, those consequences might read something like this.

Because Faisal would not go to Jerusalem as long as it was the capital of Israel, he agreed to finance Egypt's surprise attack on Israeli-occupied Sinai in October 1973. Ten days later, the Israelis had counterattacked, had entrenched on the western, Cairo-side of the Suez Canal, and had begun to approach the suburbs of Damascus. At this point, Soviet Premier Leonid Breshnev commenced an airlift of fresh military hardware to his embattled Arab clients. In response, American President Richard Nixon (embroiled in Watergate and desperate for domestic support, Jewish support included) and his newly appointed secretary of state, Henry Kissinger, started a massive reinforcement of Israel.

Infuriated that his old American friends had not bothered to inform him of their intentions, King Faisal declared "jihad" (holy war) and embargoed all shipment of Saudi oil to the United States and its allies. In 1973 and 1974 the world's stock markets crashed as they had not done since 1929, and Waste Management's stock crashed along with them. Western economies slumped. The *Financial Times,* normally not easily rattled, declared that "The Future Will Be Subject To Delay."

In the Kingdom of Saudi Arabia, the future did just the opposite. It accelerated. Before the embargo, the Kingdom had enjoyed income of $8-9 billion a year from oil, a sum probably twice what the sparsely populated nation needed to live on. By the middle of the 1970s, the black gold whose price through the 1960s had never exceeded $2 a barrel, rose to over $30. In 1975, oil earned the Saudis $35 billion, which left the Kingdom with a problem that from the West's debt-ridden perspective was, and is, a little hard to imagine. What to do with the money?

Deposited in Western banks, it would just be eaten up by inflation. If it were invested in the West's developed economies whose growth depended on cheap energy from oil, the Saudis would find themselves in the trap of pumping away their only natural resource to protect faraway investments from the opposite danger: recession caused by a shortage of oil. There was only one answer: to develop inside the Kingdom. The mountains of petro-dollars would have to be converted into modern infrastructure, modern industry, modern cities. The secretive desert kingdom cobbled together from warring tribes by Abdul Aziz in the 1920s and early 1930s would have to become a modern nation at last. It set out to do so with a fatter checkbook and a faster timetable than any other nation in history. In the process, opportunities were created for many outside helpers, Waste Management among them.

Faisal was assassinated in his Riyadh palace by a disgruntled nephew in 1975, and he never got to pray in Jerusalem. But he did change the world. As King Kalid and Crown Prince Fahad, his two brothers who succeeded him, soon discovered, he also changed the Kingdom.

The Chairman's Request

"Come on, Jerry: let's go out and have a look at the trucks."

Dean Buntrock had always liked trucks. So had Jerry Rhodes. With an easygoing, "Well sure, Dean," Rhodes, who was director of maintenance for the Waste Management/Saudi Pritchard Joint Venture for the Municipal Cleansing of Riyadh, Saudi Arabia, led his chairman out to the garage and the truck yard. There, they inspected the load-luggers, roll-offs, rear-loaders, street sweepers—two American Midwesterners (Buntrock from South Dakota, Rhodes from Oklahoma) in the middle of a Middle Eastern desert, a long way from home.

It was the autumn of 1979, and it was a good bit farther away from home for Rhodes, who had been living in Arabia since 1977, than for Buntrock, who had just flown in from Oak Brook and would soon fly out again. And it was home, not trucks, that the chairman wanted to talk about with his maintenance man.

"Jerry, I know your two years are just about up and that's what you committed to. But we haven't been able to find anybody else we're really comfortable with to take your place. So I want to ask you if you'd stay on another year."

Rhodes and his family ached for America. The romance of living in a far-away exotic land had long since worn off. It was not that Rhodes was not happy as a clam in his work, with his trucks and sweepers, but he had been happy in California before they had left (and where they had a nice house and the five horses that the company had moved around the country for him, from Oklahoma to Oak Brook and then out West). His oldest daughter was off in high school in England (there was no schooling in Riyadh for expatriates past the eighth grade). There had been sickness and death of relatives back home. He had done his time and done a good job. It was time for the Rhodeses to wind it up and say good-bye to the Kingdom. But that was not what he said to Buntrock.

"Well sure, Dean, if that's what you think we need to do. Sure, I'll stay another year."

Jerry Rhodes understood loyalty. Dean Buntrock commanded it. He had, of course, sweetened the pot: Rhodes had earned an added consideration, and Buntrock believed in paying high performers what they were worth. Waste Management was roaring along impressively at home; the Riyadh project was turning out very well. The two things were not unconnected.

Buntrock probably knew ahead of time what Rhodes's response would be, and Rhodes gave his answer right then and there among the trucks, without hesitation. Still, when he went home and told his wife about "what Dean wants us to do," there were some long faces at the Rhodes house that night. "Saudi" (as the Riyadh cleansing project came to be called) was "hardship duty," and some took to it better than others and not just because of the pay. Buntrock had decided back in 1975 when first he heard about it, that Saudi would be a good thing for the young company to attempt, and if Dean Buntrock decided it was a good thing for Jerry Rhodes to stick it out another year, well that was OK by Jerry Rhodes.

The difficulty that Buntrock felt in asking, and the loyalty that Rhodes displayed in answering, are explained by the previous three-years' experience of many Waste Management people in the Kingdom. Before 1975, none of them had ever been there. Most of them, on learning that they might go there, had to check with Rand-McNally to see just where the place was. Where it was was significant for several reasons, for both the Kingdom and the company that set out to clean it.

God's Will

To this day, no one in the West ever would have worried much about where Saudi Arabia was, but for an accident of geology. Two hundred million years ago, when the warm seas receded from what is today the Arabian peninsula, and the earth's crust crumpled to bury the rich organic leavings thousands of feet below the surface of the ground, the result was the richest oil-bearing rock in the world. "Arab-D," as this porous limestone is known to petroleum geologists, is found only beneath the east coast of Saudi Arabia and is the foundation, literally and figuratively, of the Kingdom. For decades, the House of Sa'ud, its chief beneficiaries, never knew the oil was there and until the 1950s could not, if they had known, have done much with it, anyway. It was only the conjunction of the postwar world's growing appetite for energy, and the Saudi's natural endowment of Arab-D, that has made the House of Sa'ud today one of the world's most powerful families, and their inhospitable desert kingdom a linchpin of Western prosperity worth a war to defend.

During the discussions between the author and Waste Management in the winter of 1991 about the writing of this book, chairman Dean Buntrock had other things on his mind. To-ing and fro-ing to the Kingdom and embattled Kuwait, he was preparing the way for the most recent of his company's "mobilizations" in the Middle East—to clean up after Saddam Hussein's untidy legions had been pushed back into Iraq. Although Buntrock had never before posed grimly before the smoldering shells of enemy tanks, he knew the region well. Many Arabs knew him and the reputation of his company, too. Their knowledge went back fifteen years to the time when Jerry Rhodes and other Waste Management men had lived in Riyadh and wrestled with its trash, and when Buntrock had bet the growth of his young company on their performance in a strange land afloat on Arab-D.

From Kuwait in 1991 back to Riyadh in 1975 stretches an era of immense change in the Arab world, and nowhere has that change been more radical than in the Kingdom. But for the oil, the land of Saudi Arabia is perhaps the most naturally impoverished on the planet. A very large "but" you will say, but remember this: until thirty or forty years ago, that impoverishment was pervasive. Most Saudis lived lives not much different from Arabs (or Europeans) at the time of Christ or Muhammad. Even after Western companies began to pump out the oil in earnest after World War II, the economic consequences trickled down only slowly. When, in the winter of 1901-02, Abdul Aziz and forty or so loyal followers set off on their epic raid to capture Riyadh from the al Rasheed (in Saudi history, the legend of Robin Hood, Washington crossing the Delaware, the storming of the Bastille all rolled into one), their object was the Mismak fortress, a mud-walled affair in a square of beaten mud surrounded by brown mud villas. Riyadh then was a walled oasis town right out of Bible times. There are photographs of it in the 1930s showing a mud-hut city of flat roofs and minarets and, yes, camels in the marketplace.

Mismak was still there in the 1970s, only at night it was illuminated by the neon signs of an adjacent marketplace, or souq, specializing in watches, Walkmans, and all sorts of electronic consumables. There were a few Western-style tallish buildings, but mostly there was the forest of construction cranes that violated the old flat skyline and foretold the end of the old Kingdom. The development that was the imperative of King Faisal's oil embargo was beginning to happen. Beneath the cranes, oil-rich Riyadh was becoming one vast building site. By 1991, it was all largely built, and it all looked very modern. But when you arrived at the glitzy new international airport, armed guards still rummaged your luggage for alcohol, pornography, and religious literature offensive to Islam. Christmas trees were still deemed blasphemous.

Islam is pervasive to life in the Kingdom as is no faith in the life of the West. The Western traveler or expatriate soon discovers several indicative and indispensable Arab sayings: "Alhamdulillah" (Praise be to God), "Allahu akbar" (God is most great),

"Insh'allah" (As God wills, or By the will of God). The latter especially (but they are really all the same) captures the essence of the Saudis' outlook on history, their place in it, their attitude toward the future. And it captures their attitude toward many of the things of ordinary, everyday life as well. Take garbage. "As God Wills": so it long must have seemed with the piles of garbage that had always fouled the Kingdom's cities. "As God Wills": like prayers five times a day. God willed everything, including presumably the humans (until 1962, some of them still slaves) who scavenged the garbage in the Riyadh municipal dump amid camel carcasses and offal from every abattoir in the city. God willed the shaggy goats that sorted out the edibles amid discarded packing cartons of pipe fittings and TIDE.

But in time, God willed the end of the garbage too. "By the Will of God . . . " began the contract between the Ministry of Municipal and Rural Affairs of the Kingdom of Saudi Arabia and the Waste Management/Saudi Pritchard Joint Venture for the Cleansing of the City of Riyadh. All legal documents in the Kingdom begin grandiosely in the same way. To the practical "get-it-done" types from Waste Management, God probably had less to do with it than patient negotiating, hard work, and good pay. But to their Saudi paymasters, ever mindful of where all the riyals came from, it still came down to God. What was the sole source of their wealth, anyway, but oil? And who had put the oil beneath their desert in the first place, but God?

Mining Business

For members of the first Waste Management survey teams who reached Riyadh in late 1975 and early 1976, two images among many captured the much-remarked Klondike atmosphere of those times. As inexperienced ministries scrambled to lay the pipes, string the wires, and pave the roads of a modernizing city, coordination left much to be desired. One could drive down what seemed a major city thoroughfare and find, in the very middle of it, a telephone pole. The pole may have been there first, but if that was where the road was supposed to run, the quickest answer was just to pave around it: *caveat auriga*. Chances are, the edge of the same road would be lined with the carcasses of discarded (many of them late-model) cars and small trucks. Some were obviously wrecks. The many that were not were symbols of a society trying to assimilate in a few short years habits and technologies that in the West had taken decades if not centuries to develop and comprehend. The abandoned cars signified less the Saudis' carelessness with their property than the fact that cars (and the wherewithal to purchase them) had multiplied much faster than mechanics trained to repair them. If they broke, it was not just easier, it was necessary, to replace them. Such oddities abounded.

Riyadh teemed with foreigners mining for business, all with something to sell the Saudis: hospitals, hotels, housing estates, jet planes, air-defense systems, sewage treatment plants. They packed the only first-class hotel in town, the Intercontinental, others rather less-than-first-class, and many just plain boarding houses. They all learned quickly just one thing: how different it was to do business in the Kingdom. They also learned that everything took time.

For Dean Buntrock, the prospect of joining the throngs in Riyadh first arose early in 1975, when Waste Management was four years old and with revenues of just $159 million. International tenders for goods and services were flying fast and heavy out of the Kingdom where there was limited technical know-how and even less domestic labor to meet the challenge of modernization. Not surprisingly, one of the subjects the Saudis soon addressed was the simple one of cleaning up their capital city, and learning how to keep it that way. With every new construction project, every new utility line, the mess got worse. The place looked and smelled awful. Local contractors working for the city collected refuse (when they collected it) with open trucks (when they had trucks) and dumped it in the desert on the outskirts of town.

But no job in the Kingdom was simple. When the Ministry of

Municipal and Rural Affairs called for bids to establish, from the bottom up, and then to operate for five years a complete department of streets and sanitation for Riyadh (whose population was approximately 750,000, not counting foreign petitioners lining the halls of the Intercontinental and impatiently sipping sweet tea in ministry anterooms all over town), which required hiring, housing, and feeding thousands of workers, it threw down a challenge that cut two ways. Solid waste companies in the United States were still in the process of consolidation, still relatively small and inexperienced in foreign operations. This was a bigger piece of business than any of them had ever digested whole.

The Saudis found that they too were embroiled in things they had never done before—creating vast municipal departments and supervising multimillion dollar contracts with foreign firms. And they were trying to do just about everything all at once. Add to the natural ignorance of novices on both sides the profound differences of culture and language, and the obstacles to happy outcomes would seem to have been enormous.

They were, except for the money. The Saudis had it, and they knew that if they did not plow it quickly back into the Kingdom, they would have been better off leaving the oil locked up in Arab-D. So much cash, in the presence of so much work to be done, opened yet another chapter in the ages-old history of buying and selling. Deals were struck, seldom quickly, but sometimes (as in the case of the deal that brought Waste Management to the Kingdom) exceedingly well.

No one jumped at first, but from the beginning Buntrock had a feel for the possibilities. There were several early intermediaries. Buntrock sent Peter Huizenga and Tom Frank to Minneapolis in March 1975 to talk with Lachlan Reed, a self-styled promoter of Arab-American business relations, and in May met with Bill Fox, president of American Hoist & Derrick Company, who suggested that his firm and Buntrock's consider a joint venture. Buntrock was interested enough to send materials on Waste Management to Riyadh and to request a copy of the Ministry's tender document. What he got back raised his eyebrows, both as to the scale of what was being asked and, if he were to attempt it, the difficulties even of putting together an intelligent bid.

Not uncommonly, as the Saudi government set out to buy modernization from the West, the ministry responsible for cleaning up Riyadh was already working through a Western consultant, which should have made things easier. It didn't. Watson Saudi Arabia was an English engineering firm charged with preparing the original tender documents and then with assisting in the negotiations throughout the bidding process. They had done a mediocre job, and the specifications were poorly drawn. Waste Management's operations people found them lacking in fundamental understanding of the solid waste business; the company's international lawyer, Ed Falkman, and outside counsel at Bell Boyd & Lloyd found them lacking in sophistication about the laws of the Kingdom and the ways such contracts generally were tendered, bid, and awarded.

Saudi Watson's original tender was prepared in the spring of 1975 as the basis for invitation of bids. What ultimately comprised the contract between the Ministry and the Joint Venture was formulated through a frustrating process that stretched out for nearly two years. It cost the company several million dollars and the energies of some of its best people long before there was any assurance that the Joint Venture's bid would in fact be successful. Even after they did learn that they were the preferred bidder, negotiations continued for another six months. The Joint Venture submitted its original proposal in October 1975, a revision the following April, and what it thought was a final tender in July. In the process, many miles had been logged on BOAC and Saudi Air between Chicago, London, and Riyadh. A few things were learned along the way.

Scouts

"In Saudi, there were no pleasant surprises." The observation was Fred Weinert's, the man who later directed construction of the desert cantonment that housed the project's labor force. But the theme characterized the whole adventure from the beginning. Peter Huizenga, Don Flynn, and John Melk made a first reconnaissance. They travelled via Jeddah, on the Red Sea, where 120 degree heat and primitive accommodations prompted a frustrated Flynn to declare unilaterally that they were "getting the next flight out of here—to Riyadh, Paris, I don't care where—or that's the end of the project!" Happily (in the long run) it was to Riyadh. When they came out again, several days later, they shared their judgment that indeed this was something they shouldn't too quickly say no to. Flynn told Buntrock that, yes, the Saudis really did have the money to pay for a first-class job, and Buntrock's instinct told him that the thing was worth stretching for. But he needed to know the local details. Everything depended on how the land or, more precisely, the garbage, lay in Riyadh.

He dispatched three men to tell him. Phil Rooney was by this time a senior vice president and Buntrock's close confidant. Harold Smith, a vice president, had come to the company in 1970 from Ohio with a background in landfills and packer equipment; he had worked for Waste as director of management services and done a lot of trouble-shooting, especially in the company's western divisions. Whit Hudson was a Huizenga in-law.

"Ro called," remembered Smith who was then running things for Waste in Los Angeles. "Get your passport—and you'll need a letter from your minister showing that you're Christian." Rosemarie Nuzzo had been Buntrock's secretary since the days on Spinning Wheel Road and would be the conduit for a lot of cryptic, we-need-you-there-yesterday messages as the Waste men began shipping out for Arabia. These three left in October, lost their baggage, and ended up sharing underwear. (It was Ramadan in the Muslim world, when ordinary trade stopped dead.) There hadn't been time for homework, which probably wouldn't have helped much anyway; none had ever been to the Middle East; none spoke a word of Arabic.

After fourteen hours in the air and a short nap in London, they were met at Riyadh's shambling airport by Sammy Yegen, a small-statured Syrian who reminded them of Peter Lorre and was Pritchard's (Waste's British partner) man on the scene. Yegen hustled them off to the Intercontinental and served as interpreter, not that they had much time for chatting up the locals. If the company were to try for the job, it had to enter a bid by October 20, and Buntrock needed an evaluation fast. In five days they could eyeball it at best. And that wasn't very good.

They found themselves in the midst of a densely packed, utterly foreign environment and with no perspective to judge it by. They never saw much more than downtown and something of the north side, and what they did see was hard to evaluate. About all they could get were some hunches. Walking the marketplaces, or souqs, they were struck not just by the masses of people but by their relatively orderly demeanor. True: there was trash everywhere, much of it from construction. But some of it, Smith observed, seemed to be strewn fairly deliberately, almost as if in windrows, in the narrow walled passages that separated one small souq from another. It was as if a man had shoved the stuff out but with some sort of care not to shove it too far toward his neighbor, who shoved his out, just so far, in the other direction. If that were so, Smith thought, then what Riyadh really had was a storage problem: "If we could just get these people to put it in cans, then there shouldn't be any insurmountable reason why we can't come through and collect it more or less like we do back home." Well, maybe.

Rooney and Smith found the whole thing fascinating, if more than a little bewildering. They perceived it primarily as a challenge in collection, hauling, and disposal, things they knew a great deal about. When they left town, however, they still did not know what the dimensions of this challenge really were. How big, really, was Riyadh? What areas, really, did the Saudis want cleaned? What, really, did the Saudis mean by "clean?" How much garbage lurked in those souqs, mud huts, and villas—really?

With heads crammed full of impressions, if not figures, they left the Kingdom. There was no time to go home, lay it all out, and submit carefully measured recommendations to their bosses. Buntrock and Wayne Huizenga were already airborne heading for the Kingdom, bid-in-briefcase, prepared to meet the deadline. Paths crossed in London, where they all met briefly in a departure lounge at Heathrow Airport.

"Well?" Buntrock wasted no words. "Should we bid?"

Whit Hudson, who had not taken well to the Middle East and whose journey to Riyadh that October was his first and his last, said they should have nothing to do with it. More convincingly, Rooney and Smith said they should, definitely. That was enough for Buntrock. With a simple, "We're going," he and Huizenga promptly took flight for the Kingdom to put Waste Management in the running.

Buntrock probably knew how fuzzy everything still was, but he had to trust to something and make a decision. "Saudi," as the Riyadh project came to be known in company lore, was destined to be an adventure where confidence grew in small increments. Rooney and Smith's legwork gave him a bit more than he had had when he left Oak Brook a few hours before, and he was grateful.

"Take a couple days off; you've earned it," he told them as they parted.

Sensing it might be their last opportunity for quite some time, they flew off to Dublin, where Rooney, the Irish boy from Cicero, thought he might have a look around for his roots.

Name That Street

The bid that Buntrock and Huizenga hand-carried to Riyadh in October 1975 was written to meet the specifications of the tender as originally put together by Saudi Watson. Between those specifications and the situation as it actually existed in Riyadh yawned an information gap that was filled in only by the labors of scores of Waste Management personnel, on dozens of trips to the Kingdom, all undertaken very much "on spec."

In mid-November, Ron Baker, who worked as an operations manager in Holland and Grand Rapids, Michigan, got his call from Ro. He spent the next day at the federal building in downtown Chicago (he had never had a passport before), and secured his minister's written testimony that he was a Gentile. Smith had picked him for the first operational analysis team that was about to head out to Riyadh. Everyone knew they were bidding blindfolded and that they had to get some reliable facts and figures, fast. It was one thing to decide, on the basis of a seat-of-the-pants judgment, if they should tackle this thing. It was quite another to determine how they would tackle it if they finally got the chance. Smith's team and those that followed it had to figure out how.

In addition to Baker, Don Price came as assistant team director, along with his brother Gene and Waste Management Operations Managers Walt Carlson and Duane Western. From London, Pritchard Services sent Martin Rivers, a time-and-motion specialist, and B. Workman, a dispatcher.

"My God, there are another thousand villas over there!" The words were Englishman Martin Rivers', but they could epitomize the whole run of "unpleasant surprises" that Fred Weinert saw Saudi as the sum of.

As Smith's team began to sort it out, they discovered things about life in the East that empire builders before them had wrestled with. One was that their particular corner of the East, Riyadh, for all its oil wealth, was in some ways surprisingly primitive. Saudi Arabia, unique in the Moslem world, had never been ruled by Europeans. While this no doubt was a source of great pride to the Saudis, it had resulted in certain technical deficiencies in their country, even in 1975. In Delhi, Nairobi, or Karachi, letters got delivered along streets that had names. In Riyadh, by the mid-1970s one of the richest (and most expensive) plots of ground on the face of the planet, there were no decent maps.

So, the men from Waste Management drew them. They did it the old-fashioned way: they each took a sector of the city and started walking. They carried sheets of graph paper, and using one sheet for every block (or what passed for a block) they marked every structure and the locations where trash containers should be placed. A grid was superimposed for every 500 square meter area, so that when the grids were put together on the master map, any 500 square meter section in the city could be identified by numerical coordinates along north-south and east-west axes. They pushed small odometer wheels to measure the distances. And they used their eyes and instincts to make a guess about the amount of garbage.

The process had its charms: the small Saudi children nipping at their heels through the souqs and back alleys, begging not for money (as would have been the case anywhere else in the East), but for the chance to treat these hard-working Americans to a candy bar or a cold can of Pepsi. It also had its awkward moments, as when Smith, decked out suspiciously in all his mapping paraphernalia, wandered too close to a military area and found himself greeted by two unsmiling Saudi troopers, submachine guns at the ready.

The maps, when pieced together and redrawn, measured two feet by five, and resembled, in one important aspect, the maps on the walls of countless American police departments. But on the Riyadh map, the melange of little green dots signified not the location of traffic accidents, break-ins, rapes, and robberies, but of trash containers—totems, quite as much as the construction cranes overhead, of modernization in this ancient land. From "Airport" road in the north to the sheep auction lot in the south, there were thousands of them; in the center of the old city, they blurred into a solid mass as settlement itself had done. Squiggly blue lines, none with names, depicted the warren of "mud huts"; longer, straighter lines the thoroughfares of the "western areas." There were few right angles anywhere.

The maps showed the location of Riyadh's sparse large institutions: ministries and military complexes, the power station, the university, a couple of schools, the race track, the zoo. Then those places of obvious interest to Waste Management expatriates: the passport office, the airport, the Saudi/Pritchard villa, the Intercontinental Hotel. Three large sand dunes lowered over the airport road. Splotches of "white-out" correction fluid marked where the map makers changed their minds—where they moved some byway this way or that, or decided it wasn't there after all.

Categories and quantities that filled in this landscape—the numbers of things—were what they needed to come up with: "villas," "stone houses," "mud huts," "shacks," "apartments," "commercial," "industrial," and "special" structures. They put every address in the city into a category, excluding only the royal palaces that were not part of the contract. Some of it, dubbed "western areas" where construction was relatively recent, bore some resemblance to American patterns: villas (free-standing houses) accessible by streets (unnamed) broad enough for a modern waste-collection vehicle to negotiate. Much of it was like nothing they had ever seen before. The standards that they set for all of it were high and explicit.

Apartments, flats, shops, and stores would each be serviced by 1½ cubic yard bins conveniently placed in the immediate vicinity; they would be emptied daily by vehicles operating mainly at night when congestion had thinned out. Villas were to get daily attention from a truck and crew pulling 60-gallon detachable plastic containers on two-wheel carts.

The mud/stone house sector was another matter. The Saudis rendered this section into English as the "popular" areas, by which they meant "populated" areas, and populated they certainly were. The place was already packed with thousands of foreign workers—from Egypt, the subcontinent, the Far East—busy building the new Riyadh that their oil was paying for. Housing was hard to come by and many of these "guests" concentrated in these older, already tight quarters. For this ancient huggermugger cityscape, the Waste surveyors proposed daily service by collectors working on foot and pulling 60-gallon detachable plastic containers, which they would empty into 1½-yard stationary containers at night. Industrial areas were to get larger containers, which could be served mechanically by modern rear-loading equipment.

To determine productivity standards—literally the amount of labor it would take to move the garbage—the team simulated actual work performance. With a reasonable count of how many containers they would need in each zone, and knowledge of where they would be placed, they made certain operating assumptions. This was how they built operations plan back home. Viz.: It took five minutes to dump a box. Twelve boxes could be serviced per hour. A collection vehicle could make one one-hour disposal trip per day. One collector in the villa sections of town could walk 4,005 meters and service approximately one hundred homes per hour. Villas generated 6 gallons of refuse per day.

As for the "popular" mud hut areas, they calculated that a garbageman could walk 1,830 meters per hour and tip the cans of 173 customers. The mud huts, they reported, generated two gallons of refuse per day. The stone houses fell in between the villas and the mud huts. There, a man could be expected to cover 2,500 meters and service 189 establishments each hour.

They applied the same operational due diligence to the street-sweeping function, quantifying it with crisp, engineer's precision. "Main and arterial streets: gang sweeping at ½ mile per hour per three-man crew; three miles per day per three-man crew; six hours of productive labor; containers for sweeping to be placed 250 meters apart on arterial streets. . . . Regular street: one man can sweep a sidewalk ten feet wide at fifty meters per hour; one man can sweep 300 meters per six-hour day; 175 meters of gutter per hour (one meter wide); 1,050 meters of gutter per day."

The resulting operations program described how such manpower would be mobilized. In the areas to be serviced by mechanical collection, the garbage trucks would be manned by a driver and two helpers. Among the mud huts (no-go areas for conventional trucks), a "senior overseer" would deliver collection and sweeping crews to the scene in crew-cab pickups. Crew size was not to exceed two dozen men to a mud hut area; they figured half that many, mechanically assisted, could take care of the villas.

They sited transfer stations throughout the city, many of them small walk-in affairs that in addition to holding trash for transshipment to the landfill, stored the most basic, old-fashioned tools of the trade: carts, brooms, shovels, and rakes. They compiled detailed lists of equipment—truck bodies, sweepers, support vehicles—and observed weather and desert operating conditions in Riyadh in order to fine-tune their recommendations about selection and maintenance. The contract—if they got it—was to run for five years, and preventive maintenance, which would assure the long-term life of their equipment, figured high among the priorities for these operations-oriented managers. The extreme heat of Riyadh summers—120 degrees F. was not uncommon—called for design changes that they hoped would make things last longer, such as the elimination of shutters on radiators, larger radiator capacity, and larger fan blades. Packer bodies from the Leach Company were to incorporate case-hardened and chrome-surfaced hydraulic cylinders to reduce abrasion from blowing sand. And special EMRON paint would be used on all enamel-finished equipment surfaces to provide maximum protection and attractive appearance.

The survey team recommended equipment that would come as close as possible to the "parts-common" principle that is the ideal of managers of big fleets of vehicles. They wanted a standardized fleet to accommodate all facets of the operation and recommended the White Truck with its Road Xpeditor [sic] chassis, which could mount small or large diesel engines depending upon the equipment's application. The actual refuse collection fleet would consist of single-axle Whites powered by V-555, 225 H.P. Cummins diesels. They would mount Leach 17 Packmaster bodies with container-tipping devices that would squeeze the Riyadh's garbage to a four-to-one compaction ratio. Larger units would include tandem dump trucks, tank trucks, and tractors using the same Xpeditor cabs but powered by larger Cummins PT-270 H.P.

engines with SST 6+1 transmissions. The combination, they hoped, would give their fleet good maneuverability within Riyadh's cramped collection areas, as well as long-range power and durability.

Between the time the survey team figured what it should take and when the shiny trucks and the men with brooms actually hit the streets, much changed and changed again. The company treasurer and vice president for administration, Bob Paul, ultimately headed up procurement of the nearly eight hundred pieces of equipment that were sent to the Kingdom, and the trucks ended up coming from International Harvester and the compactor bodies from the Heil Company. But the general considerations outlined in the first surveys—sturdiness, flexibility, ease of operation and repair—prevailed throughout the long procurement and operations planning process. The degree to which the experience of collecting, hauling, and disposing, as these men knew it in America, could be transferred to the Saudi setting was also subject to changing interpretations.

Harold Smith initially imagined that "running Riyadh" wouldn't be much different from running one of Waste Management's region's back home (Smith had come to the project from managing the company's eleven-state western region). In fact, he ventured, Riyadh should actually be easier because it was only eight by ten miles in area (a measurement itself subject to much contested revision), and the zones within it were nice compact little areas. As with any municipal contract, there would be no competition in Riyadh, nor any worry about unions and strikes, thanks to an authoritarian regime that forbade both.

Though not unintelligent, such conjectures proved largely incorrect. Too much, just physically, was different. The efficient operation of Waste Management companies back home depended on simple things that no one gave a second thought to but relied on utterly. In America, streets had names and addresses had numbers, but not in Riyadh. In America, communications with units on the street via telephone or radio had been commonplace for years and were key to controlling the efficient movement of men and machines. In the Kingdom, a security-conscious government permitted no truck radios, and to say the Kingdom's telephone system was rudimentary was to be kind. In the early days of the Saudi mobilization, there was but a single phone line in the company's office in downtown Riyadh; calls to Oak Brook had to be booked sometimes two days in advance. No lines at all reached the desert encampment that housed the workforce and all the equipment. And, of course, no expat had a phone at home.

Waiting

"Saudi" came in stages. The Saudis may have been hurrying to modernize the Kingdom, but Waste Management would have thought no word less apt than "hurry" to describe the process of winning the right to work there. It was one thing to hold a fat tender document in your hands and submit a bid to match. It was another to keep track of what happened to things afterward. John Melk's job was to attempt it, and he assumed straightaway the central role in Saudi that foreshadowed his responsibility in the next half dozen years for the company's subsequent international ventures. In Riyadh, a large team of people eventually would get the job done, but Melk's work—his endless one-to-one dealings with Saudis at the highest level—singled him out. In the beginning, however, the process of winning the Riyadh contract tried even his extensive repertoire of marketing skills.

It was apparent from the start that there would be serious competition, particularly from a French consortium, Plastic Omnium Semat. It was also apparent that the English consulting engineers, Saudi Watson, who had drafted the tender and whom the Saudi ministry relied on to deal with the bidders, were going to be more hindrance than help. By December 1975, Melk sensed favoritism toward the French. It turned out that the mayor of Riyadh, Sheikh Abdullah Al Nuaim, was the brother-in-law of the agent of the French consortium and that Saudi Watson was recommending acceptance of the French "alternate tender" of SR 970 million. Pritchard Joint Venture had actually submitted two bids: a first bid on the tender as it stood, which called for comprehensive cleaning and sanitation services, and a second alternate bid, which limited the specifications to refuse removal and street cleaning and was much nearer to how it actually ended up.

By the end of the month, the mayor had formed a committee, which was moving (for the Kingdom) with unusual rapidity to negotiate with the French—and was poised, in fact, to recommend awarding them the contract. Early in January, Waste's Saudi partner, Prince Abdul Rahman bin Abdul Rahman al Sa'ud, weighed into the action with a strong letter to the governor of Riyadh, to his deputy, and to the mayor, and dispatched personal emissaries to the committee members. It had the desired effect. The governor upbraided the mayor and demanded a delay in the proceedings. The mayor suddenly took sick leave, and his deputy made it plain that both bids would be examined afresh.

But what you heard depended on whom you listened to. The third week in January 1976, the Saudi Watson consultants told Melk that they had been part of "final negotiations" with the mayor's committee and the French, and that as far as they were concerned everything was finished except the formal awarding of the contract. Meanwhile, a son of Crown Prince Fahad surfaced for the first time—representing the French. The Joint Venture flew into a frenzy to convince Prince Abdul Rahman to intervene and get a fair and objective review of their proposal. Waste Management, Inc. protested directly with a letter to Crown Prince Fahad, to the minister of Rural and Municipal Affairs, and to the governor of Riyadh. The deputy mayor dissented from the pro-French recommendation of the mayor's committee, and the Ministry decided to form its own committee to sort things out. By the end of February, Melk was cautiously optimistic that the Joint Venture would have its day in court and that they had a fighting chance of getting, if not the whole contract, then some of it.

The jockeying, the frustrating communications, the to-ing and fro-ing of intermediaries, the drafting and redrafting continued into the summer. As Melk maneuvered to align the bid with what the Saudis seemed to want, the operations planners were driven to distraction, redoing specs for equipment and laying out alternate scenarios for how the work would get done, if they ever got the chance to do it. There were half a dozen operations plans before it was all over, great notebooks-full, the result of thousands of man-hours in Riyadh and Oak Brook, and the expenditure of several millions of dollars. In April 1976, the Joint Venture submitted its second, revised tender, and on July 4 a third and supposedly final one.

Back home, it was the Bicentennial Fourth. In the Kingdom, the date was Ragab 7 in the Islamic year 1396. At the office of Saleh Al Malik, the deputy minister of Municipal and Rural Affairs in Riyadh, a Saudi clerk opened the sealed envelopes containing the bids, one from the Joint Venture, one from the French consortium. In addition to Melk, Phil Rooney and Don Flynn were there for Waste Management. Englishman John Miller represented Pritchard Services. Ibrahim Kamel, an Egyptian consulting engineer retained by the Joint Venture to help navigate Middle Eastern ways of doing business, had come in from Cairo to attend.

The numbers, once the arithmetic had been checked, revealed the Joint Venture bid of SR 853,703,600. It was lower by 10 million than the French, who then offered first to match their competition and then to reduce their own bid by 2.5 million. They offered a final 1.2 million reduction, which put their bid at around 850 million. Whereupon the Joint Venture offered their own discount of 4.9 million, which left them at 849 million (848,803,600), and still the low man. Though the numbers still had to be submitted "to higher authorities," the Joint Venture seemed to have it. In August, they were formally told as much by letter from Majid Ben Abdul Aziz, minister of Municipal and Rural Affairs:

Dear Sirs:

We refer to the subject of Riyadh Refuse and to the meeting which took place in the ministry 7/7/1396 (4/7/76) when you submitted your final offer for execution of the project in sum of SR 848,803,600. We are pleased to inform you that your offer is accepted and that you will be requested to enter into a formal contract with the Ministry. The Contract shall include all of the conditions and specifications in the tender documents together with the approved amendments made before 4/7/76.

After what they had already gone through, it seemed a solid victory. It wasn't.

Counting Flies

Things are seldom as they seem, when they seem it, anywhere in the East. The British, who had long experience there, might have told them as much, but the can-do Americans from Waste Management had to learn it for themselves. Their contract to clean the Kingdom's capital still lay six long months away. Their experience during that time bore a certain resemblance to an old poem:

> Now it is not good for the Christian's health
>   to hustle the Aryan brown,
> For the Christian riles, and the Aryan
>   smiles and he weareth the Christian down;
> And the end of the fight is a tombstone
>   white with the name of the late deceased,
> And the epitaph drear: "a fool lies here,
>   who tried to hustle the East."

Looking back on it, Kipling fit the situation in Riyadh in the mid- and late-1970s to a tee. But the likeness was also apparent to someone there at the time and, as it happened, on Waste Management's behalf. Curt Everett was a securities lawyer from Bell Boyd & Lloyd in Chicago, who had helped orchestrate the company's acquisition campaign in 1972 and 1973 and who had been summoned to Saudi to help negotiate the contract. Kipling spoke from another century, but Everett thought the sentiment apt as ever. The East, and the Saudi corner of it in particular, moved to rhythms and at a pace markedly different from those the Waste Management men were used to. Just how different they learned during the six months between their notification as "the preferred bidder" and the signing of the contract.

The presence of lawyers early in the game was typical of Waste Management. Never, since their earliest acquisitions, had they skimped on legal talent. At almost all their deals, they insisted on business, financial, and legal perspectives. And Buntrock mustered his top men to get this contract: Don Flynn the financial wizard, John Melk the marketers' marketer and paramount figures in these key months, Phil Rooney the operations man who was in charge of the mobilization, and the lawyers from Bell Boyd & Lloyd. It took all their wiles—and patience that none, going into it, knew they possessed—to see the thing through. All of them, like Buntrock, were used to hustling, in the wholesome sense of "what the plan says do tomorrow, let's do today so we can do even more tomorrow . . ." The Saudis did not play that way, at least not until the time came actually to start paying someone else to hustle their garbage off to the landfill. Then, no hustle was enough.

John Blew was the Bell Boyd & Lloyd lawyer who had most helped the Waste team interpret the original tender documents and prepare their bids. He had had previous experience with other clients who had business in the Kingdom, and had traveled there several times. Starting in September 1976, he was again a regular aboard the long flights to London and on to Riyadh. From his perspective, on the outside and the inside at once, it was a daunting task.

The scale alone was greater by far than anything the young company had done before, and much of what the contract required they had had no experience with. They knew about collecting garbage and disposing of it in a landfill, but they had never done it, comprehensively, for a city of perhaps 750,000 for a five-year period. (They had never done any street-cleaning, which the contract also called for.) They knew a great deal about purchasing trucks and other equipment, but they had never had to ship them half way around the world and maintain them in desert conditions with mechanics who spoke no English. They knew nothing at all about recruiting and training thousands of third-country nationals who would serve as the labor force. They knew nothing about large-scale construction projects such as the desert cantonment they would have to build to house and feed those workers. They had no experience working with an English company and a Saudi prince in an international joint-venture.

And they had no experience in a bidding and negotiating process like the one they now found themselves in. On the face of it, the tender document seemed to say that when a company submitted a bid, it submitted the terms under which it was prepared to perform and could not deviate from them; once the bid was accepted, a one-page document would be signed incorporating everything in the bid into the contract. That would have been normal, but it didn't quite work out that way. Nothing was cut-and-dried; competition still lurked in the wings; serious, sometimes very strange, negotiating continued. Blew made seven or eight trips during this period; Rooney and Melk and Flynn took up residence. There were hours-long phone calls with Buntrock in Oak Brook, often in the middle of the night. They constantly discussed questions of business and points of law: whom they should talk to next, how they should approach them, who should make the approach, should it be in writing, should it be orally, how long should they wait.

Between the heavy phone calls home, there were periods when nothing happened at all. "I used to lie in my hotel room (not the

Intercontinental) and count the flies because I had nothing else to do," Blew remembered. Nothing to do? The Saudi's sense of scheduling was casual at best. Melk and Rooney and Flynn might have a meeting with the Ministry—and then not another for four or five days. They could only prepare so much. "We prepared, and prepared, and prepared, and talked through every provision, almost to death. There was no place to go and wasn't a lot you could do. The time lapse used to drive people crazy. If you didn't like to walk through the souqs or get in a car and drive out into the desert, you could go nuts." It would be hard to imagine a setting for which the hard-driving people from Waste Management, a company where you worked and worked and then worked some more, were less suited.

One meeting in particular captured the atmosphere: Melk, Rooney, Flynn, Blew, Ibrahim Kamel, and a translator, in a Ministry conference room with the minister of Municipal and Rural Affairs, his deputy, and four or five other thobe-clad Saudi officials. The Waste people were convinced at this point that some people in the Ministry favored them and others still favored the French (or at least didn't favor the Americans), and members of both camps were present. They began in the morning, the Americans on one side of the long table, the Saudis on the other, except for the minister who sat at the head. After two hours or so, the minister got up and without a word left the room. He did not come back. After a time, one of the deputies got up and left too. As the Waste men carried on with their presentation, it became hard not to notice that the numbers on the Saudi side of the table were dwindling. When the last Saudi drifted away, also saying nothing, a disgusted John Melk turned to the others and said: "Well, I guess that means the meeting's over."

It was, but nobody packed up and went home (or if he did, he soon came back). The crosscurrents and byplays were countless. Saudi Watson, consultants to the Ministry, continued to be unhelpful to the Joint Venture. Kamel Brothers, also consultants to the Joint Venture, raised the hackles of some Saudis because they were Egyptians and there was historic animosity between the two Arab nations. The chemistry between Saleh Hejeliam, the Saudi lawyer retained by the Joint Venture, and Prince Abdul Rahman was less than perfect.

Through that long difficult autumn they were sometimes worried sick that they would lose the whole thing. Fiddling went on into January 1977, the month the contract finally was signed. What made it worth the effort and the patience was the money. The amount—SR 848,803,600, or approximately $242 million—must be seen from two perspectives. For Waste Management, the sum was greater by $63 million than the revenues of the entire company in 1976, and the provision for advance payment of 20 percent, or $48.6 million, represented an enormous cash infusion into a still relatively small company. No single piece of business like this was to be had anywhere back home, or anywhere else for that matter. For the Saudis, it was then a sum smaller by approximately $60 million than the Kingdom's income from oil in a single day.

Ironically, the very difference in relative values may have led to similar behavior on both sides. Buntrock's men bargained long and hard because of the great leap forward it would represent for their company. If anything, the swamp of petro-dollars made the Saudis hard bargainers, too. They knew how fleeting, in the long term, was the source of their wealth—oil—and they understood that the rich man who spends his capital and doesn't get superb value for it will have few rich grandchildren. The Kingdom was also awash with petitioners hoping to channel some of the petro-dollars their way, and not all were as reputable as Buntrock's men. Dave Blomberg, the Joint Venture's first country manager, once observed a recycled Spiro Agnew waiting in line outside Riyadh's only Chinese restaurant. The Ministry may seem to have been impossibly slow, even obstructionist, in its handling of the matter, but if Waste Management had never done this before, neither had the Saudis ever parceled out such cartloads of cash for such sophisticated goods and services. Nothing makes a man comfortable like experience, and at the Riyadh conference tables in 1976 neither side had much to offer. Besides, many Saudis had gone to school in England and read their Kipling too.

Getting On with It

The contract (five volumes, in Arabic and English) was executed at last on January 31, 1977. Dean Buntrock, Peter Pritchard, and Prince Abdul Rahman signed for the Joint Venture, Prince Majid for the Kingdom. Saudi newspapers reported the agreement and ran a photograph of the parties around the table, the portraits of old Faisal, King Kalid, and Crown Prince Fahad looking down. Back in the United States, the *Wall Street Journal* reported the deal. The company's stock moved up. Analyst Kay Hahn took Waste out of her "sell" column once and for all.

"How safe is Bahrain?" Mike Rogan, a young accountant sent to Saudi to develop accounting controls and information systems for the Joint Venture, wanted to know. It was Rogan who collected "the check." Numerous lucite-encased copies of it can be found today in offices at Waste Management headquarters and at Bell Boyd & Lloyd: "SAMA," the Saudi Arabia Monetary Agency pays to the order of the Waste Management/Saudi Pritchard Joint Venture the sum of SR 848,803,600. It was in Arabic and bore only the Islamic date, 11/3/97.

Rogan, on his own, needed to know where best to put $48 million of the company's money. The money ended up at Citibank in Bahrain (a safe place he was assured) drawing 3/4 of a percent, until Buntrock and Flynn arrived a week later to parcel it out for this and that part of the project. The sums were large and getting the right exchange rate was important. Rogan spent many an hour over the next two years, whenever he had a deposit to make, at the offices of the al Rajhi, money changers since before any local currency existed in Arabia, when trading pounds sterling and Indian rupees was good business. "The banks," remembered

Rogan, "always had a way of losing your money for a day or two to get the float, but never al Rajhi." How much he saved the company, sipping tea with a thobe- and sandal-clad Saudi, pushing a calculator back and forth across an old metal desk with piles of currency all around, is lost to the record.

Behind the amiable local customs, risks abounded. For one thing, it was a fixed-price agreement with performance stretched out over a six-year period (twelve months for mobilization, followed by five years of service). There was no provision for price adjustment, which left the Joint Venture bearing the risks of inflation and population growth beyond projections. Contract disputes were to be resolved by a Saudi grievance board whose decisions were final. Termination provisions were distinctly one-sided, with the Ministry free to back out for any reason at all on sixty days notice, the Joint Venture free to terminate only for *force majeure* (which the Saudis interpreted as "physical impossibility" rather than "circumstances beyond one's control"). It could not terminate, for example, even in the event that the Ministry failed to pay. Boundaries were still subject to dispute (which prompted Waste to assign its own bright young attorney, Ed Falkman, to continuing negotiations to try to nail them down). Nor could the joint venture itself, by its very nature, be expected always to run smoothly.

Buntrock understood the risks, going in, and did what he could to hedge them. The Waste Management/Saudi Pritchard Joint Venture was to be governed by a management committee (which functioned more or less as a board of directors), through an operations committee and a managing director. Waste Management controlled a majority of the management committee (Buntrock, Flynn, and Melk; the others were Prince Abdul Rahman and Peter Pritchard), and controlled all pricing decisions and the provision of all materiel.

Melk became managing director. Rooney was director of mobilization. But if the risks kept him up nights, the prospects kept him fresh for the next day. If, like Dean Buntrock, Wayne

Huizenga, and their fellows, one were betting on growth to enhance the company's value, here was the chance to catapult it several big steps ahead. Part of nobody's long-range plan, it would take some improvising and some sacrifice even from people used to hard work and to being always "on call." It would add a new word—"mobilization"—to Waste Management's corporate vocabulary. And it would take a lot of people a long way from home. Very few ever regretted the journey.

"I want to inform you of the two large steamer trunks with contract documents and the excess baggage charge of $485.78, Chicago-Cairo, and 130.15 Egyptian pounds, Cairo-Riyadh, and to tell you that TWA lost an additional box," John Blew wrote to Don Flynn in February 1977. Flynn paid a lot of excess baggage charges over the next several years, for it became an unwritten Waste Management rule that when a man (there were only men, the laws of the Kingdom forbade female workers) set out for Saudi, he never went "unaccompanied." Very likely he would be traveling without his wife and family, but never without company goods: contract documents, spare parts, frozen sirloin steaks from London—they never missed an opportunity.

They could not afford to. They had to figure out everything from scratch, with no model to work from. They tried to sort things out by priority. "Items to be addressed on your next trip," read Melk and Dave Blomberg's instructions as they set off for Riyadh in August 1976. In the "mandatory" column were such as bloc visas, work permits, and drivers licenses for the third- country nationals, and much else just to "check out." "Locate three villas for temporary offices . . . See what food is available locally at prices less than imports (mutton, chicken, rice, fish, vegetables, flour?) and meet with the new Saudi Arabian Government Food Company which has been created to compete with greedy merchants. Observe the current sweeper/refuse collectors employed by the Ministry and make notes concerning their attire— especially as to whether they wear shoes." Before long, the Joint Venture bought a great many pairs of shoes.

A young Kuwaiti patriot proudly displays dual allegiances as he welcomes
the Waste Management crews who were brought in to clean up the mess
left behind by retreating Iraqi forces.

A box-cab Reliable dump truck from the 1920s convinced the Huizengas to give up horses. Dutch immigrants who went into the scavenger business in Chicago in the 1890s, Huizenga & Sons were one of the predecessor companies to Waste Management.

In Buenos Aires, as in all of Waste Management's city cleaning contracts abroad, Dean Buntrock worked alongside the company's top management in planning the complicated mobilizations.

Chairman Dean Buntrock (right) and Vice Chairman Wayne Huizenga in a Waste Management truck was more than a pose. Both men saw each truck as a fundamental profit center, and each driver as a basic builder of the company.

Trucks swinging out from the derricks of ocean transports symbolize the company's many mobilizations of men and machines for cleaning contracts overseas.

The 1976 contract for the cleaning of Riyadh, Saudi Arabia marked Waste Management's first foreign adventure. It required building and operating a complete self-contained city in the desert, which was home to thousands of employees.

Wayne Huizenga (right), with Dean Buntrock, was a co-founder of Waste Management. In 1975, he and Buntrock traveled to Saudi Arabia (then in the first throes of oil-boom modernization) to investigate the prospects for cleaning the city of Riyadh and doing business in the Kingdom.

Fred Weinert, reviewing plans with Saudi officials, had responsibility for building the desert cantonment that housed the company's workforce during the Riyadh contract in the late 1970s.

In Riyadh, Waste Management chefs tailored meals to the requirements of a range of third-country workers. Food and housing went with the job; most of the wages went back home.

Waste Management's Seattle Rail-Haul is the nation's first intermodal system for transporting the solid waste of a major metropolitan area to a modern sanitary landfill hundreds of miles away from densely populated areas.

People and technology fuel today's company. At Waste Management's Environmental Monitoring Laboratory in Geneva, Illinois, which is the world's largest ground-water analysis facility, an advanced robot ("Emily," after "EML") speeds analysis of water samples from monitoring wells at landfills across the country, under the watchful scrutiny of chemist Miriam Roman.

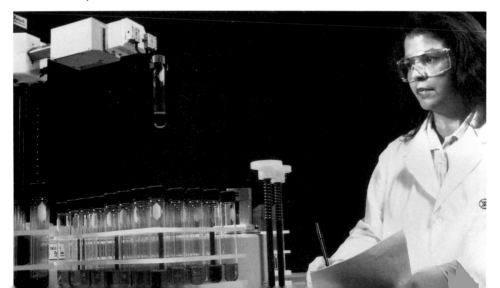

Columbia Ridge Landfill in Gilliam County, Oregon is the destination of the Seattle Rail-Haul. Covering 2000 acres and exceeding all environmental standards, the site is designed to provide safe disposal of municipal solid waste for years to come.

Garbage makes gas (methane). Waste Management helped pioneer the successful tapping of this energy resource for electricity generation.

The growth of Waste Management has offered a broad field for talented men and women to launch and build careers. Before a line-up of trucks in Jeddah, Saudi Arabia, five of them line up: Bill Reichert, Mike Rogan, Joe Jack, John Melk, and Ed Falkman.

President Phil Rooney and Chairman Dean Buntrock inaugurate Waste Management's leadership training center in Oak Brook, which will play a key role in developing leaders for tomorrow's company.

The remediation of damage done to the environment through the improper disposal of hazardous waste has become a major area of business for the company, which is today the nation's largest "clean-up" contractor.

Founder and Chairman Dean Buntrock and President Phil Rooney join Tampa Mayor Robert Martinez at the opening of Waste Management's MacKay Bay waste-to-energy plant.

Protective gear goes with the job at the company's Rust International division.

Clean water technologies are an important dimension of the company's environmental services capability. In suburban Atlanta, the Fulton County Water Treatment Plant began operating in 1991, treating 30 million gallons a day.

In Hamm, Germany, Waste Management operates a waste-to-energy
plant controlled from this console. Short of real estate for landfills,
Germany looks toward incineration with electricity generation as a
favored waste management alternative.

Located adjacent to Settler's Hill Sanitary Landfill, Waste Management's
Environmental Monitoring Laboratory is the largest in the world.

Waste-to-energy, a recycling technology pioneered by Wheelabrator Technologies, Inc., transforms an abundant commodity that no one wants (garbage) into a scarce one that everyone wants (electricity). Wheelabrator's second plant in Broward County, Florida began operation in 1991.

Envirospace Ltd., a joint venture between Waste Management and Chinese partners, is building the world's largest comprehensive hazardous waste treatment facility in Hong Kong.

Chem-Nuclear, a Waste Management company, is America's largest private handler of low-level radioactive waste. Shielded containers are inspected and unloaded at the company's secure disposal site in Barnwell, South Carolina.

Waste Management's Recycle America and Recycle Canada programs put the company in the forefront of the movement to recover resources from the nation's waste. Driver Kenneth Reid reclaims plastics and other household products on a residential route in Seattle.

Trucks have long been one of the primary tools of the trade. Today, Waste Management buys more of them than any company in America.

The WMS System, introduced in America in the late 1980s, brings smaller two-axle trucks to neighborhood streets, and has greatly increased the productivity of both residential and commercial refuse collection. Some analysts have called the WMS System the first major innovation in collection since the internal combustion engine.

During the Gulf War, flags in front of the Oak Brook headquarters signified Waste Management employees serving in the Gulf. As each returned, a yellow banner gave way to the Stars and Stripes.

One of Waste Management's longest-serving people, Leroy Elmore began work with predecessor company Ace Disposal in the 1950s.

Waste Management stock reached the New York Stock Exchange's Big Board in 1973. Left to right: Dean Buntrock, Wayne Huizenga, Harold Gershowitz and a stock exchange official (far left) were witnesses.

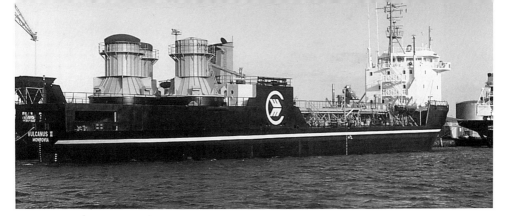

In the early 1980s, Chemical Waste Management's ships *Vulcanus I* and *II* demonstrated the technological integrity of ocean incineration of hazardous wastes, including PCBs. Nonetheless, a fierce campaign orchestrated by competitors and environmental extremists made permitting the ships virtually impossible.

Through Rust International, Inc., Waste Management is the nation's third-largest environmental engineering firm.

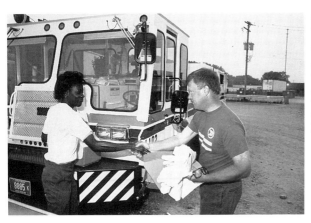

Glenda Moore of Waste Management's Oak Lawn, Illinois division congratulates Waste Management President Phil Rooney on a job well-done, Founders' Day, June 8, 1989.

Dean Buntrock and senior colleagues, 1990. Left to right: Steve Bergerson, Don Flynn, Buntrock, Phil Rooney, Harold Gershowitz, Jim Koenig.

The contract laid out the project in three phases: site improvement and construction of operating and housing facilities; supply of mobile and static equipment; and performance of cleansing services for five years. In the actual doing of it, however, everything had to be thought about at once. The Saudis stipulated that cleaning services had to begin no later than twelve months after signing the contract, which left no time to spare for mobilization. Much planning work was still done in Oak Brook with information brought back from the field, but London became the real nerve center of the project. There, from the Joint Venture's offices close by the South Harrow tube station and from Waste's own closet-cum-office near Shepherds Market in Mayfair, orders were coordinated and troops dispatched to the Kingdom.

Top on everyone's list in the late winter of 1976-77 was where the troops would come from. The contract called for a workforce of two thousand to three thousand (Waste Management employees then totaled just four thousand), and Phil Rooney got the job of investigating third-country sources of supply. They needed a wide range of skills; they needed them fast; and they needed value for the dollar. (Koreans, for instance, were much sought after in the booming "third-county national" labor market, but they were also expensive.)

Accompanied by Tom Frank, who was in charge of human resources in Oak Brook, Rooney set off in June 1977, first to Cairo, where Pritchard had contacts. But they were not very good ones, and Rooney and Frank soon concluded that Egyptians probably weren't right, anyway. As Arabic-speakers, they might prove a bit "too mobile"; easy communication with the Saudis could make it tempting for a man to work two jobs or to leave altogether for a higher paying one. So they moved on to Jeddah for a pow-wow with Buntrock and Melk, and then (after a two-day delay in Bahrain when the plane broke down) to Karachi.

There they met representatives of Mackinnon Mackenzie & Co., a British firm with a pedigree reaching back to recruiting work for the P&O Steamship Lines in the days of the British Raj.

They met Pakistan's "Protector of Emigrants," who sensed a big deal when he saw one (the Joint Venture was proposing to hire a great many people in one fell swoop), and they returned home feeling that Pakistan could fill their needs. But a month later, the Pakistanis unilaterally doubled the wage rates that the Joint Venture would have to pay, which set the Waste crew desperately looking again. To help, the Joint Venture had hired Jim Meers, a retired vice president for labor relations at ARAMCO and the man who had written much of the Kingdom's labor law. On his and Mackinnon Mackenzie's advice, they turned to India.

Tea Boys and Sergeant-Majors

Also in the spring of 1977, Tom Frank hired Jim McGrath from the personnel department at the *Chicago Tribune* to help with recruitment for Saudi. McGrath shipped out for Bombay via Riyadh in July. He met Meers at the Taj Mahal Hotel, and the two of them set about selecting from India's endless masses the two thousand–plus workers who would be right for Arabia. They set up shop under the high ceilings and dark woodwork of the great Victorian pile by the Arabian Sea that housed the offices of Mackinnon Mackenzie. From there, with Indian assistant Jim Mehta, they broadcast the word.

"MacKinnon Mackenzie & Co. Ltd., Overseas Recruitment Service, On Behalf of Their Principals in Saudi Arabia [who were unnamed] Invite Applications for the Following Posts," read the full-page advertisement in the *Times* of India on July 24. It offered posts in sixty different categories, attractive salaries together with free air conditioned bachelor accommodation and food, free medical benefits, and paid leave on completion of a two-year contract period which was renewable. The gamut of skills needed were those it took to operate a full-bore streets and sanitation department, with an apartment building, a cafeteria, and a clinic thrown in.

Under operations, they needed: "Heavy equipment mechanics (67 vacancies), proficient in diesel and petrol engines, experienced in cost and maintenance control, with valid drivers license . . . Heavy duty drivers (220 vacancies), five years experience and capable of driving rear loaders and load luggers . . . Operators transfer station (32 vacancies), experienced in operation of hydraulic compressing machines . . . Operators stoker (3 vacancies), experienced in incinerator plant . . . Welders (4 vacancies), proficient in all phases of welding . . . Lubemen (10 vacancies), with a good knowledge of servicing systems and [who] can read, write and speak English." They needed four male nurses (two doctors came out from England), seven laundrymen, two barbers, eleven fuelers, and forty-four clerk/typists (male). For supervisors—of manual labor, of transport, of fire and security—they wanted English-speaking ex-servicemen experienced at handling large groups of men who knew about chain-of-command. For the catering, they wanted chefs, bakers, commissary men, storemen— "teaboys (2 vacancies), young and energetic with minimum three-years experience in a restaurant/hotel." For the unique Saudi environment, they needed four sewage and water purification men and (absolutely essential) six air conditioning mechanics.

For days after the word went out, bags of CVs filled the mail. For two or three weeks, lines of hopeful Indians packed chock a block together, snaked along the corridors, down the stairwells, and out into the streets of Bombay. It was a massive job and even though they tried first to identify supervisors to help sort out the others, progress was slow. When Buntrock and Rooney came through in October, they ordered Tom Frank out from London with a dozen British support staff to quicken the pace. Everybody worked twelve-hour days, seven days a week. There was little time for sightseeing.

Indians were hungry for this type of opportunity, and they came to Bombay from all over the subcontinent. Wages offered by foreign firms operating in the Kingdom were several times what the same work brought at home. (The Joint Venture started helpers at $60 per month, supervisors at $300—paid, as the Joint Venture was being paid, in Saudi riyals. With 100 percent of every employee's living expenses paid for by the company, their wages were all essentially savings, assuming the money wasn't squandered on souvenirs. Much of the money went to support the families left behind—a distinct improvement over what these men could have earned back home.) None of them, of course, knew anything about Waste Management in particular, but judging by those who "re-upped" for second and third tours later on, many Indians liked what they found.

Everyone had to be vetted, as the British personnel put it: that a man said he had a driver's license did not in India necessarily mean he could drive. Elaborate testing took place at the Father Agnel School in Bandra just outside Bombay, an orphanage and trade school founded by a Catholic priest who had been excommunicated over his position on birth control. There, would-be drivers, mechanics, electricians, and plumbers were put through their paces and their scores toted up. Everyone got a physical to identify communicable or chronically debilitating conditions; they watched especially for hernias and hemorrhoids. They tested lifting strength with sandbags. They took those destined to spend ten hours a day behind a garbage truck out to a local Bombay dump to see first hand if they could stand the stench.

Tens of thousands of foreign workers have been recruited for jobs in the oil-rich Middle East in the last twenty years, a phenomenon now common to our time. They have been recruited by all varieties of companies doing all sorts of work. Virtually all have been well paid; most have been well treated. Many returned home at the first possible opportunity; some stayed on with the same or a different company in the same or a different country; some jumped ship before their contracts were up. If the man and the company were well matched, something else could happen too.

"I improved myself," was how Prassad Bhuleshwar described the consequences of his visit to the old Mackinnon Mackenzie building in Bombay. Born just after independence in 1948, in the industrial town of Jamshedpur on the other side of India, near Calcutta, he came to interview for Waste Management thirty years later. He had a trade as a diesel mechanic, a wife, and growing family. He was interviewed by Jim Mehta, scored well on his tests, and was offered a position as "Grade I Mechanic." The contract, like all the contracts, was for two years, with no furlough till the term was up. He took it and a few days later was on a plane to Riyadh. He had never flown before. He had never really been away from home before.

He still lives away from home and still works for Waste Management (most recently as a supervisor in Kuwait). He returns to India more often now, but he has also grown in ways he could not have, had he stayed behind. He speaks of all the fine "Misters," Americans and English, he has worked for—"Mr." Jerry Rhodes, "Mr." Tom Consadine, "Mr." Morris Bassingdale. "I learned many things from them all, many things that aren't even in my field."

No Greens

That was the first thing Prassad learned as the chartered SaudiAir jet carrying him and a couple of hundred other Indian contract workers made its approach to the old Riyadh airport in the fall of 1978. "No greens here," he thought.

The association of "green" with environmentalism still lay somewhere off in the future, and Prassad meant green literally. He had never seen any place but India, perhaps the greenest country on earth, and the Kingdom's burned-out landscape was quite a visual shock. Prassad, the mechanic from Jamshedpur, shared the shock with Buntrock, Flynn, and Melk, the bosses from Oak Brook. There is an often-told story among Waste Management's "old Saudi hands" of an early trip to the Kingdom when Buntrock, Rooney, Flynn, Weinert, and Melk in a rented white Chevrolet Caprice struck out into the desert off the Dammam road north of Riyadh in search of "the site." The car got stuck in the sand, and the brains trust of the company had to push and shove and swear it back onto the track (at that point, not really a road). When they got to where the site was supposed to be, they found some white concrete block markers—and nothing else.

What then was desert waste is today green with the suburbs of Riyadh. But before there were suburbs, there was "the camp." Of all the action-packed episodes of the Saudi adventure, the building of this small city in the sand to house and feed two thousand to three thousand workers and maintain 450 vehicles, evokes perhaps the sharpest memories and stirs the deepest emotions, sharper and deeper even than the cleaning of Riyadh itself. Waste Management was in the service business of making unwanted items go away; its job was well done if at the end of the day there was "less" of those items rather than "more." It was not in the construction business, where the job was done if at the end of the day the walls were up and the roof on—and well done if ten years later it was still standing and useful. Yet that was the job they did in Saudi, before they lifted a single load of garbage.

The litany of facts and figures describing it reads like one of those breathtaking "Floating City" fold-outs of the *Queen Mary* in a children's book about ships, complete with the wonderful cut-away drawing of all the little spaces where designers and builders had so ingeniously provided for every conceivable need. To get the same impression of Waste's Riyadh complex you had to look down from the air, not from the side, and if you did, the sense of a little cubbyhole for everything was unmistakable. Quite as unmistakable, viewed from any angle you liked, was its likeness to a high-class army camp.

It was the biggest and most comprehensive expatriate labor complex constructed in the Kingdom up to that time: thirty-two acres at the main site (the sanitary landfill, at a different site, occupied an additional 118 acres; thirty-one transfer stations were scattered throughout the city) with a lot packed into it. The main administration buildings were steel-framed with metal walls and roofs. Stone siding faced the exterior. A central communications center and positive pressure computer room were in the interior.

The maintenance building with its large canopied work area was a marvel for the Middle East, with sixteen large work bays, five overhead bridge cranes, lubrication pits, specially equipped areas for engine and brake overhaul, wheel alignment, body work, air conditioning, and hydraulic repair. It included a special module for working on containers and washing trucks. Dormitories for supervisory personnel, support technicians, and laborers offered degrees of comfort and privacy depending on job rank: from twenty bunks per room for sweepers and helpers, to private accommodation for senior supervisors most of whom had come out from England.

Six mess halls catered to Eastern and Western diets, with forty thousand cafeteria-style meals served per week. Kitchens included a wide range of refrigerated warehousing and storage facilities for the substantial foodstuffs brought in from abroad. A 6,500 square foot clinic, staffed by two doctors, five nurses, and a medical technician, provided medical service in four-bed wards, and examining and operating rooms. A camp commissary stocked personal care and consumer products for purchase by employees. The laundry was equipped with commercial-capacity washing and drying machines and a sophisticated double water recovery system to reduce consumption from twelve thousand to four thousand gallons per day. There were two twenty-five meter swimming pools, tennis, squash, and basketball courts, a softball diamond, soccer field, and sitting and reading rooms. In the rec hall, Prassad took up snooker.

It was like the picture of the *Queen Mary* in another way too. Floating around in the middle of the ocean is similar to surviving in the open desert in that nothing is more precious than water in a country where it rains 2½ inches per year. In Saudi, they trucked water in from distant wells in 9,000-gallon tankers and then ran it through sophisticated prechlorination and reverse-osmosis treatment systems to provide 120,000 gallons for drinking and cooking each day. Two miles of underground piping distributed it to living, working, and support facilities. Waste water, 130,000 gallons of it a day, was purified to meet or exceed World Health Organization requirements and was used to provide irrigation for planted areas within the complex. The power that drove the pumps (and everything else) came from a 4,800 kilowatt generating plant fired by six diesel-powered generators, two of which were down at all times for programmed maintenance. The underground fuel depot stored 10,000 gallons of gasoline, 53,000 gallons of diesel.

The cost was close to $38 million, and it was 85 percent complete by the day the first garbage truck rolled out, one year after the contract award.

Modify That Mosque; Alter Those Ablutions

To celebrate signing the contract, Buntrock hosted a dinner for key people at the LaGrange Country Club in Chicago's western suburbs in February 1977. Fred Weinert was seated next to Phil Rooney, and before the evening was out he had a new assignment.

> ROONEY: "Fred, we'd like you to manage construction of the camp in Saudi."
>
> WEINERT: [Awkward pause] "Me, Phil? I don't know anything about construction, but . . . well sure, I'll do it."

You did not make a career at Waste Management by telling Phil Rooney or Dean Buntrock that you "didn't know" (at least not very often), and so Weinert (who really didn't know anything about construction) had to learn fast, on the job. Fortunately, good help was at hand.

Bob Zralek, who had retired as deputy commissioner of streets and sanitation for the city of Chicago in October 1975, was promptly scarfed up by Waste as director of engineering. By November, he found himself in Riyadh evaluating the street-cleaning situation as they worked on the bids. Next, he found himself working in the Joint Venture's London office (and often on the plane to Riyadh). Today on the wall of Zralek's office in Oak Brook hangs a handsome painting of the aircraft carrier USS *Enterprise*; Zralek is also a retired rear admiral in naval reserve. Fifteen years ago he was a captain with much experience in how the Seabees got things done, which was how the Saudi camp struck him. If you had to house and support a battalion on some remote beachhead, how would you do it? He called up navy friends and soon had their plans for such a base. The Joint Venture's camp ended up looking a lot like it. (The only thing missing was the airstrip which, given the distressing condition of Riyadh's old airport, might not have been a bad idea.)

Mike Popowich was another navy man, a civil engineer who had been building cantonments with the Seabees all over the world since the early 1960s. Zralek brought him on board with Waste shortly after he himself joined up. From late 1976, Popowich was in Saudi constantly. As of May 1977, he never left. His friend Mike Curry had spent twenty-seven years as a Royal Engineer in the British army and knew Popowich when both were assigned to NATO headquarters in London in the early 1970s. Popowich recruited him to help too. Bob Keleher, who had worked for Zralek in Chicago and followed him to Waste, eventually landed in Saudi as well. There was abundant work for everyone.

Buntrock and Rooney had retained Bechtel International of San Francisco to be responsible for the overall design and engineering of the project, and J. A. Jones of Charlotte, North Carolina, as construction contractors. Jones had a presence in the Kingdom already, and Bechtel was known worldwide; together they raised the "comfort level" for Waste Management, which wasn't a construction company and had not ventured so far from home before. Jones in turn subcontracted with Korean companies (favorites in the Kingdom), and in the 120-degree heat of Saudi's high summer, they pitched their tents in the desert and went to work.

The first slab of concrete was poured on July 7. Heat and wind are the enemies of concrete, and even though they tried to pour in the morning, it was standard procedure to add shaved ice to keep mixtures from setting up too fast. In a landscape made of sand, sand of suitable angularity actually had to be imported. In sunshine that could burn a man to a crisp in no time, the Koreans worked in shifts—a few hours in the sun, a few in the shade. In humidity so low that the perspiring human body acted as a natural refrigeration machine, the only trace of sweat was at a man's sweatband. He seldom had to pee.

The dormitories, mess, and recreation halls rose on a schedule coordinated with the staged arrival of the labor from England and India; supervisors, administrative types, and support staff were needed before the men who would drive the trucks. The pre-engineered structures came from the Block Watne company in Stavanger, Norway, which had a reputation for manufacturing tight buildings for arctic conditions. But if it keeps out the cold, it keeps out the heat too, and the well-fitted and insulated Block Watne panels, along with the Norwegians who supervised their erection, worked like a dream. Other things didn't. Weinert made numerous shopping trips to Europe with a long list of big quantities: three hundred desks, two thousand beds, 200,000 dustbins (as the English, who supplied them, called garbage cans). The beds did not arrive on time, which sent Weinert and others scurrying off to the souqs of Riyadh to buy every mattress they could find. Trucks, piled high with the things, arrived at camp just as did the busloads of Indians who would sleep on them.

There were difficulties with the "ablutions," as toilet and shower facilities were called, or at least with some Indians' unfamiliarity with how they were used, a near-disaster with the swimming pool, when on opening day, a number of Indians with no experience of such amenities jumped in and nearly drowned. And the mosque that was to be built just outside the compound's perimeter required alterations: "Close the opening in the ceiling . . . modify the area allocated for ablutions," directed the deputy mayor, Musaid Al-Ankari.

The "learning curve," as they say, was steep for everybody. Weinert was as determined to make money (10 percent) on the construction phase of the project as the company was on the purchasing and cleaning operation themselves. Timely performance was everything, and when J. A. Jones fell behind (they were heavily, perhaps overly engaged elsewhere in the Kingdom), he got help from Jim Koenig, a protégé of Don Flynn from Arthur Andersen in Chicago, who, though knowing nothing about construction either, soon learned a great deal about construction administration. When Koenig arrived in October, they didn't really know if they were on budget or not. He soon learned that it was more effective to apply pressure on expatriate contractors outside the Kingdom than to get tough with the locals on the scene, and he also learned the locations of all the pressure points. Either Koenig or Weinert was always "in Kingdom" (the phrase they came to use), keeping track, watching the numbers. When one flew out, the other flew in, and many a night the two of them huddled in the airport lounge trading information and tales of woe.

Shoof

As it turned out, a small portion was finished late—but not very late—and the whole thing (with a capacity that had been increased from 2,200 to 2,340 men) was finished SR 9 million under budget. It was as if they had always been doing this sort of thing, as indeed they had been with equipment purchasing where the results were even better. The contract had allotted SR 88 million; they had budgeted SR 75 million; they got what they needed for SR 56 million. It came as a surprise, therefore, that what they knew best—collecting and disposing of garbage—was where they almost lost it. "No pleasant surprises," as Weinert had said.

"How did it go?" Jackie Jacobie spoke intently into the telephone handset in London on that January night in 1978.

A native of the subcontinent, Jacobie had emigrated to Britain

in the middle-1960s. She came to Waste Management via Pritchard Services where she had been secretary to John Miller. Tom
Frank hired her away from his new partner shortly after coming
to London to work on Saudi. He warned her: "We work real hard
here." When she was given a tiny office just vacated by an
Englishman who had not worked hard enough, and told to sort
through half a dozen mail bags full of responses to the Joint
Venture's UK advertisement for billets in the Kingdom, she
learned quickly what he meant. "Americans worked harder than
the Brits: you know, fewer people to do the same job," was how
she put it. Being neither American nor British herself, she saw it
clearly, and she has worked for Waste Management ever since.

Before she knew it, Frank had her managing the London office,
which was fast turning into a halfway house between the States
and the Kingdom. She handled everything—people, passports,
visas (she had an Irish friend who worked at the Saudi consulate
who always got her "to the head of the queue"), excess baggage,
the telephone. Rooney called every day from Saudi to talk to
Frank, to Martin Rivers (from Pritchard), to whomever, to her.

But this particular call was hers—to congratulate the "in Kingdom" crowd on startup day.

John Melk wearily barked: "Don't ask!"

There had been a comic opera air to some of it, a "right on the
edge of crisis" air to all of it. The mayor had asked for a parade
through Riyadh to show off all the shiny new trucks before opening day, but crowds broke into the column, the back lost the front,
and it took all day to get everyone back to camp. "Some of our
drivers had never even been downtown," said Jerry Caudle who
had arrived from California with his family in October 1977 to
prepare to receive the workforce and see that it was ready to work.
The first official muster at 4:30 A.M., not exactly a model of
precision, sent Caudle and Rooney (both Marine Corps veterans)
storming through the barracks not-so-gently urging their employees along. The truck marshalling area quickly turned into a
choking cloud of dust and sand, as if the Afrika Korps had just
revved up but with a bit less discipline.

The real problem was more serious. Earlier in 1977, at a Waste board meeting, a conference call had been placed to John Melk and Harold Smith in Saudi. The subject was Smith's operations plan.

"Are you sure you have enough people?"

"No problem at all: Riyadh is going to be just like Findlay, Ohio [the small city where Smith was from]."

It wasn't. What was different, in addition to the fact that logistically everything was more complicated (no phones, no radios, no proper street addresses, no drivers who spoke English), was that there was much more garbage than Smith or anyone else had suspected. The Ministry had originally estimated 100 tons a day. Waste's plan put it at 300 tons. It turned out probably closer to 1,000 tons. The difference, coupled with the Saudis' expectations that overnight Riyadh would be transformed, was what put Phil Rooney and all the other Waste Management managers in a foul humor—and kept them that way for the next several months.

"Shoof" (phonetically in English) is Arabic for "look." Expressed by numerous Ministry inspectors, always in the imperative and always serially — "Shoof! Shoof! Shoof!"—is a word that veterans of the Saudi adventure never want to hear again. There was no mistaking its meaning: "Look at the trash that still hasn't been picked up—why hasn't it been picked up—when will it be picked up?!"

There was no denying it: initially the Joint Venture forces were overwhelmed. A longshoremen's strike in Baltimore delayed both men and equipment. Richard Evenhouse, who replaced Harold Smith as operations director in 1977, was able to field only about nine hundred workers on opening day instead of 1,300. The local press jumped on the difficulties, and the danger of sliding into nonperformance was for a short time very real. The Management Committee authorized Melk and Rooney to do everything necessary to regain operational effectiveness.

Rooney met with the mayor, and got a little time. In something of a tactical retreat, he hired back, as temporary subcontractors, some of the Saudi haulers who had cleaned the city (after a manner) before the Joint Venture had arrived and put them out of business. He pulled just about everybody off every other job, himself and Melk included, and put them on a truck or, if there wasn't a truck, then on the street pushing a broom. He organized special flying squads to handle urgent trouble spots. One lone electrician was left in charge of the camp's power plant. Mechanics dropped their tools, bookkeepers and accountants their ledgers and calculators. Everybody, even lawyers, was ordered into the trenches. Mike Curry, the Royal Engineer, and Rooney cruised the night-time streets of Riyadh in the cab of a Johnson sweeper. By day Rooney and John Blew, the Bell Boyd & Lloyd securities attorney, tossed dead goats into gaping rear-loaders.

It took two or three months to catch up and be able to say they were running according to plan. The "Shoof! Shoof!" of Mohammed bin Atik, the chief Saudi inspector, and his minions never did go away. But, gradually, the systems did take hold, the cadres of foreign workers did learn their routines, and the city of Riyadh did become clean. A citizen education program, which was part of the contract and organized by Don McClenahan, helped keep it that way: "Keep Riyadh Clean" (in Arabic) litter-bags, billboards, and bumper stickers, depicting in green and white (Saudi national colors) a thobe-clad figure dutifully putting his trash in a container that bore the Joint Venture's logo, which was really Waste Management's logo doctored slightly to slip in a Pritchard "P."

Have What It Takes?

"Why do you want to go, anyway?" It was a question that Fred Weinert (who after John Melk headed Waste Management International, which grew out of the first Saudi experience) asked of prospective transfers to the Kingdom. "Because it fits into my career plan," or some other wooden out-of-the-book answer, made him wary. Saudi wasn't out of any textbook and it wouldn't necessarily advance anyone's career. But if a man said, "I want to go there to make money, and, well, just for the excitement," then Weinert felt he had the right sort of fellow.

The company deemed Saudi "hardship duty" and paid its American expats accordingly, roughly double what they would earn at home. Housing went with the job, and Riyadh was not the sort of place that encouraged much spending. A man could save most of what he earned. The company paid for two much-needed trips a year for every family, one back to the States and another as far as London.

The "excitement" was something a man either felt or he didn't, a matter of temperament mainly, but the right temperament in tough places is important, both to the individual and to any group he is part of. True: this particular tough place offered the chance to work closely with the very top people in the company—with Buntrock who traveled there almost every month, with Rooney and Melk who didn't see home for long stretches, even with Flynn who flitted in and out—and to be noticed by them. Proximity could also, of course, be a risk, if things went badly, as sometimes they did. (On several occasions, troublemakers stirred up mess hall riots and got themselves deported.)

The point was that a man needed a certain practical clearheadedness, but along with it a sense of adventure, of daring, of fun. Almost to a man, veterans of Saudi recall it with the warmth and nostalgia natural to memories of when they were younger and, in many cases, just "setting out." To some, like Don Mc-Clenahan, it was reminiscent of army days. An abundance of military types certainly did pass through: veterans of the Marines, navy, Royal Engineers, Indian army, even a crisp former group captain in the RAF, Frank Bowen-Easley. A campaign-like atmosphere suffused the whole endeavor, a "now, here's the objective, guys/we're throwing everything we've got into it" singlemindedness: "Get mobilized, get the city clean, control costs, get paid." No one who experienced it left unchanged.

Because the job was so big and required so many unaccompanied men to do it, a military-like organization was inevitable.

But something else about the experience touched the "officers," the Waste Management managers sent out to muster the troops and lead the charge. While Riyadh was thick with expats, the number of Waste Management families was small—the Blombergs, the Caudles, the Evenhouses, the Rhodeses, the Bakers, the Gencauskis, the Rogans, the Jacks, the Dudzinkis, the Reicherts—never more than ten or so.

And there were few distractions. The wives could not work, were not permitted to drive, and depended on company cars to accomplish their few shopping chores. With little entertainment outside the home, it was very different from "home," but in some ways superior to it.

"Saudi was a creative environment," remembered Jerry Caudle, senior operations manager, who spent two years there with his young family. He referred both to the challenges of the job (cleaning a place that had not been cleaned before) and to life outside it. They had videos, and sports teams were organized for the children (who through eighth grade attended the local International School). An interdenominational Christian fellowship gathered discreetly so as not to offend their Saudi hosts, and there were weekly parties around the pool with the barbecue and perhaps (again discreetly) some bootlegged booze. But what they mainly had was one another. "It was what I imagine the 1930s and 1940s must have been like," Caudle said, reaching back to the constrictedness and togetherness of the Depression and wartime for an image: "You got real close to people, dependent on them." Jim Koenig remembered: "You worked and then you talked; you worked and then you talked some more." Rich Evenhouse agreed: "We talked and we played cards—and then it was morning."

Buntrock's Bet

Money and excitement. The worthy reasons for an individual to go to Saudi, were also the right reasons for the company to go there. It would have been easy enough not to; there was no shortage of good profitable work back home. Browning Ferris, then number one in the waste industry, went later, in Waste's wake. But consider the timing in the middle 1970s. The Kingdom was in the first throes of buying a modern infrastructure. The influx of oil income that would otherwise get inflated away made it desperate to develop, and desperate to get Western companies to come and do the work of development. A measure of this eagerness (despite all the months of haggling) was the 20 percent advance payment that was part of the contract for the cleansing of Riyadh. That money, which bought trucks and sweepers for the Kingdom, also thanks to Flynn and Buntrock's artful management, fueled domestic growth for Waste Management. It shifted the balance of risk within the venture itself in a way the made Buntrock view it not just as acceptable but as extremely attractive.

But the real risks were performance risks: could they do the job they said they could, in the time allotted? If they couldn't, then— but only then—was there real financial danger? His company had never "not performed" on anything, nor has it since. Though there were some scary moments for sure, hauling trash and running landfills was what these people knew better than anybody in the world. Buntrock bet they could prove it in Saudi Arabia, and he was right.

It was a very lucrative contract, and more than that. It was exciting: it made the blood race a bit, it made a man think about where it might lead, which was Buntrock's job. Visibility was high for venturers to the Kingdom then: do a smart job there and a young company would get a lot of notice. The scale was right too. Both daunting and doable, the right sort of challenge for the right crew of talented and ambitious men. It made the company reach for levels of performance it had not achieved before. Saudi made the company and the people in it grow, and not financially alone.

It is not accurate, therefore, to say that with Saudi "Buntrock bet the company." Rather he was factoring it into a larger wager he had about the rate of its growth. Saudi, if it worked, which it very likely would, would leave the company enviably poised for

197

its next challenges. It led in 1981 to similar cleaning contracts in Jeddah (by which time the Saudis were willing to part only with a 10 percent advance) and in South America (Buenos Aires and Caracas). In Buenos Aires, where the company's success would be conspicuous even by its own high-performance standards, polls showed the highest levels of citizen approval for Waste Management (Manliba S.A. and ASEO S.A. were the local companies), and the city saved a hefty $100 million in one year alone. (When the announcement was made on the same day in 1981 of the Jeddah and Buenos Aires contracts, the company's stock rose eight points, its largest single rise ever.) In 1985, the company entered the Australian market with a large collection contract for the city of Brisbane. By the 1990s, the company enjoyed a truly world-wide presence. It strengthened the balance sheet even as it stiffened the people who had pulled it off.

Some stiffness had been evident that evening back in 1979 when Dean Buntrock, out in the truck yard, asked Jerry Rhodes to stick it out one more year, and when Rhodes replied, "Sure, Dean." Among his other duties, Rhodes helped the Saudis set up a maintenance program for their own vehicles before the Joint Venture could start up.

He recalls his first depressing tour of the city garage with the vice mayor of Riyadh, who could only wave his arms toward the forlorn vehicles and admonish the American: "Awaken my sleeping trucks." It was typical of the Kingdom then, a kingdom with the money to buy all the trucks in the world and a culture that had still not quite forgotten the camel. Rhodes and his mechanics got the trucks running. Buntrock, by going to Saudi with men like Rhodes, awakened his company to worlds far beyond it.

8

Chemical Waste

SHORTLY AFTER the end of the Yom Kippur War, American Secretary of State Henry Kissinger paid a visit to King Faisal in an effort to get the Saudis to lift the oil embargo on the West. As his plane neared the Kingdom, he is reported to have turned to his staff and reporters and joked: "Well, fellows, get ready for some of Riyadh's famous night life." Then he paused and, to several of the journalists who like himself were Jews, added with a wry smile: "Except for you guys."

Kissinger's humor underscored a sad reality of that troubled region, a reality that neither Waste Management, nor any other foreign company, could change while doing business there. To do business there meant enduring large and small frustrations: procuring, for example, all those "letters from your minister" that were as important as passports to Waste employees setting out for the Arab Kingdom. It also meant that some employees, with the wrong sort of minister, stayed home.

Matching the talent to the work has always been one of Dean Buntrock's long suits. He seldom failed to select the proper instruments to implement his vision. His relationship with Harold Gershowitz, who as the years passed became to many communities Waste Management's most eloquent advocate and interpreter, is a case in point. Gershowitz, of course, never went to Saudi (although back in Oak Brook he was the one who oversaw production and authored large parts of the Riyadh proposal), but he and many others tended just as important business at home.

For "cleaning up" was not just on Saudi minds. By the late 1970s the United States was well down the road to becoming the world's leader in environmental protection. In the fall of 1976, as the Waste team in Saudi worked and waited to nail down the contract there, the Waste team in America set about aligning the company with broad social forces that were reshaping public policy and private markets. The result, as perceived and experienced by those in the company, is, without exaggeration, almost a social contract. Cynics may sneer when Waste Management today declares that its very purpose is to preserve and enhance our environment. They doubt such words in an era when all companies bend over backward to appear "green." But in the case of Waste Management, words achieve credence from a history that did not begin with last year's annual report, and that like all true histories, covers some rough patches along the way.

The Resource Conservation and Recovery Act (RCRA) and the Toxic Substances Control Act (TSCA) were passed by Congress and signed into law by President Gerald Ford in 1976. (The regulations implementing RCRA did not take effect until November 1980.) Only a month later, Harold Gershowitz was in New York running a meeting organized by Waste Management to explain the new legislation to the investment community. Gershowitz was a good choice. His audience were financial professionals familiar with Waste's impressive early growth through acquisition and operation of solid waste companies—in solid waste alone the potential for growth remained enormous. They had less reason to be familiar with the opportunities that RCRA represented, or with Waste Management's determination to seize them. This was Gershowitz's job.

He talked about how RCRA was going to be a landmark change for Waste Management and how it would open up a whole new business down the line. He spoke of how RCRA followed logically from the country's growing anxiety over pollution in all its forms, and of how the companies that positioned themselves to manage new streams of waste (or, more accurately, streams of waste newly perceived to be a threat) would stand to prosper mightily.

RCRA, subsequent amendments to it, and TSCA, have become America's great umbrella legislation for the definition, classification, and handling of chemical and hazardous wastes. The context for their passage was rising public concern over the health and environmental effects of improper waste disposal, particularly ground water contamination. TSCA subjected the entire chemical industry to comprehensive federal control for the first time. It gave the EPA broad authority to identify and control chemicals already being produced and those proposed for the marketplace, and it touched all phases of the industry: product development and testing, manufacturing, distribution, and disposal. RCRA established the Office of Solid Waste within the EPA and provided a federal-state-local partnership to share the task of dealing with criteria for land disposal of solid hazardous and nonhazardous wastes. It required establishment of federal standards, to be implemented by the states, for the safe land disposal of nonhazardous waste, and another program to identify, track, and manage hazardous wastes, and to encourage waste-reduction and resource-recovery efforts.

Subtitle "D" of RCRA mandated the EPA to set criteria for the proper land disposal of nonhazardous solid wastes in order to protect ground and surface water, air quality, and environmentally sensitive areas such as wetlands. With federal aid, the states were to inventory and evaluate all land disposal sites. Open dumps were to be closed within a reasonable time (not more than five years), and states that failed to comply would forfeit federal aid for solid waste management programs. The law gave "interim" status to facilities that generated or managed hazardous waste, which gave the EPA the opportunity to evaluate and require changes in existing facilities before granting final operating permits.

Subtitle "C" of the RCRA legislation began a national hazardous waste regulatory program, including a definition of what hazardous waste was. The act listed some 150 wastes and waste streams and specified four "hazardous" characteristics: ignitability, corrosivity, reactivity, and toxicity. The language opened many doors: "a solid waste, or combination of solid wastes, which because of its quantity, concentration or physical, chemical or infectious characteristics may (a) cause, or significantly contribute to, an increase in mortality or increase in serious irreversible, or incapacitating reversible, illness; or (b) pose a substantial present or potential hazard to human health or the environment when improperly treated, stored, transported or disposed of, or otherwise managed." In 1979, the EPA estimated (based on a preliminary study of seventeen industries) that 10 to 15 percent of the nation's annual production of 344 million metric tons of industrial waste was hazardous.

Congress reauthorized RCRA in November 1984. These new Hazardous and Solid Waste Amendments (HSWA) went much further than the earlier legislation. In addition to new controls, they extended the law's reach to small generators of hazardous waste as well as to underground storage tanks (such as service stations), and required improved technology such as more sophisticated treatment or incineration prior to landfilling.

The growth of this legislation may have flowed logically enough from the larger concerns that had led to passage of the National Solid Waste Act of 1965 and to creation of the Environmental Protection Agency in 1970. The progression is significant. The EPA was first concerned with water pollution associated mainly with domestic waste waters. With sewage treatment plants built all over the country, the agency enjoyed a wide and firm base of political support. But by the middle 1970s, attention began to shift to air pollution, which was more difficult because the sources were more numerous. First, what were known as "point sources" (factories and power plants) got attention, and then "non-point sources" (cars and trucks). The air gradually got cleaner. But as air and water pollution controls took hold, they shifted disposal options to the last-regulated possibility—the land where wastes refused conveniently to "disappear" and where problems from improper disposal multiplied.

But for companies that had grown up in the garbage business, the path between municipal solid waste (garbage) and chemical waste, could, like some of that waste itself, be extremely "hazardous." The way Waste Management negotiated those hazards, in an ever-more highly charged regulatory and political atmosphere, illuminates the evolution of its own environmental thinking and makes its claim today of devotion to the environment more than fashionable public relations.

Pieces

Waste Management, Inc. in 1992 consists of a worldwide family of companies capable of nearly every type of waste recovery, treatment, disposal, remediation: Waste Management of North America, Waste Management Europe, Chemical Waste Management, Chem-Nuclear Systems, Chem-Nuclear Environmental Services, Wheelabrator, the Brand Companies. The pieces have gotten very large. The pieces of Waste Management, Inc. in the mid-1970s, quite small at the time, all fit under one modest corporate hat. None was smaller than what would become Chemical Waste Management—or, as known locally and across the industry, "Chem Waste."

Its origins, which actually antedate RCRA, lay close to Waste Management's home in the Chicago area. Developed by Buntrock and Larry Beck, the CID Landfill in Calumet City, Illinois, lay at the far western end of the great industrial corridor that reached up the Hudson, along the Erie Canal, across the Alleghenies, and along the lakes to Chicago—the mills and factories that from the late nineteenth century to the middle of the twentieth had made America the greatest industrial power in the world. Buntrock was the first to become convinced of the potential of the place as a solid waste disposal site, but, typically, his vision was able to accommodate the unforeseen. Today, the CID Landfill has grown into an important part of the Chemical Waste Management network of hazardous waste facilities.

It started with a "pug mill," or acid–neutralization facility offering treatment for the pickling liquors that were a by-product of nearby steel mills. It was a simple affair in keeping with the practice of the time—a pond and a couple of silos—and it was run as the chemical waste division of Waste Management of Illinois.

The people at CID began to take small steps toward getting control of what they handled. Rudimentary as it sounds today, they made a great leap forward just by segregating drums by their contents. A manifest system and sampling protocols were also implemented, and the company built its own quite up-to-date analytical laboratory to test incoming substances. The first concern in those days was safety—chiefly for the employees who handled the wastes. But "safety" in handling hazardous materials is not a divisible characteristic. Care taken for one's employees naturally became care taken for one's surroundings, and, as environmental protection regulations grew with RCRA and TSCA, a habit that had already been established helped make "compliance" an instinctive company behavior.

To support the infant operation, they added a transportation segment, using the tanker fleet of Clearing Disposal, and generally viewed all their Chicago hauling divisions as the customer base for the new chemical business. The biggest pieces of that business in these earliest days, for $3–$4 million, came from Lakeway Chemicals in Muskegon, Michigan, and Ansul Manufacturing Company in Marinette, Wisconsin, which led to an important patent for the treatment and disposal of arsenic salts. Chemical waste operations in 1977 contributed approximately $10 million to the company's total revenues of $223 million. But they were big enough to make people take notice, and early in 1978 management announced its intention to expand liquid and chemical waste hauling and disposal operations beyond the Chicago region.

The context for that decision is important, for it defined the evolving dual nature of this very special segment of the waste business. First, chemical waste was a new business, whereas garbage was an old one. At that time, virtually all of America's chemical and hazardous wastes were self-disposed, that is, handled in one way or another by the firms and factories that produced them. Today, while the regulations strictly segregate chemical from solid waste streams, self-disposal still accounts for most hazardous waste handling in America.

Then, however, companies that wished to buy the service had few reputable places to turn to. If Waste Management could position itself early to develop that small market, it would stand to profit later as that market grew absolutely, if not relative to the whole. The second characteristic of the chemical waste business that came into play was that the demand for it (at first very low, as was the price a generator was willing to pay) would be driven by a market that was created and sustained by the regulations. RCRA, TSCA, and their children made new public policy and mandated a new behavior with regard to hazardous waste. The means for carrying out that policy and of financing it remained largely within the private sector. The quickness of companies to anticipate and conform to that policy would in the future be as important to their survival and success as old-fashioned operations performance itself.

Only Opportunity Here

Throughout 1975 and early 1976, Congress held hearings in Washington and in communities across the country, gathering information and testing sensitivities prior to the passage of hazardous waste legislation. In anticipation of its expanding regulatory agenda, the EPA surveyed the country for geographically and geologically suitable sites for hazardous waste disposal. The importance of EPA's authority to bestow "interim status" (Part A permits) on acceptable existing sites during the period between passage of RCRA in 1976 and its implementation in 1980 cannot be overstated. Subsequently, all sites would have to apply for full-blown Part B permits, a process that was predicted to take five to ten years. But while that process was pending, such facilities could continue to operate under "interim status." It was essentially a grandfathering arrangement to enable the system to make the transition from the bad old unregulated days to the stringent new regulatory regime. Any site that failed to win interim status was effectively doomed to go out of business. Any facility begun after November 1980 would have to complete the years-long Part B permitting process before it could even start. It all meant that those facilities in operation under interim status by November 1980 would largely constitute the universe of hazardous waste management facilities for the next five to ten years. If a company hoped to become a serious player in this new business, this was the moment to move.

Waste Management moved, and with a quickness that recalled its first acquisition drive just after going public in 1971. EPA surveys in hand, Wayne Huizenga, Phil Rooney, Don Price, and a few others fanned out from O'Hare on Monday mornings, "write-your-own" plane tickets in hand, looking for permitted capacity that would give the company a national network of chemical waste management sites. These same men had barnstormed the country just a few years before in search of the solid-waste hauling and disposal companies whose acquisition had made possible Waste's remarkable early growth, and some of the old thrill-of-the-chase was familiar.

But the quarry was very different, the field much smaller. They needed to find disposal facilities with hazardous waste permits from state environmental agencies already in place; they were in the market for permits. On finding one, they conducted such investigation as time allowed to determine if the place was in fact what it claimed to be. Not that it was always possible to tell, or to carry out lengthy due-diligence. Peter Vardy and his engineers were called in to pass technical judgment on what Huizenga and the others' instincts said was a good site, but with competitors hot on the same trail there was no time for leisurely shopping. Don Flynn fashioned the deals and had Buntrock and the board's authority to make them happen fast. Inevitably, the process yielded some lemons. It also yielded the half dozen properties—in Emelle, Alabama; Kettleman Hills, California; Lake Charles, Louisiana; Port Arthur and Corpus Christi, Texas; Vickery, Ohio—that beyond any doubt established Chemical Waste Management (which in 1978 became a separate entity within Waste Management) at the strategic center of the hazardous waste industry.

How undeveloped that industry was on the eve of RCRA is hinted at in the experience of Waste's first men in Alabama. Ray Bock worked in sales for Don Price at the chemical waste facility at CID, and when the orders came down to spread the net nationwide for other sites, he sat down and wrote letters to the environmental protection agencies (or sometimes just the health departments) of all fifty states asking about the status of regulatory enabling legislation and probing for opportunities.

From Alfred S. Chipley, director of the Division of Solid and Hazardous Wastes in the Department of Environmental Management in Montgomery, came a memorable reply to the effect that "while we don't have much enabling legislation in Alabama yet, we do have a lot of opportunity." Bock and Price promptly paid Chipley a visit, and he put them on the path to one of those opportunities, off to the northwest in Sumter County, near the Mississippi line. Not long afterward, "Emelle" entered the Waste Management vocabulary—a synonym for the potential of the chemical and hazardous waste industry, and for the technical level and real estate investment necessary to prosper in it.

It took some imagining at first. Price and Bock rented a car with a license plate that read "The Heart of Dixie" and set off into Alabama's Black Belt, whose rich soil had once made it the heart of the Cotton Kingdom. Most of the cotton had long since migrated to Texas and California, but what they found, out on state highway 17 five miles from the towns of Emelle and Geiger, was a resource as valuable in the 1970s as any cotton plantation had been in the 1850s. They found a 350-acre hazardous waste disposal site whose sign read "Resource Industries of Alabama, Inc.," a company that had been put together in 1977 by four entrepreneurs alert to the EPA recommendation of Sumter County as geologically ideal for the management of hazardous wastes. They had complementary talents. Mark Gregory was an engineer. Jim Parsons was George Wallace's son-in-law and a man with a sense for local politics. Jim Massey was in the drum reclamation business in Memphis. David Wilder was a Tennessean with money to risk.

The package of property that they had assembled and permitted might have come right out of the EPA's ideal spec book for hazardous waste disposal. With a constant eye on the integrity of ground water supplies, the agency sought out stable formations with thick clays or highly impermeable chalks protecting underlying aquifers. If they happened to be located somewhere with slight rainfall, so much the better. Even though Emelle was located in the Southeast, which can be wet, it was close enough. What the EPA geologists had reported and what Parsons and company had acquired, was real estate set atop some of the most stable geology on the planet. The "Selma or Demopolis Chalk," locally known as limerock, is a massive homogeneous formation running through central Alabama with outcrops into Sumter County where it reaches its greatest thickness—over 700 feet from surface to groundwater. An alkaline material of calcium carbonate with a pH level of ten, the chalk has been unchanged for 70 million years and is so dense as to be almost impermeable.

The ideal had yet to be realized, however. When Price and Bock arrived, they found a lone trailer, which was Parson's office, one trench to receive waste, and two customers. Bock also saw, lying on Parson's desk in the trailer, a business card bearing the blue "BFI" logo of Browning Ferris Industries. The competition had been there ahead of them. After a couple of hours, they headed home, and for a while the car was quiet. Then, all at once, they turned to each other and, with the usually unrecorded expression of explorers who reach the mountaintop, exclaimed: "Holy s___—that's the place!"

They worried at first about convincing the brass in Oak Brook to invest some serious money (the four partners had mentioned $20 million as a suitable sum) in an obscure plot in Alabama with some nice geology and a couple of customers. They needn't have, for it didn't take Buntrock, Huizenga, and Flynn long, after having a look for themselves, to make their move. It did take some local hand-holding on the part of Price and Bock; the company brought the partners and their wives up to Chicago to persuade them that Waste Management had the sort of people they would want to come in with, and to woo them from BFI who was courting them heavily.

It all paid off in February 1978, when Resource Industries of Alabama became Alabama Solid Waste Systems, soon to be known as Waste Management of Alabama. The deal that they finally struck was (typically) mostly for stock: 120,000 Waste Management common shares. As the site developed beyond anyone's expectations and as the royalties paid out, that original figure of $20 million came to look positively reasonable.

The first permit that the company held for Emelle came out of Alfred Chipley's office in Montgomery. It authorized the holder "to collect, treat, store and recover any resources contained in and dispose of all solid and liquid industrial wastes, and all wastes categorized as potentially hazardous or toxic except waste requiring incineration for final disposal . . . and except radioactive wastes, pathological wastes and normal commercial and domestic wastes." It took effect on February 23, 1978, and was to run for five years. It was one page long.

From such beginnings grew the largest of all Chemical Waste Management facilities. The original 350 acres (still the active disposal area) became 2,700, most of which was given over not to imported waste from New York and New Jersey but to abundant local deer and wild turkey. The site became the object of heavy company investment in the fast-evolving technology of hazardous waste handling. The EPA approved it for the disposal of poly-chlorinated biphenyls (PCBs) in June 1978. Its Part B RCRA permit came through in 1988. It filled five volumes.

BFI was the company with the big customer base in the South-east, and utilization of Emelle grew slowly at first. But gradually, the market followed the regulations, and a wide variety of industries—steel and automotive manufacturing, paints, poly-mers, pharmaceuticals, agricultural chemicals—lined up to send their wastes to Emelle. The process for doing so was determined by the external regulations and a company's internal sense of prudence, and it became a ritual.

A waste generator seeking to use the Emelle facility first had to submit an initial sample of the waste stream for chemical analysis at the on-site laboratory. The sample had to be accompanied by a "waste profile sheet" describing the waste and the chemical pro-cess that had produced it. The laboratory then analyzed the sample to determine if it was in fact an acceptable material and how best to handle it upon arrival at Emelle. If Chemical Waste Manage-ment vehicles were to transport it, the analysis also stipulated the most appropriate type of hauling unit. Every shipment, however transported, was moved only in accordance with a "uniform haz-ardous waste manifest," which identified both the generator and the carrier by name and by US EPA i.d. number, and described the waste itself, tagging it with the number corresponding to its particular waste profile sheet.

For a shipment of PCBs from a generator in Kansas, for example, the manifest might offer additional descriptions—"transformers drained and flushed; transformers drained in drums; regulators"— and list the states—Pennsylvania, New York, Colorado, Tennessee, Georgia—where the waste had originated. The manifest contained the generator's certification that the contents of this consignment were fully as described and met in all respects Department of Transportation regulations for their transport by highway. Once a waste stream was "certified" by the company for handling, and received at Emelle, it was subject to "fingerprint analysis" to confirm that it matched the original sample on the profile sheet.

The sophistication of the process grew with time to where the protocol of hazardous waste handling came to incorporate redundancies similar to those observed, for instance, in the construction of commercial aircraft. From the beginning, it has been that kind of business. Commercial flying statistically is many times safer than driving to the drugstore, but the surprising number of people who "won't fly" don't believe it. However elaborate the safety procedures of a hazardous waste handler, it is impossible ever to be "safe enough." Add in the special charge that accompanies anything to do with "the environment," and the difficulty increases: "There's something coming out of the incinerator stack today; that's pollution!" or "There's nothing coming out of the incinerator stack today; I wonder what they're hiding."

At Emelle, two separate laboratories were developed, one to analyze preshipment samples and do fingerprint verifications, the other to perform more detailed chemical analyses involving compatibility tests for liquids to be stored in tanks or destined for recovery treatment. Treatment processes aim to reduce toxicity and change liquid material into a solidified form which can then be placed in lined disposal cells. In compliance with the more stringent RCRA amendments that came into effect in the mid-1980s, no liquid wastes are buried at Emelle. In the early years, regulations did not require the synthetic lining even of hazardous waste landfills, which at Emelle, with its particular geology, probably posed less of a threat to groundwater than would have been the case almost anywhere else. (One study estimated that it would take at least 10,000 years for significant seepage to penetrate the Selma chalk.) The installation of a double liner system reduces almost to nil the chance of the leaching process ever getting started.

To observe a place like Emelle is to be struck by the scale—on the surface, immense piles of earth and sand, vast rolls of black plastic, huge earth-moving machines, and piles of plastic pipe evidence engineering sophistication of a high order. But the real substance is what lies underneath: a floor of protective soil cover (2 feet), a geotextile filter, the primary leacheate collection layer (1 foot), the geotextile protective layer; a 60 mil synthetic geo-membrane, compacted clay (2 feet), another geotextile filter, a secondary leachate collection layer (1 foot), another 60 mil synthetic membrane, a final layer of compacted clay (3 feet minimum). The piping is designed to extract rainwater and keep the cells dry. Deep monitoring wells along the perimeter of the site reach all the way to the Eutaw Aquifer, 700 feet down; shallower wells probe for leakage closer to the waste and provide an early warning system for potential trouble.

Who Has the Permit?

The San Joaquin Valley between Los Angeles and San Francisco shares precious few geological or geographical characteristics with the Black Belt of western Alabama. But one of those few was the presence of an entrepreneur who had a site that had a permit. Bill McKay, a character out of the Oil Patch, owned a trucking company and had put together a parcel of real estate back in the hills and dug a couple of holes for waste disposal. He already had a bigger customer base by far than Emelle. But most important, he had a California permit for hazardous waste in a market area that had lots of potential. McKay was the sort of obsessive entrepreneur who one day wanted to join up with a "big company" like Chem Waste, and the next day didn't, and who for months after he did suffered regular spells of postpartum blues. The highly stratified and tilted geology of the site at Kettleman Hills was a challenge too.

When Don Price was left behind on Easter weekend 1979, after he and Flynn had signed a letter of intent to purchase the site based on representations that the geology was favorable, he hired local well-drillers to bore thirty-foot deep holes, and he ran a little test. He backed up a water truck and filled the holes in the hope the water would stay right there. When it didn't, Peter Vardy was summoned to render his judgment on whether or not the place would, as advertised, really work for hazardous waste. Vardy said that in fact it would, largely because of the unique stratification, and Kettleman Hills proved an excellent long-term acquisition. Flynn worked out a deal for stock, based on a formula of $2 million divided by the current trading price of $29, which left the McKays with 69,114 shares of Waste Management—and Chem Waste with a lot of work to do.

As at Emelle, what later became a fancy piece of civil and environmental engineering was in the beginning primitive, even a touch "Wild West." Shortly after the acquisition, visitors from Oak Brook were struck by the fact that all of the equipment operators seemed to be wearing sidearms, .22 and .38 caliber revolvers in nice Western holsters. McKay explained that they used them on the rattlesnakes that poured out of the hills during the region's abbreviated rainy season (dry climate makes for good landfills and in this respect Kettleman was even superior to Emelle). Being good sportsmen, they harvested what they killed, and it was not unusual to see twenty or thirty snakeskins stretched out to dry in the Western sun, and employees festooned with handsome locally crafted hatbands and belts.

The men from headquarters suggested that it might look a little better to handle the snakes differently: "How 'bout if the company foots the bill," they told McKay, "for these guys to get steel-toed high-top boots and chaps or whatever they need to keep off rattlers? It'd sure be a good idea to get rid of the guns!"

Snakes or not, California was a good place to advance the

business of hazardous waste. If you worked with wastes in California, you worked to state standards among the highest anywhere. The state saw itself as a leader in environmental regulation, and it probably regulated more hazardous materials at the state level than were initially addressed by the EPA under RCRA. The phrase "California Hazardous" referred to a whole category of wastes first defined in the Golden State which became part of the national waste management vocabulary. To have in place a major hazardous waste disposal facility there proved a key piece in Chem Waste's growing national network.

Other pieces fell close to the heart of America's petrochemical industry: the Gulf Coast. Three sites there came into the fold in this first burst of acquisition during the "interim status" period of the late 1970s. In 1978, the company acquired on a pooling-of-interests basis (for approximately 160,000 shares) Conservation Services, Inc. (CSI), of Beaumont and Port Arthur, Texas, which operated a permitted chemical waste landfill and deep-well site, and which would become the location of one of the company's most important hazardous waste incinerators.

The very night Price and Huizenga were in Texas nursing along the CSI deal, word came through the grapevine of an opportunity in Lake Charles, Louisiana, where Connie Hebert and sons ran something called Sediment Removers, Inc., spreading foundry sludge over a 160-acre site. And they had a Louisiana permit in the framework of which a hazardous waste landfill could be built. In Corpus Christi, back down the Texas coast, they gave 180,000 shares for the permit and facilities of International Pollution Control, Inc., which added an important deep-well site to the early nucleus. Wherever, the permit was the key. Up north in the old industrial belt, Phil Rooney worked hard to garner more deep-well and land disposal capacity at the Vickery, Ohio, site of Ohio Liquid Disposal Service (O.L.D.S.), for $5.5 million in cash and notes. This was a key and highly profitable acquisition at the time, ideally complementing Emelle. During this period, the company permitted no sites of its own.

The Technology's the Thing

The bet—that by taking fullest possible advantage of the interim status provisions of RCRA and garnering disposal capacity beyond the original Chicago-area operations, the "mother" solid waste company could enhance its financial performance and spur its growth—proved a sound one. In 1976, when liquid waste operations were carried out only at CID in Calumet City, the business generated revenues of just $1.5 million. With the big early contracts at Lakeland Chemicals in Michigan and Ansul in Wisconsin, this figure rose impressively to approximately $10 million in 1977. With the addition of the new acquisitions operating under interim permits, the picture improved geometrically. The focus on securing strategically located, technically superior (or at least potentially so) land disposal sites, along with expanded hauling capabilities, resulted in an early proprietary foothold for the company in a business that was being driven rapidly forward by RCRA and its offshoots. By the early 1980s, chemical waste operations were contributing close to $100 million to the company's revenues, and the company seemed to have earned a secure place for itself alongside the solid waste business.

Yet the word to describe this relationship is difficult to find. Nicely rising numbers made it an important part of the business for sure, but never quite a comfortable part. Almost as a matter of definition, managing hazardous wastes was more complex than handling solid ones. Indeed, it was in this area that the very term "management" (as opposed to "hauling," "handling," or "burying") was extremely apt. And it only grew more so as the regulations mandated more and more sophisticated solutions, making more and more hazards for the company that engaged to manage such substances. This is not a tautology. It was a highly litigious business; it posed palpable physical dangers; it confronted ideologies that judged waste management companies complicit in the creation of the wastes and therefore wicked. If ever the

phrase matched the fact, "hazardous waste management" certainly did.

In it, nothing ever stood still for long. While the acquisition of
permitted real estate, where hazardous substances could be dealt
with, was the essential first step to securing a place in the business,
it was only a platform (almost literally) on which other pieces—
laboratories, incinerators and sophisticated treatment facilities—
would have to be erected to respond to regulatory and market
demands. In one notable instance, these demands led the company
to a technology that was not land based at all and whose fate
illuminated perils that no garbage company had ever confronted.

In the fall of 1980, Waste Management announced the purchase
of the small Netherlands company, Ocean Combustion Systems,
and with it one of the world's most advanced vessels capable of
high-temperature incineration of hazardous wastes at sea, the *Vulcanus*. Prior to the acquisition, *Vulcanus* had performed three EPA-
approved "burns" from American ports, two for Shell Oil and one
for the army. In late October 1981, Chem Waste received an EPA
permit to test-burn PCBs in a designated burn area in the Gulf of
Mexico, operating out of the port of Mobile, Alabama, in close
coordination with temporary storage facilities there and the company's facilities at Emelle.

The burns were highly successful, and in anticipation of full
permitting, the company had built for it in Germany the *Vulcanus
II*, which was launched in 1982 and, though slightly smaller than
its sister, packed three incinerators to the older ship's two. It was a
big decision. The incinerators on both ships had two chambers
(one for internal mixing, the other to ensure waste-retention time
of one second or longer) and operated at combustion temperatures
of approximately 2300 degrees F. They could process 20 to 25
metric tons of waste per hour, compared to 2 to 4 tons for most of
the land-based competition. Both vessels were double-hulled.

Prospects for the ocean incineration of hazardous materials were
viewed optimistically by the company for several reasons. The
practice had been in use in Europe since the late 1960s, and it was
felt that by bringing it successfully into the American market the

company's image as a leader in advanced hazardous waste technologies would be enhanced. If it worked, it would show farsightedness in the pursuit of enlightened alternatives to land-based disposal.

Behind the strategic hopes and motives lay sound regulatory, technical, and economic reasoning for making the attempt. Tighter enforcement of RCRA rules, legislation expanding the list of toxic chemicals and restricting their combustion in industrial boilers, and pending proposals excluding certain categories of wastes from deep-wells and landfills without pretreatment, all invested incineration or thermal destruction with fresh attraction. Incineration on land was a well-established practice to destroy hazardous wastes, or at least vastly to reduce their toxicity and volume (although Chemical Waste Management as yet had no such facilities of its own). But it was not cheap. Capital costs were heavy. Volumes at that time were still relatively low. Mandatory pollution-control devices (chiefly wet scrubbers), designed to remove acid from stack gas emissions (chiefly hydrochloric acid and trace metals) added materially to the expense of the systems and helped keep prices high.

Ocean incineration accomplished the same objective but with better economics. At least for relatively clean combustible organic liquids, its costs ran perhaps a third less than land-based operations. This was because it was possible—and quite responsible environmentally—for incinerator ships like the two *Vulcanuses* to burn their cargoes without scrubbers. The dilute acid mist, not acceptable over land, was neutralized at sea by the naturally alkaline ocean water. An interagency report of the EPA, the United States Coast Guard, and the United States Maritime Administration praised the technology and the *Vulcanuses* in particular. Its only reservation was that it was in the national interest for such a ship to be American-owned (*Vulcanus I* was owned in The Netherlands), a problem solved when Waste Management bought the company that owned *Vulcanus I* and commissioned the building of *Vulcanus II*.

Under the Marine Protection, Research and Sanctuaries Act of

1972, the EPA regulates ocean incineration in the United States; it is also signatory to the Convention on the Prevention of Marine Pollution of 1972, 1978, and 1981 (the "London Dumping Convention"). The agency's tests had demonstrated that the *Vulcanuses'* incinerators destroyed principal hazardous organic wastes with an efficiency of over 99.99 percent, and that the stack emissions of hydrochloric acid and metallic oxides fell safely under marine water quality criteria and posed no threat to the ocean environment. Even though RCRA did not apply to ocean incineration, the EPA adhered to the same performance-based requirements and concluded that both ships were satisfactory.

Under the test permits granted Waste Management, *Vulcanus I* in two burns, December 1981 and August 1982, successfully destroyed 1.5 million gallons of liquid PCBs. Waste Management attorney Frank Krohn headed up the daunting permitting effort. The permits that the company then applied for would have authorized both ships to transport wastes from Mobile to an area in the Gulf some 150 miles from the nearest land, and there to incinerate over a three-year period 300,000 metric tons of liquid organics, including PCBs at less than 35 percent by weight, and dioxin at a maximum concentration of two parts per million. The permitting process consumed three-and-a-half years and tested the company's persistent hopes for the process. They showed off the ships to customers and the public in Mobile and worked through the grueling public hearings there and in Brownsville, Texas, where political and emotional objections outweighed technical ones and foreshadowed a negative outcome.

In such confrontations, the parties talk past each other. If one accepted the results of the EPA that said the alkaline ocean neutralizes acid mist, then the *Vulcanuses* truly were the better mousetraps. If, on the other hand, one believed that any man-made substance "dumped" in the sea "polluted" it, then the *Vulcanuses* had to be stopped. Concerning the objections about the potential for accidents, one was either impressed by *Vulcanus I*'s spotless operating record since 1972, or one dismissed it because "that was then, but what about now?" The amount of waste—300,000 tons over three years—sounded large, until it was set against the approximately 400 million tons of chemical and petroleum material that moved every year along the Gulf Coast.

Numerous special interest groups lined up against the project—shrimpers, farm laborers, people alleging that emissions would cause further damage in Nicaragua and El Salvador. Environmentalists split, with Greenpeace predictably and adamantly opposed (perhaps anticipating a news-rich high seas encounter between the *Vulcanus* and *Rainbow Warrior*), but with the National Wildlife Federation (in a press release, but not in person) in support of the principle and of this particular application. No one at the hearing, besides representatives of EPA and Waste Management, actually spoke in favor of the permit, and the National Wildlife position mirrored the ambivalent feelings on the subject of even the most rationally inclined observers.

Destruction of persistent toxic materials, they argued, is vastly preferable environmentally to their storage or disposal, and incineration by the *Vulcanuses* would see to that. While avoiding waste generation was always preferable, wastes that already existed must be responsibly dealt with, and with only a limited number of options available, it would be environmentally counterproductive arbitrarily to preclude any of them. The risk of an accident seemed negligible considering the enormous traffic already plying the area in trucks, trains, and coastal vessels. Yet, oddly, what most appealed was the symbolism of the *Vulcanuses* as a high-tech, relatively high-cost alternative to least-cost and increasingly objectionable disposal practices like landfilling. The higher the cost, ran this logic, the more impetus there would be to cut back on waste generation. Or, as more radical voices would put it in years to come: constipate the waste system, and you clean up the planet.

It was competition, however, as much as ideology, that defeated the *Vulcanuses*. Rollins and Ensco, companies with large land-based incineration capacity along the Gulf, wanted the *Vulcanus* permit to fail for reasons that had nothing to do with the environment, and they skillfully orchestrated all manner of opposition voices. Bogus environmental organizations—the "Alliance to Save the Environment" and the "Committee for Tourism in the Bay Area"—were orchestrated to stir up opposition by telephoning unsuspecting citizens of the coastal areas to urge them to protest at the hearings. The regulators took fright, and the permit finally was denied in May 1984. Buntrock hated to give up. Financially, the consequences were not great. The two ships eventually went back to Europe, then still a viable market. *Vulcanus I* eventually was sold off and retrofitted as a tanker; *Vulcanus II* continues to incinerate waste in the North Sea, although that too will cease in 1995 under EC regulations.

Enter the Chemists

Landfills make money, but high-technology was the wave of the future. Even though the attempt at ocean incineration came to naught, the image of the two ships for Chemical Waste Management was important. They were portrayed as sophisticated technological solutions to difficult waste problems, which indeed they were. How much money they would have made in the larger scheme was another question. (There probably wasn't enough "waste fuel" out there anyway to support both them and the land-based competition.) Certainly it would not have been much compared with landfills like Emelle and Kettleman Hills. But the movement, in what was still a very young industry, to ever-higher requirements of technical expertise and performance was inexorable. It shaped the growth of the company and revealed tensions between the chemical and the solid waste businesses that have proven a challenge to resolve.

The company decided in 1975 to build an analytical laboratory at the CID landfill, even though the regulations did not require elaborate testing. Co-disposal of chemical waste with municipal solid waste, as it was carried out there, was widely deemed a sound practice. But the time soon came when the ability to determine exactly what went into a landfill would be as important as crude capacity itself.

Buntrock and Peter Vardy believed that a modern laboratory was essential if the future justified the $250,000 investment. Not all of their colleagues saw it that way, and indeed for a time one could stand at the new facility and watch the trucks pass by heading for cheaper disposal sites where they just poured the waste into the ground. But before long the laboratory became something of a showplace for the company, and an absolute necessity under the new regulations.

In 1980, Chem Waste invested yet again, this time in a 40,000 square-foot laboratory and technical center in Riverdale, Illinois, near Chicago and staffed it with chemists and technicians who began to bring a chemical-company mentality into the business. George VanderVelde, a PhD in bio-physics and analytical chemistry, was hired by Milo Harrison to improve analytical programs and quality assurance at the bench. Mark Marcus, another PhD, from Stauffer Chemical, soon joined him. The purpose of the facility was waste analysis and process-oriented research to determine what was coming and how best to treat it.

The standards of laboratory practice established there, which became standards for the EPA itself, aimed toward an analysis so thorough and well documented that it would stand up in court: it was a very litigious business. This required the appropriate paper trail on each sample to connect it with the actual waste stream, and to be able to track it all the way through the laboratory (or trace it in reverse if need be). Analysts had to be trained and certified. Equipment had to be precise and provably so.

In the early 1980s, analytical work consisted largely of waste analysis for sample approval. But as RCRA amendments took hold after the mid-1980s, receiving-analysis work at the disposal sites skyrocketed in quantity and sophistication. With the increase of analytical work at the disposal sites, the concept of regional laboratories was embraced to do the sales sample analysis and special projects. The first regional laboratory was the Riverdale, Illinois, facility. Then, by acquisition, they added a laboratory in Modesto, California, for the Western Region, another in Denville, New Jersey, for the East, and designated the laboratory at the Port Arthur site as the regional laboratory for the South. The number of analytical chemists rose in ten years from about fifty in the early 1980s to more than three hundred, all highly qualified people who sorted out into several groups.

A systems group at Riverdale, unique in the company, was also initiated to develop a laboratory information management system to provide information directly from the instruments. And a methods development group was set up to develop methods specific to the handling of hazardous wastes. While surprising, it is important to remember that many EPA-adopted methods had been developed in water-analytical programs. Another analytical group was constituted specifically to deal with the regulatory agencies in the course of preparing the waste analysis plans that were part of the RCRA Part B permitting process.

The other side of the operation was "process." In 1984, a research and development capability was established within Chemical Waste Management to look at the process technology then in use and to prepare the company to meet the latest regulatory road map. The 1984 RCRA amendments established among other things requirements for treatment technologies and standards to be met on wastes prior to landfilling. The law established the general framework, leaving it to the EPA to establish specifics for each individual waste stream. The challenge for the company (and for the whole industry) was to meet the requirements, and to see that those requirements could practically be met. The EPA, at that juncture, lacked a database of process technologies in hazardous waste, and much of the company's work went toward helping the agency establish such a database in terms of "Best Demonstrated Available Technologies" (BDAT) specific to hazardous materials. The company had the advantages of being able to obtain waste, perform analytical work on it, characterize and treat it in various ways in the laboratory, and then determine the effectiveness of the treatment. Several major areas emerged.

The ability to treat organic materials would be directed, largely, toward incineration, which had two advantages. First, it was a generic process (not, it is true, as generic as a hole in the ground, but still capable of handling a wide variety of materials), which is essential in a business whose job it is to perform chemical processes on materials that carry no precise specifications. Second, it was highly destructive of the wastes, as the company tried unsuccessfully to explain in the *Vulcanus* episode.

For inorganic wastes, the process group concentrated on chemical fixation and stabilization treatments prior to disposal. Dr. Peter Daley was hired in 1984 to head Research and Development, and smaller groups coalesced around different disciplines: chemical processes, waste water and biological treatments, advanced waste systems, and mechanical handling and systems. This last group developed a drum-opening system in anticipation of the EPA rule that as of May 1985 said no containerized liquids could go into landfills. As mundane and low-tech as it sounds, it addressed a major problem, given what the company received in drums—everything from dirty rags and soiled uniforms to electric motors and volatile liquids. Some drums were corrugated cardboard, some fiber, some plastic, some stainless; some had detachable tops, but most did not. To open the things and remove their contents without injuring personnel or generating additional waste was extremely important, and the system installed at Emelle became the prototype for many others throughout the company from Holland to Hong Kong; it set the standard for the industry.

Another group looked at a wide range of processes for waste remediation work, out of which came the X★TRAX™ Process for removing contaminated organics from solid materials. Another worked on biological treatment. Another still on waste-water, which developed the PO★WW★ER™ Process for the recycling of difficult waste-water streams. In staffing all these areas, the company was well served by the coincidence of heavy merger and acquisition activity in the chemical and oil industries and the dissolution of numerous technical and engineering groups, which made some exceptionally good people from Amoco, Arco, Borg-Warner, and Stauffer Chemical available at just the right time. At their new home in Chem Waste, they became a world-recognized group in hazardous waste processing technology.

"Technology," not "science," is the proper word. Though many of them were highly trained scientists, the people in Research and Development at Chem Waste did not do "pure research." No one indulged in scientific whimsy. Everyone looked for answers to concrete current problems and probed toward processes that might give the company an edge tomorrow. They served the same master—the market—that everyone else did.

Pits, Ponds, and Lagoons

The conjunction of rising regulatory fervor and technological innovation produced, in chemical waste management, a remarkable new industry. The industry symbolized a sea change in popular attitudes toward industrialization. Anxiety about "pollution" was first expressed legislatively with regard to air, water, and solid wastes. By the 1980s, it had homed in on the hazardous substances that were the by-products (and sometimes the products) of the industry that for decades had fueled America's economic growth and its wondrously rising standard of living. During the 1940s and 1950s, DuPont, the largest chemical company in the world, had a corporate slogan that masterfully captured the spirit of the age: "Better Things for Better Living through Chemistry."

As it turned out, all the better things that everybody wanted also produced some not-so-nice things that nobody wanted and could not ignore forever. RCRA, TSCA, and their successor laws and amendments expressed a broad cultural consensus that henceforth we would have to do better, that in the future the challenge of American industry would lie not just in producing goods and finding markets for them, but in reducing the byproducts and finding safe ways to manage them. On the public policy and private markets that resulted, the success of Chemical Waste Management has been built.

At the same time the country seemed to be saying "enough is enough—tomorrow has got to be different from today"; it was looking back on yesterday's sins and seeking to repair the damage. The key enabling legislation was the Comprehensive Environmental Response, Compensation and Liability Act of 1980—CERCLA or, as it has entered the vernacular, "Superfund." The law gave the EPA the authority and funds to clean up abandoned hazardous waste sites deemed environmental or public health problems, and it assigned perpetual liability to responsible parties for the safe management of hazardous wastes. Its intent was to deal with the past, which was tricky. In the course of ascribing guilt, apportioning responsibility, and then actually cleaning up, Superfund turned into a very tangled process. But it spurred another line of business that Chem Waste used to good advantage.

In 1981, the company formed its Environmental Remedial Action Division, or "ENRAC," and received EPA's first clean-up contract for a hazardous waste site under Superfund. The site, in Gary, Indiana, involved removal of fifty thousand drums from the Midco Chemical Company, decanting and treating the contents, and then excavating and transporting contaminated topsoil to company facilities for secure disposal. "Hog and haul," in the argot of the trade, was repeated many times at hundreds of locations across the country in the early years of ENRAC. In 1985, ENRAC was designated by the companies responsible for a Superfund site in Greensboro, North Carolina, to clean up two former PCB recycling facilities. The $4.5 million project required removal of 2,500 tons of PCB-contaminated processing equipment, oils, capacitors, transformers, and packaging materials; all of it had to be processed and shredded and then destroyed in one of the company's high-temperature incinerators. In 1989, ENRAC disposed of approximately 90 percent of the debris and contaminated materials from the Exxon *Valdez* tanker spill in Alaska.

The chemical waste remediation business was a good example of legislation stimulating market demand for a service that ended up far exceeding what was mandated by law. Superfund work continued through the 1980s (in 1987 the company won the contract for the largest ever privately funded cleanup of a federally designated Superfund site, at a former recycling center in Seattle: a $40 million, five- to seven-year piece of work). But the mechanisms for triggering the cleanup of chemically contaminated sites were various. New Jersey and other states stipulated that for contaminated real estate to change hands it first had to be cleaned up. And the internal pressures for polluters to clean, or have cleaned, past untidiness increased as the definition of a "good corporate citizen" came to include ever-heavier doses of environmental good character.

When the company acquired Chem-Nuclear Systems in a hostile takeover in 1983, it added low-level nuclear wastes to the list of materials it was equipped to dispose of, and a new kind of site to those it was equipped to remediate. Although the nuclear waste business is very different from the chemical waste business, the acquisition was subsumed under the Chemical Waste Management umbrella. Remediation projects ranged from the decontamination of a single house in Philadelphia, and a building used by a radiation sterilization business in suburban Atlanta, to massive undertakings such the Department of Energy's long-term Uranium Mill Tailings Remedial Action Project begun in Colorado in 1983, and the Denver Radioactive Superfund project that called on the company to transport and dispose of half a million tons of radium-contaminated soil and debris from forty-four separate locations.

The place of Chem-Nuclear within Chem Waste is at once perfectly plausible and curious. When Wayne Huizenga pushed hard for the acquisition in the early 1980s, he, along with Buntrock, saw it as a natural part of the picture, if the aim was to create a company with total waste management capability (which it was), and if new markets and revenues were needed to fuel the company's growth (which they were). It was not an easy acquisition to make, but once made it was not a difficult one to run. (The opposite might be said of Chem Waste itself.) Esoteric as it may be, the low-level nuclear waste business was actually a simpler business, in the sense that the dangers posed by low-level radioactive waste were relatively short lived and easily measured. (Most low-level nuclear waste handled by Chem-Nuclear is of relatively low activity to begin with and decays down by 90–95 percent within a hundred years; its dangers are measurable with technology no more complicated than a Geiger counter.)

The nuclear waste business was also older than the chemical waste business, dating to the 1950s and 1960s. Springing from the history of nuclear power itself, it was from the start hedged in by a pronounced cautionary culture: the margin for error in weapons production and power generation was small, the consequences of error conceivably catastrophic. This attitude of great care carried over, as the uses of lower-level radiation spread in industry and medicine. In the business of low-level nuclear waste (which is Chem-Nuclear's business; high-level wastes from power plants and weapons remain the responsibility of the federal government), there were numerous personnel with experience aboard nuclear submarines. The navy operated more reactors than anyone else in the world, and the men who had tended them and depended upon them brought to a company like Chem-Nuclear habits of work learned in the most unforgiving of environments.

With the acquisition of Chem-Nuclear in 1983, Chem Waste acquired at Barnwell, South Carolina, one of the only three low-level nuclear waste disposal facilities in the country. At the time, Barnwell had operated continuously without mishap since opening in 1971, and it was destined to do so for many years to come. Its monitoring equipment, whose purpose was to keep track of canisters buried in nearby trenches, easily detected trouble at Chernobyl half a world away.

Biggest Buy

Adding to the network—operating facilities that actually did the work of waste management in new markets—was the motive behind Waste Management's acquisitions from its earliest years. It bought in order to grow, and not to strip down and sell off. In a growing industry, demand-driven by regulation and the inexorable rise of environmentalism, such a policy was a happy combination of imperatives. Necessity, prudence, and an instinct for right timing conspired to make it happen, in the early 1970s, and the 1980s, as it does today.

If an acquisition netted important new capacity across several "fields," then so much the better. Waste Management's acquisition in 1984 of Service Corporation of America (SCA), the third-largest handler of solid and hazardous waste in the country, is the most striking example of this, and is something of a tale in itself. It was by far the largest addition to Waste Management accomplished up to that time. It added several key chemical waste handling and treatment facilities and great capacity in solid waste, simultaneously. It was an acquisition that was also more than the sum of its parts. It boosted the company firmly ahead of Browning Ferris Industries as the country's number-one waste manager, a position it only strengthened in the years that followed. It made Waste Management into a major company and gave it forward momentum that it never has lost. It helped the company shake off the doubts that plagued it as a result of 1983 press allegations of environmental mismanagement (subject of the following chapter). It was the sort of turning point from which no one at Waste Management looked back again. It also demonstrated again the company's good fortune in counting Chief Financial Officer Don Flynn among its leaders.

Somehow acquiring SCA had been an idea that the company had long contemplated: from a market strategy perspective it was an exceptional piece of business. SCA had gone public shortly after Waste Management and, across the country, had competed heavily with it for acquisitions and market penetration. While SCA had faltered by the late 1970s and lost some of its market allure, the obvious antitrust obstacle in an acquisition remained: number two buying number three and then eliminating number three from the market and becoming number one. It was Flynn, however, who hit upon a concept that made it possible.

In 1983, he suggested trying to acquire SCA in a partnership mode that would entail the spinning-off of SCA businesses directly competitive with Waste Management's existing businesses and retaining only those businesses where there was no market overlap. Flynn initially had in mind Pritchard Services, the British firm that had been the company's partner in Riyadh and that was then looking to expand its presence in the United States. Pritchard turned out not to be a viable contender, but the concept stuck. General Counsel Steve Bergerson was intrigued, and Buntrock agreed to go ahead, if there actually was a reasonable chance of surmounting the antitrust problem. Confidence gradually grew, and other partners were explored (one of which was what is today the Wheelabrator group, which backed away for fear that the situation might become hostile). As discussions proceeded, it became clearer that they needed more than just a financial partner who would likely be viewed askance by the Justice Department as a buyer and seller unlikely to maintain its share of the business and really compete. The company needed an actual operating partner.

In Genstar, a Canadian company headquartered in San Francisco, which owned numerous cement and limestone quarries and trucking operations, they found the right match and put the deal together. The key to it was defining (at first on a preliminary basis, for it would all also be negotiated with the Justice Department), which businesses Waste Management would be able to take, which it wouldn't, and which fell in the middle.

Despite the simplicity of the concept, deals like this had not been done before, and this hurdle stopped them. Laboriously, they worked out a pricing mechanism for the parts, which factored in revenues, profits, and asset value, and which seemed to work in whatever business they applied to it. The negotiations, with Flynn, Rooney, and Bergerson in the thick, were not easy. It was a complex challenge: taking a large publicly held entity and breaking it into two pieces in a way that made business sense and that would pass antitrust muster. They were helped by the probusiness environment of the Reagan administration, and they anticipated that part of the SCA's defense would be to claim antitrust violations and sue, which they did.

"Hostile" for a time, the situation ended up "friendly," as over a process lasting two months SCA succumbed. Browning Ferris actively competed for the acquisition. Indeed, at the last minute (over the weekend after Buntrock, Flynn, and Bergerson thought they had a deal nailed down on Friday; the SCA board had passed a resolution and everyone had shaken hands), they came in with an unsolicited offer over Waste Management's price and almost took it away.

The episode prompted one of those "Dewey Beats Truman!" headlines, as the *Chicago Sun-Times* reported on Monday, August 13, 1984, the imminent merger of SCA and BFI. But the deal had not yet been signed, and Flynn told Buntrock that if they wanted to save it they would have to go back in over BFI. They did; they were offering cash (BFI which did not have WM's balance sheet was offering stock); this time they let no one move until the ink was dry. On Tuesday, August 14, the *Wall Street Journal* got it right, announcing that SCA would be acquired for $423 million ($28.50 per share) and that its assets would be split between Waste Management and Genstar. Waste Management's share amounted to approximately 60 percent of SCA's business and operations, for which it paid $220 million in cash. On the solid waste side, they achieved new presence in New England, Texas, southern California, and other important markets. In chemical waste, they acquired their first hazardous waste incinerator (in Chicago), an industrial waste water treatment facility, and a landfill permitted for the disposal of PCBs in Model City, New York (near Niagara Falls), and a double-lined hazardous waste landfill in Ft. Wayne, Indiana.

Positioning

The annual reports of Chemical Waste Management, Inc. since 1986, when the company became a separately traded entity on the New York Stock Exchange, are crafted with a powerful image in mind. They are filled with photographs of shiny plants—colored pipes, valves, uniformed hard-hatted personnel—of fancy laboratories with scientists in white coats, and of large computers and control panels. Though posed, as is much of this genre, they are genuine depictions of a technology-driven business. It takes nothing away from their authenticity to observe that these same pictures might be transposed directly to the annual report of Dow or DuPont. But it does help make an important point. What one puts together, the other takes apart; what one leaves behind, the other reduces to an acceptably innocuous state. Ever-stricter rules about what is innocuous continually redefine the threshold of technological competence required to do the job.

The desire to reap the market's reward for such high-tech orientation was what lay immediately behind the initial public offering in 1986 that spun-off Chem Waste into a separately traded entity. Multiples then enjoyed by much smaller publicly owned chemical waste companies were higher than that of Waste Management as long as Chem Waste was tucked into the much larger parent. Don Flynn conceived and engineered it, and the IPO of nearly 18,900,000 common shares in October 1986 raised capital of some $300 million. Waste Management itself retained approximately 81 percent ownership. Buntrock was chairman, Flynn was CFO, Rooney and Peter Huizenga were directors. Jerry Dempsey became the first president and CEO of the free-standing company, which in its first independent year had revenues of $418 million and a pretax income of $104 million. Value was enhanced for everyone.

Operationally, the spin-off had no great impact. Thematically, it signified the recognition that the chemical waste and solid waste businesses were quite different businesses, a recognition that had been present all along but for which the IPO was a fitting symbol. It also signified the rapid-growth, no–looking-back quality of that business and the optimism that saw a future in terms of 25 percent growth rates. Such optimism was justified by the actual performance, which was due to the added technological challenges posed by the handling of hazardous wastes; it was perhaps even more remarkable than the analogous early growth of Waste Management itself. By the time of the IPO, the company had achieved a breadth of technology and geographical positioning that made it the industry leader. What began in 1975 simply as a way to bring more revenue into the solid waste company, became a strategy for the full-service provision of hazardous waste services to both industry and government.

The functional positioning of the different components was such that the company could adjust to, and profit from, shifting waste streams and regulatory developments. The relation among incineration, treatment, and landfilling was vastly important. Incineration, for example, was regarded as an essential piece of this strategy, but a piece also linked to landfills. The concept was to have the capacity to burn incinerable wastes, as EPA-stimulated demand grew for high-temperature destruction of organic materials. The recycling and fuel-value related to liquids, however, called for the ability to handle increased quantities of solids and sludge that, unlike the liquids, left behind substantial quantities of ash. Under the regulations, ash carried the same characteristics of the original waste and so required more treatment and double-lined landfills to deposit it in.

The so-called "Land Bans," started in the late 1980s to divert more hazardous waste streams away from land disposal, required increased treatment and stabilization of dangerous substances. But more elaborate treatment services required higher prices for them. Both incineration and treatment activities tried to accommodate a wide spectrum of waste streams. This protected the company from "internalized competition" from large producers of relatively homogeneous wastes, who might handle the waste themselves on site in their own permitted facilities and then market their excess capacity.

The performance of the company also depended on two other kinds of "positioning." The first was the quality of service to the customers. Obviously, quality service had been paramount ever since Buntrock brought together the first garbage companies back in the 1960s, but in Chemical Waste it had an added dimension. To the old service of "picking it up and responsibly putting it down" had been added a sort of information or educational service to waste generators. As the regulations grew ever more lengthy and complex, the company could claim (rightly in most cases) that it knew the ins and outs of these things better than anyone else, and that from that knowledge flowed superior service and reduced liabilities.

The second sort of positioning was presenting the company to the regulators and the public as a responsible steward of the environment. Buntrock and Wayne Huizenga spoke of care for the environment in their very first letter to shareholders of the newly public Waste Management, Inc. back in 1971, and quietly had made it a part of their company's ethic from that point on. But, again, when the subject was the less forgiving one of hazardous waste, everything ratcheted upward.

The executives who have served at the top of Chemical Waste Management since the late 1970s—Don Price, Phil Rooney, Milo Harrison, Joe Knott, Jerry Dempsey, Pat Payne—have all been talented men. But as telling as their talents is their number: it is not an easy job. It is a symptom of intense outside scrutiny and internal pressure, and of a natural tension between Waste Management and Chemical Waste Management, between the solid waste business and the hazardous waste business that is historical in origin.

Solid waste landfills and hauling companies, some would say, always did and still do lend themselves to decentralized operations, albeit backed up (as Don Flynn long ago conceived it) by centralized financial controls. Hazardous waste operations, others would say, cry out for centralization of operational control and of in-house technical capability. The single greatest crisis in Waste Management's larger story of success involved the handling of chemical waste. The legal, financial, environmental, and public relations questions it raised laid bare this tension. As they were sorted through, the culture of the entire company, not just of Chem Waste, was changed.

9

As Others See Them

A DOZEN years into its corporate history, Waste Management had established a track record highly pleasing to its managers, its employees, and its shareholders. By all measures, it was a study in the creation of value. Revenues ($965 million in 1982) had grown an average of 26 percent a year, net income ($106 million in 1982) 35 percent, and earnings per share 29 percent. (Only once— during the recession of 1975—did earnings per share fail to climb, and that was attributable to wastepaper recycling operations that the company soon exited.) Even in recessionary 1982, earnings rose robustly by 23 percent. The company began paying dividends in 1976 and never since missed a quarter. The stock market rewarded the predictability and consistency of this performance handsomely. In January 1983, Waste Management shares were trading at a hefty fifty-seven. Waste Management enjoyed the highest pretax margins in the industry. Its balance sheet sparkled. Following a 2 million-share equity offering (at 49½) in November

1982, it had no short-term debt and its long-term debt represented approximately 20 percent of its total capital. Return on equity was running about 25 percent.

Financial strength rested solidly on operations know-how and strategic positioning that enabled it to benefit from the myriad opportunities blossoming throughout the country. RCRA and Superfund fueled the growth of Chem Waste (CWM). Though less in the public eye, the problems of properly disposing of the nation's 200 million tons of solid waste without contaminating groundwater, fueled the growth of Waste Management of North America, the new subsidiary set apart in 1981, which served over 2 million households and consolidated all North American solid waste operations. Of the then-twelve thousand landfills in the United States, more than half could not meet forthcoming standards and were destined for closure. As the disposal side of the waste business consequently consolidated, implications for well-located and properly designed sites were striking.

Waste Management's early heavy investment in real estate was paying off. It had the largest disposal capacity (some sixty sanitary landfills with an estimated useful life of fifteen years, and a unique national network of fifteen chemical waste disposal facilities) and the broadest range of technical capabilities in the industry. These strengths, particularly in disposal and processing, as opposed to simple collection, gave it enormous operating leverage considering the high-fixed-cost/low-variable-cost character of such large increasingly hard-to-locate facilities. The operating experience of its technical staff and the expertise they developed soared past the competition's, enabling the company to perform virtually all of its quality control and testing in-house. In collection too, the trends were only favorable for private providers who already hauled an estimated 60 percent of the country's residential refuse at perhaps 30 percent lower cost than did public agencies. Even in resource recovery (recycling), where markets were always fickle, the company positioned itself to take advantage of opportunities as they developed.

Waste Management had exclusive American license for the Danish "Volund" system of mass refuse incineration and was building a large facility in Tampa, Florida. It was also expanding its system for methane recovery from major landfills. Although still a small contributor financially, the company's international operations, which had begun in Riyadh in 1976 and included other city-cleaning projects in Jeddah, as well as Buenos Aires and Cordoba, Argentina, and Caracas, Venezuela, provided a proving ground for a whole cadre of managers who ran the company through the 1980s.

And it was this intangible—the quality of management—as much as anything else that distinguished this company from the others and made its stellar performance possible. Since 1971, once people came, they tended to stay. All of the founders were still there, and they had assembled from within and without the industry a team of remarkable scope and depth in operations, finance, and technology. With Buntrock leading, they developed the ability to identify trends early and strategically position the company to ride them, such as in chemical waste, and in international and low-level nuclear operations.

Capitalizing on near-term opportunities where they could (the trend toward privatization of refuse collection, for example), they seldom let the long view slip. They had been at it long enough to have gained confidence in one another, but not so long as to have forgotten that the proof still lay with each individual's own performance. Pressed to describe their "style," one would have to say they had two. As if by a formula (which of course it wasn't), they had nurtured a genuinely entrepreneurial spirit, while constantly learning how to manage a larger and larger organization.

They didn't quite walk on water, but they shared in the universal weakness of extrapolating past experience (especially if it were as pleasant as theirs) into the future, while forgetting how the present sometimes stood up and slapped you in the face. True, they could look at their company squarely and say that what they saw made them proud: they were the professionals who did a good job, who served customers best, who made investors and analysts purr, who followed the rules and treated the environment with all the care that the rules, and common sense, said were due it. This was dangerous. It was too commonsensical, too rational, by half.

Markets, however, in general do behave rationally, and it was in this world that these and other good businessmen functioned most comfortably. Dean Buntrock, it is often and rightly said, is a businessman of great vision, amply testified to by the way he has led his company from obscurity to the heights. But not even he could have foreseen, in 1971 or even in 1982, the irrational or antirational world that this particular business would find it had to navigate in henceforth. A new political culture was dominating markets and changing forever the way American business would operate—no business more so than waste management. It was a culture that changed the meaning of risk.

This was true all across the industry, but was felt perhaps most sharply in chemical waste. On the one hand, real operational risks were remarkably low. The combination of well-located and de-signed disposal sites (geologically and hydrologically), state-of-the-art analytical and treatment processes, quality controls with high degrees of built-in redundancies, and extensive sudden and non-sudden liability insurance, gave companies the tools to do a good job responsibly. On the other hand, the perceived risks multiplied, far outpacing the real risks and making everything about the business controversial.

Glossy or Grainy: As You Like It

Perceptions had never mattered much to the men who built Waste Management. Not that they didn't care how others viewed them, but they were convinced—their experience had shown them—that how they were perceived correlated directly with how well they performed: do a good job, they believed, and everything else will follow. There never has been anything glamorous about hauling garbage to a hole in the ground (or to a new landscape being contoured above grade). But a great deal has become, if not quite "glamorous," then decidedly "in vogue" about being certain that the hole in the ground or the fill above it does not leak, that it accepts only designated wastes, that indeed alternatives are sought to burying wastes there in the first place. During the 1980s, garbage and other waste (understood as a threat to the environment) and the management of that threat, achieved new status in the continuing war the nation was waging against pollution. Today, this new status has become a commonplace—but a commonplace with a stiff ideological charge that does not have a lot to do with performance alone.

We live in a visual age where judgments are rendered, and products pushed, with the power of pictures. It is not an oversimplification to say that pictures of Waste Management consist of two types, and only two. First there are the sort of pictures that the company (indeed any company) uses to illustrate itself to the outside world. They fill every annual report. They are carefully selected, sometimes posed, and always produced with great care: landfills that look like golf courses; garbagemen spiffier than chauffeurs; incinerators that resemble rocket-launching pads—all hard hats, white coats, gray suits. Then there are the sort that the media use to illustrate a company (and an industry) that they have never quite understood and often seemed wary of. Figuratively, and often literally, such pictures are grainy, shot from unflattering angles, composed with the photo-journalist's eye for clashing images that will get a viewer's attention and make him remember.

On March 21, 1983, the New York Times launched an exposé, now famous within the company and the environmental community, of alleged lapses in Waste Management's environmental performance. The photograph (shot at Waste Management's Calumet City, Illinois hazardous waste treatment plant) of acid waste recovery towers and a sinister cesspool-like lagoon behind a chain-link fence, had force equal to the headline: "Leader in Toxic Dumps Accused of Illegal Acts." Nine years later, at this writing,

239

little has changed. On April 13, 1992, *Business Week* ran an article about Chem Waste's troubled hazardous waste incinerator on the South Side of Chicago. The photograph is an excellent piece of work with a clear editorial purpose: stack and tower emblazoned with a large Waste Management logo and the words "Safety First" viewed across the barbed wire and "Danger Unauthorized Personnel Keep Out" sign. The angle is askew; power lines crisscross; everything looks ajumble. It too "sticks," like the headline: "The Ugly Mess At Waste Management."

Words and graphics like these pain Dean Buntrock greatly, particularly today, after his company has made enormous strides and leads the industry in environmental good citizenship. But he and his colleagues have become used to them. Nine years ago, they were shocked as they had never been shocked before. The "events of 1983," revolving around serious allegations of environmental misconduct, and the company's reaction to them, were a watershed in the company's evolving understanding not just of how the waste business worked (they thought they knew that well enough), but of how public opinion could be molded, given the great urgency Americans had come to attach to environmental issues. It was at this point that these two things—waste and the environment—converged for good in the history of Waste Management.

At this point too, the entrepreneurs and good businessmen who had founded Waste Management realized that their responsibilities were broader, their accountability greater, than before. They had chosen a highly regulated line of work, where the relations between private business and public policy grew every day more intricate. Regulations drove the market that made them thrive; regulations also made them vulnerable. The company had moved into the management of chemical and hazardous waste just as the regulations were taking form—quickly enough, for instance, both to take advantage of "interim status" under RCRA, and to demand of people who had "grown up" in the culture of solid waste, a very quick adjustment to what turned out to be a very different kind of business.

At the same time, the revelations surrounding Love Canal in Niagara Falls and other abandoned dump sites effectively joined the politics of hazardous waste. Campaigns in the election of 1980 resonated with "stump the dump" rhetoric, which raised considerably the public anxiety over real and imagined "ticking toxic time-bombs," and the political investment of officials, elected and unelected, in environmental enforcement issues. The early Reagan years also saw scandal in the Environmental Protection Agency leaving in its wake the surprising revelation to some within the administration that the environment's constituency was broad and deep. At stake, all of a sudden, was the credibility of government to enforce the regulations. At stake was the credibility of EPA inspectors to demonstrate that they were doing their jobs. Doing their jobs meant unearthing violations and writing tickets.

By the time the EPA's house was cleaned and William Ruckelshaus succeeded Anne Gorsuch, it was vital that the agency behave, and be seen to behave, like an enforcement giant. Waste Management, by then already the country's leading player in the commercial handling of hazardous waste, became an obvious target for scrutiny. It is important to remember that, at the time, this was "new business" for everyone. Most hazardous waste was then (and still is) "self-disposed," that is, handled one way or another by whoever generated it. Dow, DuPont, General Motors—pick a big company in a heavy industry—each was probably a bigger "handler" of hazardous waste than Waste Management. They also represented heavier political constituencies—more jobs and more votes—than the still relatively small commercial waste companies. As the regulators felt their way, it was understandable (if unfair) that someone should be first to feel the government's wrath.

Thus began, in 1983, a curious chapter in the history of Waste Management that, ten years before, its founders had not anticipated and that, ten years later, dogs the company still. In the beginning, it was attributable to the politics of a new regulatory world. Its persistence today can only be ascribed to the self-declared mission—the ideology—of a certain segment of the environmental movement. It is a chapter with a dynamic all its own of innuendo, suspicion, deceit, indictment, and, on Waste Management's part, painstaking rebuttal.

Good reporters dig. Excellent reporters explain. The reporters who over the years have followed Waste Management have dug incessantly. In the beginning, their work had the air of fresh revelation. As time went on, it sounded increasingly forced. One fact once unearthed, one allegation once made, never quite goes away. For an example of the perverse power of sheer repetition, no better example exists than the experience of Waste Management with the press. To many people at Waste Management, rightly proud of their company's record of corporate citizenship and environmental compliance, this is disheartening. The best consolation, however, comes with the longer perspective—it is still early in the game. A hundred years from now, when Waste Management will still be only about half the age of a DuPont today, and the world will no doubt be changed in ways no one now can guess, it may all may look very different.

"The country's largest handler of chemical wastes for private industry and the Defense Department," intoned the *New York Times*, March 21, 1983, "has violated state and Federal laws in disposing of dangerous chemical wastes at half a dozen or more sites around the country, according to government documents, court records and former employees. . . . Harold Gershowitz, the Company's senior vice president, called the . . . assertions 'patently untrue or extreme misstatements' and said they were motivated by 'strong vested interests in making the Company look bad.' He said the allegations of wrongdoing had not been brought to the attention of corporate headquarters." Thus began the "dialogue" that continues today. It is like a play with two actors talking past each other to the audience. Whom to believe?

That depends, it seems sadly, mostly on where you stand (or sit) at the start of the show. The theatrical metaphor is apt in that initial appeals to the emotions frequently achieve greater dramatic effect than any reasoned arguments later on. Chances are that if, with a critical eye, one were to rummage through the history of any company over a ten-year period, something would "turn up." It is not a perfect world. In a young industry particularly, where the rules are still much in-the-making, it is sometimes hard to know just where you stand.

Waste Management was built through acquisitions, and built quickly. It was reasonable, though unfortunate, to discover that a facility bought today might be found to be out of compliance with new rules tomorrow. It was also reasonable, and unfortunate, to get slammed in the newspaper for it, no matter how often one said (as Waste Management did many times): "OK, it's a problem we inherited; just give us a chance to fix it." For regulators with the need to make themselves important in the eyes of their constituency, it was reasonable as well to behave like litigators suing for big damages—"We're going to fine Waste Management $1 million!"—and then negotiate. But it was the headlines that stuck.

That original *New York Times* story carried a map to mark the location of three problem sites. A detailed accounting of the history of those problems is significant, as is the company's confidence in recounting it. It has done so over the years in many forms and venues (white papers, press releases, letters to shareholders, letters by officers to the editorial pages of offending newspapers), but never so completely as when in early 1992 the company commissioned an investigation by the Los Angeles law firm of O'Melveny & Myers under the direction of senior partner and former Under Secretary of State Warren Christopher, of all the environmental, antitrust, and corruption charges ever made against it. The "Warren Christopher Report," May 28, 1992, was commissioned in response to a hostile report on the company issued by the San Diego District Attorney's office that relied heavily on information disseminated by two environmental advocacy groups, Greenpeace and Citizen's Clearinghouse for Hazardous Wastes. The O'Melveny & Myers report, coming from a source whose integrity would be considered by many to be above reproach, constitutes the most thorough rebuttal yet to the endless assaults made upon the company. The local context for the report (rumors circulated by opponents of a landfill proposal the company had made to the supervisors of San Diego County, and the views of a local public official philosophically opposed to "privatization" of municipal waste services) are less important than the report of Christopher and his investigators as a historical document. Composed by lawyers in a crisp charge-and-rebuttal format, it attempts to answer emotion with fact, to deflate innuendo with argument, to expose special pleading with full context. It is correct, comprehensive, and remarkably revealing of the lengths to which the company's adversaries have stretched to distort the record and malign the organization.

Its impact remains to be determined. Opponents of Waste Management will of course dismiss it, no matter the name it carries, because it is a commissioned work. Money changed hands. But money does not necessarily, and did not in this case, buy endorsement. What it bought in this case was a sophisticated, workmanlike record of how reckless the opposition can be—and with relative impunity. Consider the three "problems" that first caused the company trouble back in 1983, which are recounted here along with many others.

Vickery

Ohio Liquid Disposal, Inc. (O.L.D.S.), in Vickery, Ohio, near Lake Erie, was incorporated in 1971, having originated ten years earlier as Don's Waste Oil, a recycler that also accepted industrial wastes such as cutting oils, hydraulic fluids, and solvents. Retention ponds were added through the years, as first the Ohio Water Pollution Control Board and then the Ohio Environmental Protection Agency permitted the facility to accept additional chemical process wastes, including highly acidic pickling liquors used in the steel industry. CWM (as Chemical Waste Management, Inc. is notated in the Christopher report) acquired the facility in 1978 by which time three permitted deep injection wells were in operation. Between 1979 and 1981, CWM closed one well and opened three others, and treated oils to sell as recycled product. The waste oils were deposited in a retention pond along with the pickling liquors. The acid caused impurities to separate from the oil, which were then skimmed from the surface, heated in tanks to remove aqueous materials, and sold to industrial customers for use in fuel for high-temperature boilers.

In 1983, Peter Phung, the former chief chemist at Vickery, who had recently been dismissed, alleged to the New York Times, among other things, that CWM had received wastes from Hammermill Paper Company that contained impermissible levels of PCBs and had improperly diluted them in retention ponds. Phung also alleged that waste with arsenic concentrations was improperly disposed of in an injection well.

CWM, upon learning of Phung's allegations from two New York Times reporters (Phung never reported his allegations to company headquarters), immediately embarked on a preliminary analysis of the site, and the Ohio EPA in turn immediately ordered CWM to provide it with the results of its analysis and to retain an independent environmental consultant to investigate alleged leakage from injection wells. The analysis revealed that sludge at the bottom of some of the retention ponds had impermissibly high concentrations of PCBs. A New York Times report indicated that CWM confirmed that perhaps 135,000 gallons of PCB-contaminated oil waste were present at the facility in 1980.

CWM stopped all waste receipt and disposal at Vickery and notified both the Ohio EPA and the EPA of the existence of PCB concentrations in excess of fifty parts per million (ppm). CWM remained in constant contact with state and federal regulators to obtain approval and oversight of CWM's investigatory and remediation activities; meetings were held at least monthly until 1985; and the plans developed during this period were to a large extent incorporated into the regulatory agencies' orders and consent decrees.

CWM proceeded to examine the facility's soil, groundwater, injection wells, ponds, and air emissions. It confirmed that several ponds were contaminated and that injection wells were disposing of fluids in unpermitted, although equally secure, geological strata.

In the judgment of Dr. Richard Shank, former director of the Ohio EPA, who was involved in the proceedings at Vickery, the mistakes made by CWM were in part due to the fact that CWM had expanded quickly and allowed employees hired by the facility's prior owners to continue operating the facility without sufficient supervision. He also attributed some of the cause of these mistakes to a general ignorance of technical issues that was prevalent at the time. For example, the EPA should have realized that there was an injection well leak by reviewing the records provided by CWM. Shank states, however, that a decision had been made by the then-general manager (who had previously managed the predecessor company, Don's Waste Oil) to dilute the PCBs in the ponds on the site.

Ohio brought action on twenty-three counts against CWM, which can be summarized as follows:

1. Industrial wastes disposed of in certain injection wells were not injected into the permitted zones.
2. CWM failed to close Pond 4 by March 30, 1983, in violation of its permit. It partially closed Ponds 4 and 10 without submitting a written closure plan. It allowed odors to emit from the facility.
3. CWM maintained a nuisance by disposing of PCBs on the premises, and failed to test for PCBs in wastes accepted at the facility or accepted wastes containing PCBs in violation of its permit.
4. CWM failed to obtain documents from its customers identifying the waste streams accepted at the facility, failed to verify the nature of the waste streams, and failed to update its analysis of such waste streams.
5. CWM failed to submit a hydrogeologic assessment as required under its permit.

6. CWM failed to maintain appropriate security measures at the facility, and failed to maintain a personnel training program.
7. CWM failed to obtain permits to install and permits to operate air pollution sources, viz., reactor tanks, storage tanks, and ponds.

Intense negotiations resulted between CWM and the Ohio EPA to craft a consent decree, and the testimony of negotiators for the regulatory agencies shows that CWM was cooperative and totally forthcoming with everything the other side wanted. In the 1984 Consent Decree, CWM agreed to pay a civil penalty of $5 million over a ten-year period to the state's Hazardous Waste Cleanup Special Account; to reimburse Ohio in the amount of $3 million for administrative expenses; and to pledge a $2 million contribution to the Sandusky County Commissioners over a ten-year period.

The decree also imposed a range of remedial and operational responsibilities on the company. Injection wells were to be rebuilt. CWM also agreed to undertake extensive groundwater monitorings, to cease the sale of oil products until reclamation procedures had improved, to improve its waste analysis plan, and to conduct annual environmental compliance audits at the Vickery facility. Penalties were stipulated for violation of the decree. Shank monitored the company's compliance and developed "a real respect" for it. He used the rebuilt deep well at Vickery as an example of how a good disposal well system works.

The federal EPA filed its own administrative actions against CWM in seven counts. They alleged the improper discharge of PCBs into ponds in violation of regulations requiring disposal of PCBs in an incinerator; the improper mixing of PCB oils with other oils; the sale between 1980 and 1983 of 6 million gallons of recycled oil containing detectable concentrations of PCBs; and the improper storing of PCBs and contaminated materials in open ponds with inadequate labeling and inventory controls.

In fixing on a penalty for the violations, the EPA weighed the general dangers of handling PCBs and the estimated financial savings of $20 million achieved by CWM by selling the PCB-tainted oils for destruction in high-temperature industrial boilers rather than incinerating them. On the other hand, they also noted that CWM "had initiated various control measures at the facility since discovery of the PCB problem and has cooperated with the EPA in controlling and removing additional PCB oil that was not sold in commerce." They proposed a total settlement of $6.8 million. The Consent Agreement and Final Order (CAFO) required various operational improvements beyond those stipulated in the Ohio decree, and ultimately settled on a civil penalty of $2.5 million.

The CAFO also stated that the alleged violations of TSCA and RCRA at the facility resulted in no known threat to public health or the environment. Only thirty customers bought contaminated oil, and CWM tracked down every one of them. Twenty-two had burned it in industrial boilers. Samples taken from the other eight revealed PCB concentrations of less than 10 ppm, well below the level subject to federal regulation. Only one customer had used the oil for dust control in streets and alleys, which were tested and found clean. None of the oil was used for home heating. Nor did the deep well problems threaten the environment. Approximately 8 to 12 percent of the 450 million gallons injected at Vickery was in unpermitted but secure disposal depths of 2,500 to 2,700 feet, instead of the permitted 2,800 feet. All deposits were at levels considerably below the deepest freshwater-bearing formation (the "Big Lime" at a depth of 600 feet), which meant that no contamination of potential drinking water had occurred or was ever likely to occur. Horizontal migration was perhaps 6 inches per year. The area was not seismically active.

Since 1985, three other incidents involving the Vickery facility have been reported. Two involved minor or technical violations that were reported by CWM itself to the Ohio EPA and promptly remediated. The third involved a dispute over the language and effect of the federal CAFO, which was settled for civil penalties of

$750,000. None of these violations posed any threat to health or the environment.

Pursuant to the 1984 decrees, Vickery has had annual environmental compliance audits conducted by Arthur D. Little, Inc., an outside environmental consultant. Their reports identify some limitations in environmental compliance systems, but state generally that the site's compliance procedures are effective for environmental management and in some cases meet or exceed prevailing procedures in the waste management industry. Edward Kitchen, an enforcement officer for the Ohio EPA who had supervisory responsibility at Vickery since the first 1983 incidents, lauds the company's improved compliance procedures. Obviously the facility is not perfect, but it is safe. It is "almost impossible," he observes, "to operate this type of facility perfectly."

Emelle

CWM's 2,730-acre hazardous waste treatment, storage, and disposal facility in Emelle, Alabama, is the largest in the world. Some 360 acres are currently used for waste disposal purposes. There are twenty-three capped, inactive landfill trenches, plus an active trench, container and tank storage areas, a fuel recovery area, and a solvent recycling unit. Allegations about Emelle have centered over the years on the improper storage of PCBs and on evidence of migration of hazardous substances from the landfill into the groundwater. They began in 1983, when a former employee accused CWM of improper dumping and storage practices that resulted in a consent decree between CWM and the EPA in December 1984.

The issues related to CWM's application in 1981 for permits for incinerator ships *Vulcanus I* and *II*, which were to sail from the port of Mobile, Alabama, and were designed to incinerate liquid wastes, including PCB waste, at sea. Research permits for test burns were granted in October 1981, and CWM accordingly began accepting liquid PCBs for storage at Emelle prior to movement by truck to Mobile. The first test burn was conducted between December 22, 1981, and January 2, 1982; the second occurred between August 15 and 31, 1982. The EPA reported that destruction efficiency of both burns exceeded the permit requirement of 99.99 percent, and concluded that "there were no apparent environmental impacts from incineration of PCBs under these operations and performance conditions." The third test burn (deemed unnecessary by the EPA as it began to feel heat from protests) was canceled and the research permit expired on October 12, 1982.

The process appeared to be going well, and CWM was under the impression that operating permits would in fact be forthcoming. It therefore began accepting additional PCBs at Emelle. On October 21, 1983, the EPA gave public notice of its intention to grant the permit applications for both ships. Over the next seven months, however, politics and the competition derailed the process. The result was the opposite of what the findings of research had indicated they would be: the permits were denied on May 22, 1984. This turn of events led to the "storage" problem that led to regulatory action against CWM.

On July 2, 1983, CWM notified EPA that as of January 1, 1984, some of the PCBs stored at Emelle in anticipation of ocean incineration would have been in storage for more than the one year permitted under federal regulations. CWM requested a waiver and was told that none was available. The Toxic Substances Control Act (TSCA) requires that liquid PCBs be disposed only through incineration, a capability the Emelle facility did not have. CWM attempted, and failed, to find another facility that could dispose of the wastes. Therefore, as of January 1, 1984, CWM was in technical violation of the one-year storage regulation. CWM and the EPA entered into negotiations leading to a consent decree on March 23, 1984, that contained a schedule for disposal of the PCBs.

The state of Alabama then intervened. The director of the

Alabama Department of Environmental Management (ADEM), without notice to CWM and without a hearing, ordered Emelle to stop accepting PCB wastes and to dispose of those it already had, on a schedule that was in conflict with the EPA consent agreement. That prompted the federal district court to enjoin the state from enforcing its April 16 order. It was the federal judge's language, however, that cut through the political posturing of state officials, and went to the heart of the matter.

The court said that there was not "one shred of evidence to indicate that there [was] any immediate or even potential harm to the public that might arise by violation of the April 16, 1984, order." There had been "no showing of improper storage of PCBs, of PCBs leaching into the soil, of PCBs being released into the atmosphere, or of any other danger, *real or imagined*, to the public health, safety or welfare." (Emphasis added) And the court further drew attention to the essential context of the "violation." At no time had there been any "allegation of wrongdoing on the part of the plaintiff other than the charge that some PCBs were retained in storage in excess of the one-year limitation period," and this was because CWM had reason to believe that the EPA intended to license the *Vulcanus* ships. ADEM's action, the court concluded, "manifests harsh over-reaction to this set of circumstances and can only be categorized as arbitrary and capricious."

The Alabama motion nevertheless went forward and negotiations began to reach another consent agreement. In the course of that development, the EPA's National Enforcement Investigation Center (NEIC) conducted an intensive on-site investigation of the Emelle facility. It uncovered violations of certain regulations, including record-keeping requirements and improper location of groundwater monitoring wells. CWM offered affirmative defenses. The consent decree among CWM, EPA, and ADEM of December 19, 1984, called for improved procedures and for payment by CWM of $450,000 in civil claims to the EPA and $150,000 to the state.

The "migration" of toxic substances has also been an issue at Emelle. During 1984, a citizens' group contesting CWM's efforts to permit a landfill in neighboring Mississippi took samples from two drainage ditches outside the Emelle facility. Laboratory analysis, confirmed by CWM, discovered trace amounts of PCBs. The background concentrations of 1 to 3 ppm were, again, well below the level regulated by the federal government. Regardless, the company undertook to excavate the tainted soil and dispose of it in a permitted landfill. CWM also concluded that the source of the contamination (if it could be called that) was not leakage from any disposal cell but rainfall run-off from a parking lot used by trucks transporting PCB materials to Emelle. To prevent a recurrence, CWM constructed a series of collection basins to capture runoff and established a program to test sediments in the basins for PCBs. Detection of PCBs in the ditch resulted in no enforcement action by regulatory authorities.

Also in 1984, detection of volatile organic compounds (VOCs) in deep monitoring wells designed to detect migration of toxics toward underlying aquifers, again illustrated the danger of "facts" disconnected from their causes. As part of the process of granting CWM a federal hazardous waste permit, the EPA considered groundwater issues exhaustively. The draft Part B permit, issued in 1986, was subject to extensive public scrutiny. The final permit, issued in 1987, exempted CWM from the requirement to monitor groundwater in the uppermost aquifer, and in response to public comments, the EPA explained that due to the hydrogeologic characteristics of the 700-foot thick "Selma Chalk" formation (a "confining unit" that does not transmit significant quantities of water), there was no potential for migration of leachate materials during the active life of the facility or during the postclosure care period. The agency added that, using conservative assumptions, no landfill contents could penetrate to the nearest aquifer in less than three hundred years, and they noted CWM's analysis demonstrating that penetration could not occur for ten thousand years.

The five shallow wells used by residents in the vicinity were deemed by the EPA to be cisterns rather than wells, drawing their water mainly from rainfall. VOCs that were detected in Emelle's eight deep monitoring wells, the EPA concluded, did not migrate there through the Selma Chalk, but had been introduced into the groundwater during construction. When CWM drained the stagnant water, further sampling revealed no contaminants. Similarly, shallow test wells were found to contain traces of chloroform, which it was determined had been introduced in tap water supplied by the county that had been used as a drilling fluid during installation of the wells. Once the wells were cleaned, further sampling revealed no chloroform.

Other incidents at Emelle have received publicity equally disproportionate to their environmental significance. In April 1985, a fire involved flammable solvents that were being emptied from drums in the drum-processing unit. Within five minutes, general manager Roger Henson evacuated the entire facility. The local fire department was summoned, and within twenty-five minutes the fire was extinguished. All spills and leaks, which were confined to the drum processing unit, were contained and remediated. ADEM and EPA, which were notified at the time of the incident, took no enforcement action.

In 1985, a spill was caused by a broken hose of 600-700 gallons of acidic wastes as it was being pumped into a solidification unit. When it was determined that some of the material had run under the perimeter fence and onto neighboring property, CWM with the permission of the landowner removed the liquid, excavated, and disposed of the soil in a hazardous waste landfill. ADEM filed an action criticizing CWM for failing to notify the agency for thirty-four hours after the incident and for incomplete follow-up reporting of the spill, and it ordered CWM to install a backup containment system for all piping that might cause another such release. CWM complied.

Emelle has also been criticized for noxious air emissions. But some scents mislead. On March 4, 1987, CWM accepted a load of waste soil from the Texas Eastern Gas Pipeline Company. Excavated from three feet below ground, it gave off a rotten smell associated with anaerobic conditions, plus the smell of mercaptan, a compound commonly mixed with odorless natural gas to serve as a warning agent. There was no threat to human health and no conceivable damage done to the environment.

Chicago

Waste Management's involvement with hazardous wastes began at its Calumet Industrial Development Landfill (CID) in the 1970s. A four-hundred-acre site on Chicago's southeastern edge, it sits in a Ruhr-like landscape much abused by a century of heavy industrialization. Area residents are tired of pollution, and touchy about anyone seen to be connected with it. The distinction between waste generator and waste disposer, between the problem and the solution, is not often observed. When the regulatory and press criticism of the company broke in the spring of 1983, many on the Southeast Side were happy to say, "I told you so."

What they were referring to was the accusation by the former laboratory manager at the facility that, from 1976 to 1981, the company illegally disposed of thousands of gallons of toxic wastes at CID. Coinciding with the newspaper charge, the Illinois attorney general's suit against the company contended that at CID for a five-month period in 1980, Waste Management affiliates had accepted and disposed of a waste stream containing dichlorobenzidine (DCB), a hazardous substance not authorized under its permit. The suit further alleged that the company had failed to file proper manifest forms on the DCB wastes, and that they operated another waste stream illegally for a one-and-a-half month period after one permit had expired and while the renewal was still in-process by the state.

One of the company's responses to the accusations was to retain outside counsel (the law firm of Karaganis, Gail & White) to conduct an independent investigation. The Karaganis Report to Waste Management's board of directors concluded that CID did in fact have a valid permit in effect for the relevant period authorizing receipt of DCBs, and that the inadvertent failure to file manifest forms in a timely manner, while a violation of Illinois EPA regulations, did not appear to stem from any deliberate plot to conceal information from the regulators. Equally important, the attorney general's suit alleged neither the improper treatment or disposal of any waste streams, nor that the disposal of any waste stream at CID had been dangerous to the public health or in any way damaging to the environment.

The original suit demanded a pressworthy $2.2 million, and it hung on for years. Finally, on August 12, 1991, it was dismissed for want of prosecution. On February 14, 1992, the attorney general's office agreed to settle for payment of a (relatively) small $50,000, pursuant to an agreed order in which Waste Management denied any violation of the law.

Compared with CWM Chemical Services, Inc., which is its neighbor, the troubles of the CID landfill seem tame and long past. One of just three facilities in the entire country licensed to burn PCBs, this hazardous waste incinerator was acquired by Waste Management when it bought SCA Chemical Services, Inc., in 1984, and so was not part of the company's early credibility crises. But ask a Chicagoan today, especially one on the Southeast Side, what he knows about Waste Management, and chances are high he will recite something about "that incinerator." What he knows may well be incorrect and will certainly be incomplete.

Both before and after the plant was operated by former SCA personnel, several compliance issues troubled it. In 1987, the Illinois EPA (IEPA) filed a complaint about inadequate groundwater monitoring, alleging that scrubber water in several surface impoundments "may be affecting groundwater quality." A consent agreement was signed in 1988 providing for payment of a civil penalty of $18,240 but constituting neither an admission of wrongdoing nor a finding of violation of the regulations. In fact, the company contended quite plausibly that any groundwater contamination that could be proven (none was) was likely the consequence of other longstanding activities in this highly industrialized area.

Other problems were less conjectural but came to light from within the company and were then reported by it to the regulators. In January 1988, a former employee of SCA Chemical Services informed CWM that between the fall of 1986 and June 1987 he had disconnected the incinerator's carbon monoxide monitor so that waste could be fed faster (if carbon monoxide levels exceed a set limit, the incinerator automatically shuts down). In fact, solid PCB wastes were fed faster than the permit allowed. The company's immediate investigation confirmed the information, and it reviewed data on both the emissions and the effectiveness of the burns during the times when the monitor was shut off. They discovered that the feed rate for solid PCBs had been exceeded for the period of one hour, but that even then the combustion removal efficiency for the PCB waste was greater than 99.9999 percent, and that no excess stack emissions occurred during the monitor outages.

The operations of the incinerator never threatened community or environment. Nor, however, did they meet CWM's own standards for ensuring full compliance. Old staff departed. A new general manager was put in charge. A full-time inspection team was assigned to the site to provide internal review during all operating hours. An outside evaluation of the facility was commissioned. And plans were accelerated to install a direct-access computer-monitoring system to provide real-time operating data directly to the state EPA. As part of a consent decree approved on June 2, 1988, the company agreed to a civil penalty of $53,000 and to pay $300,000 to fund additional oversight at the facility. The company also reported subsequent difficulties to the regulators.

On December 23, 1988, the new general manager, Kurt Frey, reported to Illinois EPA's enforcement manager Joseph Svoboda that during a power outage that had rendered emission monitors inoperable, waste had continued to feed into the incinerator for thirteen minutes, which constituted a permit violation. Consequently, CWM consented to payment of an additional $87,500 per quarter until January 1, 1994, and to an additional civil penalty of $340,000. The same self-reported violation prompted the EPA to file an administrative complaint under TSCA seeking to impose a $4.47 million penalty.

Additional allegations ranged from scrubber water not having the proper pH level during certain periods, to deficient record-keeping. An EPA scientist at the time, however, said none of the infractions threatened the public health, since the incinerator continued to operate at temperatures high enough to destroy all PCB wastes. The suit was settled in September 1990 with CWM Chemical Waste Services agreeing to a civil penalty of $3.75 million; it neither admitted nor denied allegations other than those which it had itself reported. An EPA spokesman at the time of the settlement said none of the violations endangered the environment.

In this context, the EPA had denied the company's revised application for a Part B permit under RCRA in September 1989. CWM appealed the denial to the Illinois Pollution Control Board and was able to continue operations under "interim status." It also submitted a revised Part B application, which addressed issues raised by the EPA. Additional problems reported by the company involved an explosion on February 13, 1991, of laboratory wastes, including tetrazole, in the incinerator's rotary kiln. The Illinois attorney general brought suit, and CWM Chemical Services entered into an interim consent decree on July 1, 1991, calling for $350,000 to fund additional oversight by the EPA, and payment of $2 million in civil penalties.

A final decree was delayed by the discovery, and report to the authorities by the facility's general manager, of the intentional mislabeling of drums containing hazardous waste generated at the facility. A provision of the interim consent decree had limited the volumes of wastes that could be accumulated on site, and the labels were changed, apparently by one or more employees who believed that the wastes being accumulated exceeded that limit. The company fired the most senior employee believed to be involved (a materials-handling supervisor). At the time of the drum-labeling incident, the company ceased accepting waste at the incinerator, and offered to continue the hiatus until its permit status was finally resolved. The Illinois Pollution Control Board accepted their proposal on April 23, 1992, and most of the facility's employees were notified that they would be laid off.

Compliance and News

There is a problem of perceptions here. The regulatory "violations" of Waste Management can be said to fill volumes. The Warren Christopher Report, which recounts and analyzes most of them, fills three. Continuing violations of some sort are a certainty, and so too their meticulous rebuttal and attempts to place each incident in some kind of perspective. Yet there is danger even in writing a sentence like that—it might be quoted in isolation, one more black mark on a record filled with them. How, then, to weigh these things?

Two requirements are essential to getting at the truth. The first is to acquire at least as much perspective on the history of the industry as has been shown by David Ullrich, the EPA official with jurisdiction over another of CWM's troubled incinerators at Sauget, Illinois. He notes, for example, that the industry has been forced to change from operating incinerators that were essentially involved in burning garbage, to operating complex plants that must be run with clockwork precision, and where the necessary level of performance will be "very, very difficult to achieve." To his knowledge, no one in the business has yet achieved it. The other requirement is to retain a rudimentary sense of proportionality. This sounds a cliché, but it happens to be true: bad news gets broadcast; routine successes do not. In a business beset by controversy, the distinction between allegation and verdict is easy to overlook.

The original case at Vickery, Ohio, remains perhaps the most striking example. The first phrase that contained a number—"$2 million fine"—was the language that stuck, not the civil penalty of $750,000 that the action was settled for. Seldom noted outside the company, moreover, was how Vickery and the other 1983 incidents galvanized Waste Management into action, motivating it to turn the sites in question into model facilities and to become industry leader in environmental compliance. Beginning immediately with the twin revelations of compliance problems and the enormous damage they wrought on the company's standing in the eyes of the public and investors, radical steps were begun to formalize companywide the process of environmental compliance, and to suffuse its young culture with an ethic of environmentalism.

Joan Bernstein is currently Waste Management's vice president of Environmental Policy and Ethical Standards. In 1983 she was a practicing attorney in Washington, D.C., in environmental issues and former general counsel to the EPA in the Carter administration. When in the spring of 1983 the company considered engaging, for the first time, full-time Washington counsel, general counsel Steve Bergersen approached her. On the plane to Chicago, she read the first of the *New York Times* articles and, as she recalls, arrived in Oak Brook amid the consternation of executives watching their company's good name, like their stock, fall and fall and fall. Perception, to a market, is reality. And the perception being conveyed just then by government investigators and a hungry press portrayed Waste Management in a way that the hard-working entrepreneurs there did not recognize as their company.

"We never did have a discussion about whether we'd be retained [as Washington counsel] or not," said Bernstein. "We simply went into the board room, and we didn't come out until four o'clock in the morning because we quickly made a decision that there would have to be a press conference the next day to try to deal with this and then a meeting in New York with the financial community."

The figure "toxic shock" was used at the time with a certain black humor to describe the atmosphere of those first days. But there was no panic, no stampede for the door, no searching around for excuses and others to blame. Looking back, Bergerson sees it all as something that probably had to happen; the lesson for the future lay not with the accusations themselves but with how the company reacted to them. He and Gershowitz spent hours talking to the press, trying to put things in the proper perspective. Among themselves, the attitude was "how do we learn from this and grow." "We tried to get rid of the false allegations and tried to deal with facts," recalls Bergerson. "The whole focus was not to get real defensive and hunker down. We recognized we could never hunker down again." He and Bernstein (and her former Justice Department colleague Angus Macbeth) worked intensely to craft a defense. Joe Karaganus worked independently to assess the charges made against the company. The annual shareholders meeting in May was tense and marked with protest. The Karaganus Report was ready for the board of directors in August.

Buntrock was in deadly earnest about restoring confidence, but not through a quick fix. The lawyers each reported separately to him and Phil Rooney about sensitive matters: judgments about people and their adequacies for handling the complex regulations that henceforth would shape Waste Management's operating world. Buntrock asked for recommendations for someone to fill a new post in environmental management at CWM and appointed Bernstein's old colleague at the EPA, Walt Barber. Peter Vardy had already set up environmental audit and compliance functions for the whole company, and Barber now sorted through the 1983 complaints and defined new procedures to deal with the issues they raised. The results were revolutionary for such an operations-oriented company, and an acknowledgement that in the fishbowl that the waste management business was fast becoming, form was as important as substance and inseparable from it.

For the next two years at least, the company, especially CWM, was the EPA's target for reasons that were largely political. But in the process, and as the new company policies to improve compliance and restore investor confidence took hold, a dramatic reculturing began, which in time would make credible Waste Management's definition of itself as an "environmental services company."

That first year, 1983, the company established an environmental audit program. Bergerson speaks for the company when he says, "It changed us forever for the good." It provides local, regional, and corporate management with comprehensive information on environmental compliance at all facilities owned or operated by the company. Environmental audits, involving both visual and records inspections, are performed by a unit of Waste Management and are independent of operating subsidiary management. The department has a heavy complement of professional engineers, whose technical language is increasingly entering the business.

The environmental audit system is used as a practical management tool. "Basically," Buntrock explains, "what I want to know after every audit is, did they do better this year than last year and if so, in what ways. If not, I want to know what the reasons are and what needs to be done to fix it. I want to know that they are tracking the audit exceptions and monitoring the fixes to the exceptions and being sure we know whether or not they get done." He also uses the audits more philosophically. They make people vigilant, and vigilance is a virtue generally. The audits enforce a culture of compliance; they push the culture down from the very top. When Dean Buntrock visits a Waste Management site today, what he will witness, however, from drivers and helpers will be more than a command performance.

It has taken a number of years, but the culture has taken root, from the bottom up as well. Ask the driver of one of those thousands of burgundy trucks what he likes about Waste Management and chances are he will speak of three things: the good pay, the good benefits, and that Waste Management is good for the environment. A wall plaque at every Waste Management location around the world summarizes the company's aims and environmental principles. The truck driver does not pause to read it when he arrives at work in the wee hours, but he does know what it says, and that what it says affects his job: whether he personally will have his job tomorrow, and whether Waste Management will be there to provide thousands of jobs like it. His job is to deal with dirt, and he must be careful. Today, everybody is watching, and when his truck hits the predawn streets and hoists its first smelly container filled with the plate-scrapings from yesterday's restaurant-goers into the noisy maw of his rear-loading compactor, he must leave no litter behind. It may be a high-tech age, but his burgundy truck still packs a shovel—and a broom.

Employees of Waste Management of North America and Chemical Waste Management and their subsidiaries receive initial and continuing environmental training. Everyone must "keep up." Programs are designed to instill respect for and understanding of environmental policies, regulations, and compliance programs. They are tailored to the level of employee education and responsibility, but they have in common the message that this is no "add-on"—something to think about second to winning business and making money. "Pay attention!" This is the heart of the matter when working for Waste Management. "This is the way we win business, grow, and profit."

Don Wallgren, currently vice president for Environmental Management in Waste Management of North America, was hired from the federal EPA in 1979 as director of Environmental Management reporting to Vice President Peter Vardy. Coming out of the government, he jokes, "I was hired as a novelty—there was a misconception by some of my new colleagues that government workers were lazy and maybe not even very intelligent!" Today, Waste Management views the federal and state regulatory agencies as valuable talent pools from which to draw some of its best environmental personnel.

When Wallgren came on board, he and Vardy had perhaps five engineers to deal with all the company's facilities. Today, engineers are legion. Environmental training related to landfill operations, for example, has undergone a sea change. In the 1970s, many of the company's best landfill operators (many of whom were acquired with other companies) were very good men with heavy equipment, "with moving dirt," recalls Wallgren. But between then and now, some big changes occurred.

Gradually, they began to supplement regional and site staffs with environmental/engineering-types in a sort of side-by-side arrangement. But it was hard to get around a "them-and-us" atmosphere, and it was important that the people responsible for the actual operations learn these things themselves. The result was a program wonderfully titled "Landfill University," which is conducted twice a year and aimed at landfill managers. Some of them may have been hired because they were good men with bulldozers, but most are now engineers and are constantly taught—and will be evaluated for—a wide range of skills. Faculty includes senior members of the company's technical, legal, and business staffs, academics, and environmental consultants. Do they know their technology? How good are they at dealing with politicians and neighborhood leaders? Can they stand up at a public hearing and speak convincingly? Do they know how to talk to regulators? New managers being attracted to the company bring the new sensibilities with them. "Not too long ago, we hired a couple of managers with engineering and masters degrees from the Kellogg School of Management at Northwestern, a totally different breed of cat," observes Wallgren.

In 1989, Waste Management established the Waste Management Executive Environmental Committee. It is composed of the chief environmental managers and the most senior environmental attorneys from throughout the company and its subsidiaries. Its purpose, as set down by Buntrock and Rooney, is "to review and propose policies to ensure continued environmental compliance and minimize potential liabilities and to advise the [Waste] Management Committee on environmentally related issues that are significant to the continued growth of Waste Management." On March 7, 1990, the board of directors approved a fourteen-point environmental policy for the company that was developed by the Executive Environmental Committee. The preamble, void of public relations verbiage, is a work of exemplary concision:

"Waste Management, Inc. is committed to protecting and enhancing the environment and to updating its practices in light of advances in technology and new understandings in health and environmental science.

"Prevention of pollution and enhancement of the environment are the fundamental premises of the Company's business. We believe that all corporations have a responsibility to conduct their business as responsible stewards of the environment and to seek profits only through activities that leave the Earth healthy and safe. We believe that the Company has a responsibility not to compromise the ability of future generations to sustain their needs.

"The principles of this policy are applicable to the Company throughout the world. The Company will take demonstrable actions on a continuing basis in furtherance of the principles."

The way they write reflects the way they think. Their "principles" are similarly straightforward. They will perform their services in ways that protect the environment even if not required by law, and train all employees in environmental matters. They will work to reduce waste, to promote recycling, and to provide safe treatment and disposal of the wastes that remain. They are committed to conservation and a policy of "no net loss" of wetlands and biodiversity on the company's property. The company will promote sustainable use of all natural resources, and will endeavor to use environmentally safe and sustainable sources of energy. They still will strive to reduce risk and operate in a manner that minimizes environmental, health, or safety hazards. They will take responsibility for any harm they do cause to the environment. They will support research and development, provide information to the public on the environmental impact of their activities, and help support environmental organizations. The board of directors promises ongoing environmental policy assessments and will commit the resources needed to implement the company's environmental principles, and the company will prepare annually a public environmental report, a self-evaluation of its environmental performance worldwide.

Much is made at Waste Management of the term "compliance." "Compliance" is the specific subject of point six of the company's environmental policy:

"The Company is committed to comply with all legal requirements and to implement programs and procedures to ensure compliance. These efforts will include training and testing of employees, rewarding employees who excel in compliance, and disciplining employees who violate legal requirements."

It sounds cut-and-dried, almost "minimalist." It is not. All large companies operate through policies and procedures, and Waste Management's manuals are as heavy as anyone's. Its policies and procedures, its systems of penalties and rewards, are the tools, the means, that make compliance possible. But before it can be implemented, it must be enlivened. The quickening spirit at Waste Management resides, first and last, at the top.

Dean Buntrock prefaces the company's second annual environmental report (1991) as the visionary and pragmatist that he is. The idea of "the environment" moves him as a human being, and he keeps that idea dangling in front of his company: "We, as a society, now know that the Earth's capacity to support human and other life in all its diversity is not infinite." The measurement of "environmental progress" moves him as a businessman, and increasingly shapes the behavior of his company. Waste Management will grow and return value to its investors to the extent that it makes—and helps the world make—environmental progress: "The Environmental Policy of our Company is among the most progressive in all of industry, but environmental policies are of limited significance in measuring environmental progress. Environmental practice is the only relevant measure of the effectiveness of environmental policy."

Smartly Now, Let's Save the World

It seems so reasonable. They sound so responsible. Nor do they just say it of themselves. Arthur D. Little, Inc., the leading firm in the field of environmental auditing, which performs two hundred environmental compliance audits per year for over forty different companies including several of Waste Management's larger competitors, says for the record that "the environmental management systems developed by Waste Management, Inc. provide an appropriate framework for effective environmental management and establish WMI as the leader in this area in the U.S. waste management industry. Further, in our opinion, certain of these systems reflect management approaches which are state of the art and which place WMI firmly among the leaders of industry as a whole with regard to corporate environmental management." State and federal regulators who have worked with Waste Management on compliance problems echo their approval of the company's attitude toward tackling problems that need work, and in general getting things right.

And yet this company is reviled by a body of managed and manipulated opinion that dismisses offhand anything positive said by its chairman, by lawyers commissioned to examine its record, by consultants charged to evaluate its environmental performance, by totally independent observers, institutions, and even federal and state courts that have found the company innocent of most of the charges brought against it, and by the author of this book. How large this body of opinion is, it is hard to say; it is most assuredly very vocal, very unjust, and a source of great sadness to the company. Compare again the messages conveyed in two contradictory pieces of evidence. Headlines in 1983 and in

1992 (and countless occasions in between)—"Leader in Toxic Dumps Accused of Illegal Acts" . . . "The Ugly Mess at Waste Management"—tell one story. The lawyers' and the regulators' measured phrase—"no environmental damage"—contained in virtually all compliance actions ever taken against the company, tells quite a different one.

The story that you choose to believe will likely depend on prejudice—a prejudgment based on a general understanding and unrelated to a particular situation. This is because the environment has taken on an emotional charge that has become hard to control. It preempts much intelligent discussion, and is far from conducive to making intelligent distinctions.

The stance of Greenpeace, Waste Management's archnemesis, illustrates the difficulty. Television viewers and headline readers know Greenpeace as the courageous or outrageous (pick your adjective) operator of the *Rainbow Warrior,* a "protest ship" that gallantly takes on Japanese whalers, Norwegian seal hunters, Dutch ocean incinerators, and French nuclear testers, in the name of protecting the environment and saving the world. Both on and off camera, Greenpeace also takes on large American waste companies, and Waste Management, the largest, is the archvillain of Greenpeace's villain-filled world.

Greenpeace is a large and well-funded organization. It is nonprofit and knows little outside scrutiny. The primary impetus for its relentless hostility to Waste Management, the organization admits, "is philosophical. Greenpeace believes that landfill and incineration technology is inherently flawed and its promotion by Waste Management and other firms only makes it easier and cheaper for waste generators to ignore recycling and other programs designed to reduce the production of waste at their [sic] source. . . . Waste producers who can't meet on-site disposal regulations now hire commercial disposal firms, such as Waste Management, Inc., to take wastes off their hands, instead of looking for ways to eliminate wastes entirely through prevention" (*Los Angeles Times,* May 10, 1991).

In making the case for its philosophy, the organization generates a lot of paper. "Greenpeace Reports," as they are known in the environmental world, are scripture, or screed. Dean Buntrock's company is the subject of one of the fattest (285 pages): "Waste Management, Inc.: An Encyclopedia of Environmental Crimes & Other Misdeeds" (third edition, December 1991). If one came of age in the 1960s and yearns in a nostalgic moment for the sense of righteous outrage for virtue violated that suffused "the movement," then read this document. You will warm to the idiom of the antiwar protests of yore, to the "our cause is right/ you are either for us or against us" attitude of the students and professors who forsook the hard daily work of teaching and learning in order to occupy the dean's office and "stop the war now!"

Greenpeace also brings to today's environmental movement a strong whiff of Luddism. The rainbow warriors of today's environmental movement have as the object of their wrath much of the drift of history since the Industrial Revolution. For two hundred years, it seems, we've gotten everything wrong. The moment of crisis is now at hand. The action demanded is radical. Its report on Waste Management is a universal indictment of everything the company does, of every place it does it (" 'Burn as Much as Possible': CWM's Land-based Hazardous Waste Incinerators"; "DOD/DOE Cleanups: The Last Refuge of Scoundrels"; "The Empire Expands: International Operations"). The particulars can be argued. The general premise behind them is the problem. If true, then Waste Management, Inc. from the name on down is a dangerous fraud. If not true, then Greenpeace needs to find some other way to save the world.

The premise is that the wastes of modern urban industrial society cannot be safely managed once they are created. Greenpeace words it well: "No incinerator, landfill or other method of waste disposal can protect future generations and the environment from hazardous chemicals, including the hazardous chemicals used in our homes every day (oven cleaners, paint thinners, pesticides, and so forth). The laws of physics dictate that disposal equals dispersal. Everything must go somewhere, and sooner or later, all wastes that are created will be released into the environment. . . . " When, or as, this happens, poisoning occurs.

Greenpeace is much concerned about poisoning, a nasty practice perpetrated by only the most wicked criminals—like Waste Management. "[W]aste disposal has caused steadily increasing contamination worldwide. The deepest oceans are contaminated; wildlife in remote Antarctica is contaminated; human breast milk is contaminated. While still in the womb, babies are contaminated." This flood of hyperbole sweeps reflection aside. There is not much hope it seems: "If humans are to survive, we must diminish out releases of chemicals into the environment. This means we must rely less and less upon waste disposal technologies and eliminate the creation and use of these harmful substances to begin with."

Someday, decades or centuries hence, this may come to pass. If it does, then the business rationale for a company like Waste Management will indeed vanish and, barring changes in what services it provides, its history will be over. Companies begin, and end, because the world changes. For now, it is essential to reach prudent relative judgments about these things, not to take absolutist stands. Despite its own rigid stand, Greenpeace's words are not illogical: "Everything must go somewhere, and sooner or later, all wastes that are created will be released into the environment." "Sooner or later" is the defining phrase. (Indeed, all industrial production, from the moment it rolls out of the factory, becomes *part of* the environment; "waste" is just one part of it.) How far must we, can we, see ahead?

At Emelle, Alabama, the EPA figures say it will take at least three hundred years for any potential leachate from CWM's hazardous waste landfill to penetrate the Selma Chalk and reach the aquifer underneath. (No liquids have been placed in the landfill for ten years.) CWM's scientists put the figure at ten thousand years. Three hundred? Ten thousand? Something in between? The garbage deposited in one of Waste Management's elaborately engineered solid waste landfills will almost certainly stay put for centuries.

But nature is filled with surprises. Earthquakes happen. Wind erodes. Water eventually moves everything. Both Waste Management and Greenpeace profess deep concern for the "generations yet unborn" who will inherit this earth. Both share concern that this present generation not further abuse its environmental patrimony. Greenpeace, like a tent revivalist, thunders warnings that the hour is nigh, that repentance must be immediate and total. Waste Management quietly does deeds that, added up, will do much more to save us. "Generations yet unborn" have always inherited risks, and future ones will too, our wastes inevitably among them.

True to its own logic, Greenpeace contends that by its very existence Waste Management creates waste, the very problem it professes to solve. Waste Management, reasoning quite as straightforwardly, says it doesn't. Every man, woman, and child creates waste: if you would ascribe true responsibility, look around you. You will find only "we the people," including thousands who fill the collection plates of environmental faith movements like Greenpeace.

Greenpeace judges and condemns Waste Management as a "bad actor" driven by "bad ideas." The world today, and tomorrow, would be better off, the environment healthier, without it. Greenpeace cannot afford to credit all those regulators (many of whom, it says, go out the "revolving door" to work for Waste Management) who render all those "no environmental damage" judgments in favor of the company. And even if such judgments were true, wouldn't it amount to pretty faint praise? If the best that can be said about a company is that it is successful at *not* doing something, then how much have you said?

Quite a lot, actually. Consider something that economic historians like to call "the counter-factual." What would something be like, if something else that shaped it had never happened in the first place? How, for instance, would the great open spaces of the American West have developed after the Civil War, if there had been no railroads? More slowly for sure, which would itself have had various consequences. The tall grass prairie, the buffalo, and the Indians would have lasted longer. There would also have been less beef on Eastern tables, and the price of bread would have been higher. Immigrants from Europe, with less access to Western homesteads, would have crowded already crowded Eastern cities.

What, then, would the waste situation be like had there been no Waste Management? Given the existence of the same regulations, would other waste companies have grasped the market opportunity that Buntrock saw? Very likely. Would any of those companies have performed, every day on the street and every quarter on Wall Street, as Waste Management has done? Harder to say. Possibly, the waste industry would have been consolidated less ably and would not have been able to command the capital and develop the technology to meet the challenge of handling more waste under stricter rules. And perhaps, without good landfills and high-capacity incinerators, waste generators (all of us) would have become more frugal with our trash. Or maybe trash generation would have increased anyway, piling up in dumps or "over the back fence."

To the faint praise of "no environmental damage" must be added the conjecture of the environmental damage that might have occurred had Waste Management not been there, diligently doing its unglamorous job, every day of every year. To the charge that Waste Management landfills, like all works of engineering, will one day fail must be added these questions: What constitutes failure? Can it be anticipated? If so, can it be managed? How far into the future can responsibility conceivably extend?

All actions have unintended consequences, some quite soon, others farther off. If a landfill leaks in three hundred years or ten thousand years, does that mean that it was a "bad idea" to have built it in the first place? Yes, says Greenpeace. Certainly not, says Waste Management, especially if the leak is directed through advanced engineering to proper treatment and safe disposal or discharge. Sanitary landfills and waste-to-energy plants are excellent solutions to a monumental problem today, and they are built for long life. They are not perfect solutions. Neither is recycling.

271

Besides, straight-line extrapolations of present trends into the future are notoriously treacherous. In addition to unforeseen challenges, the future also holds unforeseen solutions, which, after all, is what will make it different from "now."

Enemy of the People

The problem of Waste Management, for Greenpeace, has another dimension. Among its many "crimes and other misdeeds," Waste Management makes money. Dean Buntrock, Phil Rooney, Don Flynn, and the others have made a great deal of money. A thousand shares of stock purchased and held since 1971 would have resulted in a handsome sum. A single share originally priced at $16, would today fetch nearly $3,000. Where there is such money, surely there must be much wickedness.

The nineteenth century, with a grander language than ours, would have used the phrase "Malefactors of Great Wealth." The crude graphic on the cover of the "Greenpeace Report on Waste Management" conveys the same crude idea. It is a knockoff of the company's swept-back "W-M" logo with three embellishments. From the upward pointing legs of the "W," toxic air emissions represented by hand-drawn squiggles foul the air. From the downward pointing legs of the "M," toxic effluents represented by smooth ribbons foul the waters. To the right, at the end of a menacing black pipe, dollars spew forth. "Economic Malpractice for Profit," the report dubs the company's behavior: a litany of "deception, corruption, monopolism." Its sins of price-fixing, bid-rigging, and other such illegalities are as numerous as the company's violations of the environment, the report charges. They are also as meticulously rebutted by the company, including in the Warren Christopher Report, which, among other matters, has this to say:

On the company and the mob: The insinuation "that Waste Management, operating in the environment it does, has maintained a secret relationship with organized crime dating back to 1962 is irresponsibility. We have seen nothing even remotely linking Waste Management and organized crime. All the evidence we have seen and all the accounts of law enforcement officials who have truly looked into the matter indicate that no such connection exists."

On company-sponsored political corruption: "In its twenty-one year history, neither Waste Management nor any of its subsidiaries have faced political corruption charges. The SEC's case against the company shortly after it was formed was based for the most part on the practice of a subsidiary's landfill manager to make political contributions from unrecorded cash. The company discovered the practice, reported its findings to the SEC, terminated the improper practice, and instituted appropriate accounting procedures and policies to ensure that nothing of that nature would occur again. The Company has not faced a similar problem since." Only two employees in the company's history have been convicted of charges of political corruption. One was found by federal prosecutors to have been acting on his own, and the other actually defrauded the company to make an illegal payment on behalf of another company for which the employee was moonlighting. "[T]he Company has never been found to have made improper payments or to have improperly influenced public officials."

On the company's antitrust record: "[T]he activities giving rise to the antitrust violations were directly contrary to Company policy and were the product of unauthorized acts of local employees. . . . [T]he Company as a consequence of those violations has acted vigorously to bolster its antitrust compliance program to avoid recurrences. . . . Waste Management now assures that its management and sales personnel receive regular antitrust training so that employees, including those joining the Company by acquisition, are aware of the Company's requirement of full compliance with the antitrust laws."

The "crimes" are often exercises in hyperbole; the "misdeeds"

are usually misrepresented. Consent decrees and financial settlements with one's accusers, without admission of guilt, are part of
the conduct of any controversial business. They will continue at
Waste Management as long as controversy embroils environmental issues. The insinuation and innuendo against the company will
also continue as long as other "bad ideas" hold sway at Greenpeace. A deeper prejudice than mere disgust at gains allegedly ill-
gotten is at work here. The prejudice is against gain itself, when
gain is associated with the environment.

Profit and the environment, to Greenpeace, do not mix. Landfills are landfills, but they are not quite so awful when they are
publicly owned. It is the old rhetoric refurbished for a new cause—
the "them and us," the big corporation versus the little people (or
versus the self-appointed spokesmen for the little people). In the
late nineteenth century, it was the railroads, their menacing tenta-
cles reaching everywhere, versus the small farmers, who were told
by the Populist party that the railroads should be nationalized and
operated not for profit but for the "common good." In the late
twentieth century, it is the waste companies versus "real people in
real communities"—anyone who lives or might have to live in the
shadow of a landfill or an incinerator, anyone committed to the
environment not as an abstraction but as "a tangible and diverse
ecosystem that is integral to [their] lives and neighborhoods"
(Greenpeace "Report").

Greenpeace makes much of "communities," and with the word
"grassroots" it vests them and itself with special sanctity: "The
grassroots movement for environmental justice works to protect
the environment by practicing democracy. . . . WMI not only
destroys the natural environment, but also undermines demo-
cratic decision-making at the local level. Many grassroots leaders
can attest to the truth of this latter point."

This is the romantic leftist world of direct community organization, much revered by practicing "activists" and their academic
fellow-travelers, who stand fiercely for "social change" and warm
to spacious terms like "environmental justice." Always trust the
activist; always suspect the businessman.

In such an atmosphere, it was probably inevitable that the Waste Management malefactors should find themselves in the dock for racism. In 1991, the California Rural Legal Assistance Foundation filed a state suit alleging violations by CWM and Kings County of the federal civil rights statute—providing inadequate Spanish translations of the environmental impact report for a proposed hazardous waste incinerator to be located at CWM's Kettleman Hills facility. The same plaintiffs also filed an action in federal court, alleging among other things that CWM and Kings County had violated the federal civil rights statute for deciding to locate the incinerator in a predominantly Latino community. The allegations were dropped in the state court action and dismissed in the federal court, but the taint stuck. "Environmental racism!" shout the activists. It is a novel idea that combines the two darkest sins acknowledged by our times: environmental degradation and racial discrimination. Count on hearing more of the same.

In Greenpeace's grassroots world of earnest activists and abused little people, Waste Management plays the perfect villain. It is big where they are small, corporate where they are "community," hi-tech where they are green, profitable where they are struggling. (To receive a copy of their report on Waste Management, Greenpeace requests a "donation" of $20. However, "[w]aivers may be granted to grassroots groups in uncertain financial circumstances. For-profit companies will be charged $50" (Greenpeace "Report," flyleaf). Also, one might add, Waste Management is the perfect enemy because it represents the unpleasant and untidy world of imperfect solutions, of half-way technologies, of motives that mix altruism about the environment with personal ambitions to profit and get ahead. Reality always offends myth. Deceit is not the exclusive preserve of capitalists. Everyone has a right to ask why any past deviations from perfection have occurred at Waste Management facilities, just as they have a right to ask why Greenpeace prints allegations made against the company while deleting references to the exculpatory conclusions.

Examples abound of Greenpeace's penchant for incomplete reporting of Waste Management's "sins," a word whose theological flavor fits the work of the organzation remarkably well. Hell hath no fury like the wrath of an angry Greenpeace report. The 1987 report on Waste Management, for example, persists with the allegation of serious environmental misconduct (in particular that toxic chemicals had leaked into groundwater used for drinking by local residents) at Waste Management's Laraway Landfill near Joliet, Illinois, after the Illinois Pollution Control Board determined that the concern of the state environmental protection agency was unsupported by the evidence, and after both state appelate and supreme courts had upheld that conclusion. Or again, Greenpeace makes much of the 1982 closure by the Kansas Department of Environment and Health of a hazardous waste facility in Furley, Kansas, which Waste Management had acquired late in 1980 from National Industrial Environmental Services, Inc. State authorities had detected leakage of contaminants into a nearby creek, a situation which when discovered prompted Chemical Waste Management to undertake clean-up procedures and to sue the former owners for breaching their warranties that the site was in compliance with existing laws and was not leaking. The United States District Court in 1985 found in favor of Chemical Waste Management and awarded damages to cover remediation costs. Chemical Waste Management may have bought a "pig in a poke" and regretted it, but that was not the point. Judge Patrick F. Kelly tried hard to be clear about what was. Waste Management and its subsidiaries "are wholly innocent in this matter. They have not caused nor contributed to any part of the circumstances which has given rise to the leak. . . . They have responded from the instant of first notice as a responsible company should. They have done all that is reasonably contemplated to alter or remediate the situation. They are not deserving of any part of that which has unfortunately befallen them." It is as if one were dealing with two different orders of value, two entirely different understandings of how one measures the truth.

Absolute or relative? Free to choose. The choice no doubt is a matter of temperament. If you have a taste for categorical demands (reminiscent of those made by students with bullhorns in the 1960s) and would like to pull the plug on the machine of modern economies (like the counter-culture of the 1970s), you will send a tax-deductible donation to Greenpeace:

"Because clean technologies to dispose of waste do not exist, Greenpeace and Citizens United for Environmental Justice are presenting the following demands to public officials: 1) Publicly elected officials *must* enact an immediate moratorium on all new types of disposal facilities . . . 2) Industry and government *must* recognize that disposal of hazardous waste is unsafe and *must* respond by enacting policies that reduce the use of persistent toxic materials . . . Bans and phaseouts of chemicals such as organochlorine solvents and other halogenated hydrocarbons *must* be enacted to turn the toxic tide toward preventative solutions to the toxic substance crisis. 3) Industry and government *must* enact policies to reduce the volume of sold waste (garbage) and to reduce the toxic materials commonly found in garbage . . . 4) Citizens *must* be allowed meaningful participation in decision about the environment . . . 5) Public officials at all levels *must* enact and enforce laws that preclude government from conducting business with companies, or with any subsidiaries of companies, that have been convicted of a felony. . . ." (Emphasis added)

Or, if you have a taste for practical solutions today that will probably wear reasonably well into the future, and are not offended by a regular dividend check, then you will buy shares in Waste Management.

If you are moved most by appearances, the choice may be trickier. The Greenpeace Report on Waste Management is printed on "non-chlorine bleached paper, which does not contribute chlorinated toxics to the environment." The Waste Management 1991 Annual Environmental Report "uses soybean-based inks, [and is] printed on recycled paper containing 10 percent post consumer waste and is recyclable."

Green is a game that everyone can play.

⊛ 10

Familiar Visions Far From Home

L'ambiente é Il Nostro Futuro

The first half of Dean Buntrock's vision is to make Waste Management the world's most important provider of environmental services. The second half is for Waste Management to become one of the world's great companies. It is a good time for such an aspiration. "Global economy," like "green revolution," has become a defining cliché of the age—but one of enormous significance. To aspire to greatness, for a company built on the green revolution, necessitates global ambitions. Greenery respects no boundaries. Differing stages of economic development, country to country, may result in differing rates of policy formation and differing levels on enforcement of environmental matters. But the contemporary yearning to clean the place up, and keep it that way, seems nearly universal.

Now that the Cold War world is over, what goals should move us? Most of today's humanity seems to be in remarkable agreement on a few broad themes. Most people agree that freely elected governments are the only legitimate ones, that market economies are the only productive ones, and that human rights should be guarded. And no one, it seems, wants to live in a fouled-up environment, locally or globally. The environment ranks alongside other more venerable causes and packs an emotional kick that may even surpass them.

The consequences for a company whose business is environmental services are difficult to overstate. It means that markets, once shaped locally by the age-old problem of garbage, are reshaped according to the new moral dispensation governing greenery. Much of the "waste business" is and will remain fundamentally local in its operational characteristics: to give good service, the garbageman always has had to know the neighborhood. The "environmental services business" calls for local, plus other kinds of knowledge derived from other levels of experience that are useful on broader fields of endeavor. The environmental services business grew out of the waste business, and its fundamental service—waste management—remains unchanged. What has changed is the cultural context in which it must go about that business, and especially the level of our expectations about anything to do with "the environment."

Waste Management's corporate slogan, "The Environment Is Our Future," perfectly captures the mood. It is grand—in the sense of being a large claim—but Waste Management is a large company, and the claim fits. It also translates well, not just literally, but culturally into the different countries where the company today finds itself: *L'ambiente é il nostro futuro* as the Italians put it; *Miljön är vår framtid*, to the Swedes. This is important, because the business environment of the wider world is where corporate greatness increasingly will be judged—especially in the environmental business.

Not surprisingly, therefore, Dean Buntrock's vision for Waste Management has been putting down roots far from home. Twenty years after the launching of Waste Management as a public company in the United States, international operations are Buntrock's special interest. European operations, in particular, recapitulate an earlier history. They also point toward challenges that the company has never faced and must learn to master.

Abroad

Europe in the spring of 1992 is an exciting place to be, especially for Waste Management International plc. The East is tasting freedom, and barrier-free trade—a true "common" market—may soon be upon us. Europe is also crowded and prosperous. And it is dirtier than many Europeans like.

In the spring of 1992, Waste Management International became Waste Management International plc, headquartered in London, with its own publicly traded shares, a pan-European company with a worldwide presence. The initial public offering, in which the mother company sold 20 percent of its international business, brought in $770 million and was one of the largest IPOs ever handled by Merrill Lynch. For the "road-show" when the shares were floated, the company's top leadership all took part: Chairman Buntrock, President Phil Rooney, Senior Vice President Harold Gershowitz, Chief Financial Officer Jim Koenig, and former Chief Financial Officer Don Flynn. Ed Falkman, chairman of Waste Management International plc, was everywhere.

Falkman, forty-eight and a lawyer by training, has been "everywhere" for years. A native of Chicago, he has worked for Waste since 1977 and is a veritable commuter on the British Airways flights from Heathrow to O'Hare and back. He carries an American passport, has a Swedish wife, and has not lived in the United States for fifteen years. He inherited the mantle of the international operations from his peripatetic predecessors, John Melk and Fred Weinert, who set up the first company offices in London during the company's mobilization to clean Riyadh in the late 1970s. He has stuck with it through the lean 1980s when the European market for Waste Management's products seemed not quite ready, and when in Oak Brook the bloom seemed definitely off the international rose. "It wasn't a lot of fun going back to the States in those years and getting asked, again and again, 'What have you got for us?' and not being able to come up with anything."

But Falkman hung on, and the world did change. The Single European Act of 1987 took hold, and green consciousness raised the value of the environment. When the moment arrived, Falkman had the contacts and knowledge of European ways that enabled Waste Management International to move more quickly and with greater surety than if it had been a "mere American" company dealing abroad. Today, Falkman has almost become a European himself; this is his neighborhood, he knows who is who on every block. And he has distinguished helpers.

Frank Schroeder, another longtime American expat, worked for Alcoa in Switzerland for sixteen years before Falkman persuaded him to head up corporate development at Waste Management International. Working at first out of his house in Lausanne with a fax machine, a wallet full of plane tickets, and his wife as secretary, Schroeder prowled the continent for acquisition prospects, learned fast about the waste business, and never stopped learning about the ways of Europe and of doing business there. Talented colleagues accompany him: Ian Bird (vice president and general counsel), Bo Gabrielson (vice president-legal affairs), Larry Glasscott (vice president-finance), Joe Holsten (vice president and controller). Next to Falkman, Mike Collier (vice president and chief operating officer), a twenty-year company veteran, shoulders an enormous load and has the biggest job.

All these people inhabit a warren of oddly shaped offices and crooked hallways in St. James's Street in London's West End. "Windsor House" (55/56 St. James's), as it is called, is the sort of place where it is hard to find a right angle and sometimes hard to find the right office. There is a rooftop bridge between Falkman's office and Schroeder's, and stray computer terminals and fax machines hinder a visit to the loo. Charlie Powell, the English director of administration, was also director of administration in Jeddah where he had four thousand employees to look after. In London headquarters the numbers are of course smaller—when Powell came in 1990 there were thirty on three floors, grown today to perhaps ninety on six floors in two buildings.

But the challenge lies in the movement as well as in the mass. A third of these people are, on any given day, somewhere else, usually out of England. A controller may fly off to Denmark for a day's look at the numbers. An environmental engineer may head for Spain to evaluate a landfill. A vice president may disappear to Brazil for three weeks to look at an acquisition project. It is hard to find people even when you know where to look.

Windsor House is a fashionable address that one might expect of a blue-chip company with a fancy prospectus and a big future, the sort of location that beckons the business luncher. In St. James's, pubs, clubs, and restaurants abound. But Waste Management International plc, somewhat in the mold of Waste Management, Inc., is not famous for its lunches. It is more famous for staff who come to work on Saturdays and eat at their desks. There was talk in the spring of 1992 of leaving central London altogether. The rents are among the highest in the world (a tempting target for the company's ever-so-cost-conscious controllers), but there was something else too. The company's chief driver, Dave Evans, who once ran a car-hire company at Heathrow, has made the run out Cromwell Road to Terminal 1 and Terminal 4 more often than most men living: "It's the executives' time, you see: the trip just takes up too much of it. It'll be much better if we can get out a bit, into our own modern building, and closer to the airport."

Flags and Stars

Pick a desk at Windsor House, regard the coffee mug, and read there the geography of modern Europe. Beside the flags of the eight countries where the company presently operates in Europe (Britain, Holland, Germany, Denmark, Sweden, France, Italy, and Spain) are embossed, in eight languages, the company motto: "The Environment Is Our Future." (Or, if you miss the mug, the fax machines are programmed to transmit the same message along with a pastoral, dot-matrix graphic of birds, trees, and streams.) Try wrapping your tongue around one or two of the tricky ones, like Dutch: *Het milieu is onze toekomst.* It is a reminder that this is Europe. Things sound different because they are different.

For the busy executive trying to get out onto a plane, Heathrow may as well be O'Hare—with this difference. The Waste Management North America executive, setting off from Chicago, may fly far but he will land someplace like Boston or Atlanta or Seattle. The Waste Management International executive setting off from London may fly not far at all, but he will land someplace like Rotterdam or Madrid or Milan. From London, most flights lead to other countries—other sovereignties, other cultures—to somebody else's place, where the roads twist and turn in a particular way because that's how the sheep made the track centuries ago, and where the twists and turns of business reflect various national habits with their own long and devious histories.

In 1992, Europe is abuzz with "EC," the twelve-state (at-the-moment) successor to the original European Economic Community of six launched with the Treaty of Rome in 1957 (the original Common Market). This year will see internal customs barriers fall, passport controls vanish (except perhaps in Britain), and momentum increase toward monetary and, so hope European federalists, political union (the Maastricht Treaty). The scene is rich in subtleties and wrapped in the history of twentieth-century Europe, in particular the French fear of Germany and the determination to avoid another Franco-German war. Europe is indeed at peace and its western half is wonderfully prosperous. But resurgent Germany economically dominates the continent, and the newly free states to the east press at the gates. Although publicly committed to being at "the heart of Europe," the British across their Narrows Seas still are wary.

Pressed for a single word to describe it, perhaps the best one is "convergence." It is not perfect, but it is better than another commonly used: "integration." Consider one image. The country-hopping executives of Waste Management International plc are familiar faces in the business-class cabins of every airline in Europe. Most of those airlines—Air France, Lufthansa, Alitalia, SAS, KLM—are the flag-carriers of their countries and have for years literally shown "the colors" on the fuselage, frequently beside the cabin door. Today they fly other colors in addition: the EC's circle of twelve gold stars on a dark blue field that proclaims the bearer to be, in addition to French and German and Italian, "a good European." (British Airways is an exception; it also differs in that alone among the "flag-carriers," it is privatized and profitable.) This modern banner reminds Americans of a very old one: the first flag of the new American nation in 1776 whose upper left quadrant bore a circle of thirteen stars on the same blue field.

In the New World, it took many years to work out the precise relation among those stars—the equation of rights, responsibilities, and interests and the nature of the center. In the Old World two centuries farther on, working out the convergence of Europe's stars will probably also take many years. Should the "new Europe" follow the vision of European Commission President Jacques Delors and become a federalist superstate, tightly regulated and governed by a bureaucracy in Brussels, and imposing uniform standards across the continent? Or should it follow former British Prime Minister Margaret Thatcher's hope of a loose confederation of many sovereign national states, where power is decentralized and where competition flourishes among the different national systems of taxation and regulation within a free market?

However Europe chooses, Dean Buntrock's vision for Waste Management will likely prove the right one. Whether more and more power flows to the center as Mrs. Thatcher fears, or adheres to the edges as she hopes, a common assumption by all is that trade—business—is what will make it all run. Business must expand, economies must grow, standards of living must rise, if peace and freedom and unity are to be secured, extended, and enjoyed. As this happens, pressure on the environment will grow too. And in technically advanced, highly educated countries like these, the market will demand the products and services to care for it, the very "environmental services" that Waste Management International plc is now superbly positioned to supply.

Gruppo Waste Management

The Italians like to talk. It may be one of the reasons why Waste Management Italia S.r.L. developed more quickly and is today larger (with 5,200 employees and over $700 million in revenues) than any other of the company's operations outside North America. Italian subsidiaries include S.A.R.I. S.p.A. (Florence), IGM S.p.A. (Milan), Sacagica S.r.L. (Milan), Sirtis S.r.L. (Oleggio), Ecoservizi S.p.A. (Brescia), Nova Spurghi S.r.L. (Brescia), Italrifuiti S.p.A. (Turin), and P.I.T.E.F. S.r.L. (Venice). Country Manager Antonio del Sorbo oversees it. President Pietro Gennaro, seventy-two, speaks of it, and of Italy, with two minds. He is a scholarly man, founder of the prestigious firms P. G. A. and Strategia é Organizzatione and is regarded as the father of Italy's management consulting industry: Italy's Peter Drucker. His offices, in Milan's Corso Sempione, are cool and dark and sleek with Italian design. He came to Waste Management in 1989, after its major acquisitions had been put in place by Frank Schroeder and Ed Falkman, and he brought the Italian seniority needed to establish the image of the company in a country where it was still largely unknown. The second part of his mission was to maintain relations with the Italian "partners":

"You know the formula that I'm told Waste Management has used all over the world: they buy control of a company but ask the minority shareholders (who are often the founders of the company) to stay on and to continue to contribute their entrepreneurial ability. I was fascinated by this. This is a very intelligent policy," Gennaro maintains.

This "intelligent policy" is an old theme used by Waste ever since it began to take in other companies back home twenty years ago. But, as is often true in European business, it is a theme with a national, in this case an Italian, spin. You have to know the neighborhood, the local contacts, the peculiarities of the cultural landscape. In Italy, much of this comes down to the kind of relations a company has with public authorities, of which Italy—where 41 percent of all economic activity is directly controlled by the state—has more than any other country in Western Europe:

"This is more critical than anything else—than technology, finance, anything. You can't invent that or have managers in a short time acquire this kind of ability. The best thing to do is to take the people who have already demonstrated those abilities and get them to work with you."

It is a matter of local sensibility. Gennaro, with his unassailable prestige and unmatched knowledge of Italian business and governing circles, was brought in partly to repair damage when the wrong American managers were rushed in to run what had suddenly, in 1988 and 1989, become a very big Waste Management company (one-tenth of its total revenues). It is one of the dangers inherent in rapid growth: people are scarce, and the right ones sometimes hard to pick out. But the difficulties lie on both sides of a deal. Waste Management pays well for its acquisitions and it has certain expectations—particularly in the area of financial control and reporting, where its controllers really do "control." Country controllers are mostly American, and they report up and out to London. Moreover, after the IPO established a free-standing European company, watched on its own (and not just as a part of the big mother company in the States) by analysts looking for clear quarterly gains, financial performance and the operating productivity that fired it assumed even greater urgency. The new owners also had serious environmental expectations; they were serious about compliance.

Waste Management has never bought a company anywhere that wasn't already profitable, and the companies it bought in Italy had all made more than good livings—even respectable fortunes—for their previous owners. Wealthy men and women in their own right, they are also Italians to whom personal relationships are very important. Deals in Italy take time, and not all the work is done at the office or over a couple of drinks. Frank Schroeder has spent countless evenings over elaborate Italian dinners in the best restaurants in Milan, Florence, and Venice—with every second spent productively.

These people are obviously used to making money and enjoying it, and in the past have always done so with a certain individuality. Says Gennaro: "They used to be independent operators. Becoming a part of a big multinational corporation with all their rules and procedures was maddening for them. They had to be educated; they had to be soothed."

Two of these men, from opposite sides of the waste business, are studies in the entrepreneurial side of the Italian national character. Gianni Gremmo is Waste Management's partner in and the founder of Italrifuiti in Turin. He began work in the waste business in France for Compagnie Génerale des Eaux, a large water company that diversified into waste management and is today a major competitor of Americans. In 1970 he opened Italrifuiti, in joint-venture with the French, as a commercial, nonhazardous waste hauler. They started out tiny and had to fight hard not against the competition (there was hardly any), but to convince industry of the need for some sort of proper waste disposal:

"At that time," Gremmo recalls, "there weren't any laws regulating the system and, well, you could just throw it anywhere." Pay somebody to haul it away? No one had heard of it. But France was ahead, and Gremmo was sure that Italy would follow in time. The first national waste legislation establishing categories of waste and guidelines for handling it was not enacted until 1982. He had gotten into the business "perhaps a couple of years too early" and consequently had to educate his market in advance of serving it. It wasn't easy, but eventually it did put him ahead.

Italrifuiti built the first lined landfill in the heavily industrialized Piedmont region, and one of the first in all of Italy. His French partner sold out in 1977 when it appeared the Communists would come to power in Italy (they didn't), and slowly Gremmo, on his own, grew his company internally. Whatever Turin's industries chose to dispose of directly came to Italrifuiti's fleet of green and orange trucks, compactors, transfer stations, and landfills. The rate of his growth was due more to the will of local industrialists to dispose correctly of their waste than to any legislation, which wasn't enforced anyway.

Frank Schroeder found Gremmo late in 1986 and began a long courtship. Gremmo knew about Waste Management, again because of his French experience, but in Italy where as late as the mid-1980s the culture and business of waste was singularly underdeveloped, the American company had no reputation. He had dabbled, again with the French, in establishing a small hazardous waste company in the early 1980s but found it too complicated and the market not yet ready. But the experience taught him the increasing handicaps of small companies in the waste business: "It was a matter of capital, access to technology, and the increasingly difficult administrative and legislative atmosphere. The small company has no future."

He sold to Waste Management in 1988 and, "like in every good family, there have been differences." He thinks the Americans underestimated the difficulty of mastering the difficult Italian market, dominated as it has been since World War II by huge state monopolies like IRI (Institute for Italian Reconstruction), a public dinosaur that wholly owns many of Italy's largest concerns. On the other hand, the bloated public sector meant that when it came to shopping for good private operations, the best among them could be identified in relatively short order. In the waste business, there were probably only six or eight first-rate private companies, and they all affiliated with Waste Management. By the time the competition came shopping, everything good was operating under the Waste Management banner.

Joining up, for Gremmo's company, meant the disciplines of

new policies and procedures, but at Italrifuiti the shock of integration was minimal. Gremmo, for instance, already had in place computer software capable of supplying all sorts of data on a real-time basis—just the sort of thing Waste Management loved. It also meant being in a position to compete for new opportunities, such as Italy's first private waste-to-energy plant in Chivasso. Italrifuiti bid for it enthusiastically in the spring of 1992, which would not have been possible without the technical prowess of Waste Management's family of companies.

Gremmo jokes about his thinning gray hair—the price of building Italrifuiti—and hopes he won't loose the rest of it working with Waste Management. He believes that EC incentives for better enforcement of already advanced Italian waste legislation will put a new premium on technological solutions to waste problems—fewer landfills and more high-tech solutions, for instance—foreshadowing a happy future for his association with the Americans. Besides, "Italians like Americans!"

He also knows their differences. "In Italy, it is not enough to have technology, money, potential, and capability and just to say 'We are the best.' You have to prove it every day."

Prima è Meglio Che Poi

Gremmo's business is nonhazardous commercial waste, but the advantage gained from associating with Waste Management applies across the industry. "In this business you can be alone, by yourself, for a certain amount of time, but beyond a certain point you can't grow by yourself." The warning is Andreino Calubini's, president of Ecoservizi, Italy's most respected hazardous waste transportation and treatment company, which became part of Waste Management Italia in 1989. The negotiations that eventually brought him in were a roller coaster of emotional highs and lows, of expectations and exasperations. What made him finally say yes was the clause in the shareholder agreement that stipulated that one-half of the profits would be reinvested in the company. "This convinced me that with this company I could grow."

What Calubini has grown from gives his biography an authentic entrepreneurial luster. After the war, his father made a living hauling gravel with a horse and cart, and had a tiny subcontract to collect garbage from a tiny corner of a tiny town in Lombardy. Calubini started sweeping streets at age eleven and he learned to be a mechanic; at eighteen he got a truck and carried trash. He married at twenty-three, worked night and day, and ten years later bought the shares of a competitor and moved from his native Lake Garda to nearby industrial Brescia. The new company was a branch of Gianni Gremmo's commercial waste operation in Turin. By 1975, Calubini was branching out on his own, treating sludge and industrial wastes. He saw a big opportunity in a market ripe for development—if three or four companies could effectively join together to command the capital and the service capabilities necessary to establish a national presence. In this he failed, but his own company did not: he diligently plowed profits back into operations and with bank financing made things grow.

Calubini met Schroeder first in 1986, and another long and arduous mating dance began. He had other offers, but it was not the money alone that decided him. It was an entrepreneurial attitude evident in what he knew of Waste Management's history and of its entrepreneurial founder and chairman, and the fact that Waste Management did exactly what the name said, and nothing else: it managed waste.

That was important because Calubini is a "the glass is half full not half empty" sort of fellow. Whatever irksome controls he would have to adjust to with the sale of his company to Waste Management, he knew the opportunities to learn from the Americans would be tremendous. The old Italian saying, *prima è meglio che poi*, "better sooner than later," had been the motto of Ecoservizi, and with Waste Management, Ecoservizi learned how to stay ahead.

Calubini traveled to the States to see the company's operations and was especially struck by the new environmental monitoring laboratory (EML) nestled in the Fox River Valley near Geneva, Illinois, where the company analyzes ground water from landfill sites. Back in Brescia, he built a lab of his own, for chemical waste analysis, adjacent to his offices and treatment facilities. It is a masterpiece of Italian design in glass and black-and-white tile—like EML, as close to the picture in an annual report as reality ever gets. It also works: white coats, colorful flasks and test tubes, computer terminals, the very latest instruments.

Brescia lies at the heart of the most heavily industrialized part of Italy (and one of the most heavily industrialized parts of Europe), and although Ecoservizi's services are nationwide, the plant clearly enjoys what the economists call "place utility." But Calubini takes nothing for granted; he started out too low to forget how hard success is to come by. On the wall of his office hang two small plaques on this subject which, next to his wife and daughters, is the thing closest to his heart. It is what made Ecoservizi possible and what attracted Calubini to Waste Management. One plaque, by the famous economist and president of Italy in the 1950s, Luigi Einaudi, reads:

"Millions of individuals work, produce, and save money notwithstanding all that we can do to disturb and discourage them. It is their natural vocation that pushes them, not just the thirst for money. The pride of seeing their own company prosper with an ever greater number of customers, of expanding their plants, beautifying their headquarters . . . this is as powerful as the money that you make. If this weren't so, you could not explain the entrepreneurs who give all their energies and invest their capital to get back profits that very often are more modest by far than they could earn in some other way."

The notion that money is the product, not the motive, behind successful enterprises like Calubini's is something one does, or does not, accept on faith. Waste Management's Italian partners were wealthy people before Waste came along, and they have become wealthier since. Calubini believes that in addition to knowing how to make money, you have to know how to spend what you make in ways that help the business. The other wall plaque speaks to this point: "If we exchange a lira, each one of us remains with that same lira. If we exchange an idea, each one of us has two."

Ideas shape public opinion, which is all important in a business like waste management that is ever-fraught with controversy. To keep the ideas flowing, Calubini with several others subsidizes *ECO: The Ecology Magazine*, a handsomely designed and produced publication appearing ten times a year and conceived as a voice for the business. But this one reaches a level above the usual trade magazine; it is not just a piece of corporate public relations. *ECO* has 1,200 paid subscriptions in Italy, and Calubini would love to see his magazine, like Waste Management International plc, go "pan-European."

Calubini, moreover, produces museum-quality books on nature and environmental subjects, filled with serious texts and superb photography, to give away at Christmas instead of the usual cases of fine Italian wine. He prints one thousand copies and believes that if they spark a positive emotional response in just two hundred people, the money eventually will come back in other ways. He also produces highly designed "ecology" playing cards, the idea of Angela Cocovilli, an editor at *ECO*. Every card carries a graphic message: hearts are the environmental idealists; clubs are those who do the dirty work of picking up the trash; diamonds are speculators; spades are polluters. On Lake Garda, where he lives, Calubini originated the "Ecoservizi Sailing Trophy and Regatta." Today large posters proclaim it the "Waste Management Cup."

The North

It is a half-serious axiom of all sociology that "the South is different": the southern hemisphere from the northern, Italy from Germany, Mississippi from Michigan. Southern sunshine breeds a

293

gregarious race that spends a lot of time in sidewalk cafes. Northern winters breed a dour but enterprising race that works harder just to survive. The truth, of course, holds some surprises. True, Italian public administration is notoriously inefficient and corrupt; the country's undisciplined public finances on the eve of greater EC economic integration have put it at risk of being classified the "sick man" of the new Europe. Yet Italian entrepreneurs like Gremmo and Calubini rank with the best private businessmen anywhere. All the old North/South imagery is, however, a reminder that diversity reigns, even in the homogenized age of easy jet travel, the ubiquitous fax, and the international MBA. Waste Management's operations in the north of Europe afford pertinent illustration.

German history—some old, some very recent—provides the context. The country offices of Waste Management Deutschland Gmbh are located in Essen, at the heart of the Ruhr Basin, since the late nineteenth century the most heavily industrialized region in the world. This was industry in the old style—coal, steel, chemicals, armaments, railways—the sort that countries like Russia, China, and India still labor under, and whose environmental consequences have been devastating.

"I lived here for six years in the fifties, just down the road, and you would never go to Essen and beyond: you would close the windows in the car because you could hardly breathe the air," says Hellmut Kirchdorfer, Waste Management country manager for Germany, who remembers what the place used to be like. "Today they have cleaned it up pretty nicely, but the point I want to make is that the German environment has been raped for a century. People are finally waking up to it and are very distrustful of anybody who threatens to do something more."

The result, in what was formerly the Federal Republic, has been some fast-paced, stringently enforced environmental legislation that will extend to the East as well. "I think this is good," says Kirchdorfer, "because we've got the environment only once, and we'd better take care of it because we know how to do it."

Waste Management certainly knows how, and in a rich and industrious country like Germany it stands on the brink of enormous opportunities—accelerated by recent history. German reunification—which only a few years ago seemed a far-off dream—is costing far more than West Germans were led or wanted to believe (as the public-sector strike in the spring of 1992 made plain). As D-Marks drain out toward the East, fiscal pressure will increase for the privatization of a variety of public services, and for efficiencies that only true competition achieves.

Competition is not something the German waste business has been famous for, but Kirchdorfer is convinced it will happen soon and that Waste Management will be a big factor in making it happen. An excellent example of the company's approach to managing its foreign operations, Kirchdorfer is a native German who left in the sixties to work for another multinational—Sweden's Tetra-Pak, pioneer, ironically, of laminated one-way packaging material. He worked with Tetra-Pak's international operations for sixteen years, opened the American market for them, ran his own consulting business in Dallas, and joined Waste Management in April 1991. Having worked for "another great company but one that happened to be a great waste-producer, I had experience on both sides of the water, so to speak, and knew what the debate about waste was all about." He also of course knows the language, the temperament, and the culture of his birthplace. He speaks English with a smooth Texas drawl.

Ed Falkman hired Kirchdorfer after a dinner in London, and he got an experienced international operator who sees himself as a translator, not just of language, but of corporate objectives and cultural perceptions, whose goal is profitability and growth in Europe. The challenge matches the opportunity, for while history is almost certainly on his side, Germany's welcome for Waste Management's brand of private enterprise competition has not been particularly warm.

Kirchdorfer describes Germany's waste industry today as "very set in its ways," but adds with conviction that it will be totally restructured in the next five years. About 50 percent of munici-palities do their own waste servicing, which he sees as a terrific market share to conquer. The 50 percent of the business that is private functions more or less as a cartel, whose days he believes are numbered. The market is divided among the "Five Big Sisters" (Alba, Altvater-Sulo, Edelhoff, Rethmann, and Otto), twenty-five or thirty medium-size companies like the Schreiber Company headquartered in Soest, which Waste acquired at the end of 1989, and numerous small family operations with limited capital and technical capability. Private sector operations currently concen-trate on hauling; treatment and disposal in Germany (landfills and incinerators) are still in the public sphere. (One of the few excep-tions is Waste Management's trash-to-energy plant in Hamm.)

Kirchdorfer's job is to implement a "full-service" strategy: to stay in the collection business, but to build a future on treatment and disposal. In Germany, that will mean sorting and recycling, and incineration. It will not mean landfills. In all of the old Federal Republic there are permitted only about 340 solid waste landfills, and their average remaining site-life is eight years. This means that by the end of the century, unless new sites are permitted, everything will have somehow to be reused or burned up. But new sites are not at all likely, both for the usual political reasons (not in my backyard with all that trash, the "NIMBY Syndrome"), and for geographic ones: 80 million people live in united Germany, and they are in no mood to spend what little land they have on trash.

Germany's commitment to recycling appears more radical than anyone else's; one joke has it that the Germans think they can legislate waste out of existence. They have not, however, man-dated the use of recycled materials, and the world market has no greater appetite for recycled *Die Zeits* than it does for *Chicago Tribunes*. New regulations stipulate that no material may be land-filled that has an organic content higher than 5 percent. Stringent new air emission controls will soon be implemented as well, and incineration has become "the way to go," even for some greens. With the waste-to-energy plant in Hamm, acquired by the company from its German builders in 1985, Waste Management entered the German market. This may prove prophetic. Hamm, which began operating in 1985, was the first private incinerator anywhere in Germany. In the spring of 1992, Kirchdorfer's team achieved its own major breakthrough, winning the contract to build, and operate for twenty-five years, another waste-to-energy plant in Gütersloh. They hope there will be more.

Less Land Yet

Lack of space and lots of people are a great incentive to finding good solutions for waste problems. The Netherlands has extremely intensive agriculture, an extremely intensive petrochemical industry, and a population density greater than anywhere in Europe. Environmental consciousness is high, and money is available to assuage it. It should be a good place for Waste Management.

It must, however, learn the Dutch way. Most residential solid waste is the responsibility, by law, of the municipalities, and privatization of this sector is very slow in coming. Private companies compete largely for commercial and industrial customers. The government has set strict targets for waste reduction, separation, and recycling. Landfills are too few, but the permitting of new ones has become almost impossible. Waste transportation to disposal sites away from the populous western coastal area, where two-thirds of the population lives, is all by rail, which is deemed more environmentally friendly than trucks. All new waste disposal facilities in the province of South Holland must incorporate access by water into their design.

Waste Management Country Manager Peter Dessing sees himself, like Kirchdorfer, his German neighbor, as a translator of both national and business cultures. He graduated from the University of Amsterdam at twenty-two and had to choose between going for a PhD or getting a business degree from a good American school. He picked the University of Chicago (MBA, 1972) and says he has never regretted the decision. In the years since, he has worked for American companies (Borg-Warner for sixteen years, Waste Management since 1990), has spent half his time living in the United States, and has a wife from Wisconsin. He and his family are now as comfortable back in Rotterdam as they used to be in Pittsfield, Massachusetts, and Charleston, West Virginia.

"I think Waste is doing this very well: they realized that to move into a new geographic area you need to have individuals who can translate the American success story to the local group of people, individuals who have an appreciation for both cultures. You can minimize your transition costs by putting people in who have been through it once or twice before." Like Dessing who brings with him just that kind of experience and perspective, along with strong financial and general management skills. Waste Management gave him quick but intensive training in Oak Brook and around the States in the particulars of the waste business. Now it is up to him to bring these things together and make Waste Management grow in The Netherlands.

Not just growth, but profitable growth is Dessing's aim, and the simple acquisition of hauling operations and landfills (if he could get them, which he can't) is not the answer. Rather, the greatest value-added in a country like The Netherlands today lies in interim processes—what you do to waste between generation and disposal. "Unlike twenty years ago in the States, when the company was first built, there are today many waste reduction schemes, prevention and recycling, which are really the areas where we can earn our money. Anybody can collect and transport garbage. But what can we do in that middle area to reduce the volume, to take certain products out? That's where the value is."

An example of this is the company's subsidiary Afvalstoffen Terminal Moerdijk B. V. (ATM), situated on the "Hollands Diep," in the Rhine Delta country southeast of Rotterdam. ATM provides an array of services to handle and process waste and the thermal decontamination of polluted soils and liquids. There are facilities for ship-cleaning (tankers), sludge volume reduction processing, and treatment of paint waste, which efficiently recovers metals and solvents. "In the difference between what we can collect this material for and what we can get for the product we turn out, is quite a bit of margin"—enough, hopes Dessing, to pay the company for the cost of building the new paint-waste plant.

The paint waste facility—just permitted in 1991 and due to come on line late in 1992—demonstrates the intermediate kinds of processes where true value lies. In an ordinary chemical waste incinerator (there is only one in Holland, in Rotterdam), everything to do with paint waste, including the cans, gets burned up, and the metals end up in the ash. At ATM, the process is more refined. First, everything gets shredded. The liquid is then drained off, the shredded metal is washed with solvents, and the clean pieces are separated into metals and plastics. The metal is sold for scrap, the plastic is waste. The paint residue is processed into a substitute fuel which goes back to the chemical incineration company.

Frits Jellema, the general manager of ATM, jokes that if the new paint treatment plant shouldn't work, it would be because of a faulty foundation. He points to one of those "groundbreaking/first-shovel-of-dirt" photographs of visiting dignitaries in suits and hard hats, posing for the annual report. These particular brass are none other than Dean Buntrock and Ed Falkman, attending the first "pour" of concrete for the new facility in 1991, a photograph any general manager would boast about. Jellema, in fact, gets a yearly visit from Buntrock, who, after reviewing the progress of the business, stays to hunt the nearby Biesbosch wetlands with Cees Mourik who is 30 percent partners with Waste Management in ATM.

General managers, like Jellema, are the people who make it work. Even in the age of the "EC directive," knowledge of the local scene and of politicians, of who the neighbors are, is key in determining success or failure. Dessing explains that, in this respect, the company has moved into The Netherlands with a light tread. In terms of size, Waste Management actually plays second-fiddle to Browning Ferris Industries (BFI), which got in first, bought thirty or so companies, promptly obliterated the old names, and painted everything that moved BFI blue. Waste Management, in contrast, is not an overwhelming visual presence here. Brochures on individual companies and executives' business cards do not even carry a discrete little corporate logo, or reference to the fact that this is now a "Waste Management" company.

"We don't advertise as Waste Management, but as Icova, ATM, Van Vliet, whatever," Jellema states. "We have left it in the hands of the local companies, saying, 'Use our name if it helps you, don't if it doesn't.' With some customers it obviously helps: Icova in Amsterdam does a lot of business with IBM, and there it makes sense. But most people couldn't care less who the shareholder is; what they care about is how well the service is being performed, and are you cost-competitive." Frank Schroeder in London, who has watched all the European operations unfold, echoes this: "It doesn't matter if the trucks are burgundy or not [in Italy they are not]; it matters if they're on schedule—and clean."

The business card of Jos van Vliet proclaims a family business that goes back to 1931. Today, Van Vliet Groep: Milieu dienstverleners in Midden-Nederland offers solid waste and container services, chemical and medical waste management, recycling, technical consulting, and administrative services. Van Vliet sold to Waste Management in 1990, and (entirely to the good as far as he is concerned) he sees no difference in his operation before and after the changeover. Before, he made decisions after talking with his banker. Now, he makes them in consultation with the Waste Management people who provide the capital for the growing business. "The difference is that now I can speak with guys who know how this business really works."

It was still not an easy decision. It is never easy for a family man to "give up his baby," and such traumas are something Waste Management has had to deal with since it began acquiring family businesses back in the States in the early 1970s. But here in Europe, culture inevitably intervenes. New policies and procedures may for a time be irritating. Good businessmen who have agreed to a deal, however, respect a new owner's expectations, the necessity of integration, and the unrelenting drive in a public company watched closely by the analysts to show growth and performance.

"What is happening, in fact," explains Dessing, "is that we have entrepreneurs who fight for their causes and get what they want; if they are right most of the time, we leave them alone. If they are not right most of the time, things get tightened up. . . . But in this business to tighten it up too much, is to stop it dead in its tracks. The longer we know each other, the better it works. Building a new company takes time."

Broader philosophical issues are more nuanced yet. Take the idea of "work." Van Vliet, who is a very hard worker, believes that America and Holland's styles are different. His English may not be perfect, but his meaning is clear. "I want to work happy, and all my people. I am not a horse, or a horse driver. Here we are working five days a week, eight or ten hours a day, with twenty-nine days holiday. It's our way of life here. You can't change that. You can't say just 'work, work, work'; that's no way of life."

He and all the other Europeans have nevertheless chosen to work for people from a country (America) that does not have a way of life apart from its way of work. If there is a trait that the people of Waste Management in North America universally agree on as the preeminent strength of their company, it is that Waste Management people have a great "work ethic." By this they mean, simply, that people work terribly hard, that they work long hours and weekends, that they will do whatever it takes to get the job done—done right and on time. Very few of them get, or would dare take, twenty-nine days of vacation. They like what they do, and they work for people who appreciate their effort.

Ever since American multinationals started doing business in the welfare state democracies of postwar Europe, some American managers have felt that Europeans just don't work very hard. How does the "great work ethic" fare today? Peter Dessing, half-Dutch and half-American, speculates that Americans "have a cultural bias toward working themselves to death. They think: 'Work, work, work.' The Europeans, since the Second World War, have gotten used to their long vacations, and to them leisure time and other things are more important. But even for an American company, I find the 'work ethic' in Waste is incredible. Anyone who is worth his salt is working all his time and more." Partly it has to do with the market mandate for growth, which requires rather different work habits from managing a nice easygoing family business. "We have to encourage people at all levels to find new challenges and to seek new opportunities."

Dessing and Van Vliet are conversing on the subject. Van Vliet interjects, with a laugh: "Only one thing is sure, and that is, we die. You cannot take it with you. Why always more, more, more? What's important? Health. Family. When those things are OK, then you can do a lot of work."

Dessing replies: "Yes, Jos, but you are one of those people who works his tail off, day and night; 90 percent of your waking hours go to work. I am in exactly the same position. I joined a golf club this year, and I have been there exactly one time, for one hour."

"But," says Van Vliet, "that's a part of our job. That's what we get paid for. But we have to do our job to create the right atmosphere for the other guys to do their job on their wages."

Culture or, more precisely, the patterns of work and incentives in an "advanced social democracy" like The Netherlands are different from what American managers are used to. They are in a sense as immutable as the market itself. Here, the differential in financial reward for many wage-earners, between working and not working, is minimal. Getting and holding the right people under such circumstances is not easy. Waste Management's Dutch companies have to advertise five or six times for driver positions, and come summertime when the weather turns sunny, turnover predictably goes way up.

Dessing, however, views it all with equanimity, through his old University of Chicago lens. "Remember: you have to think in terms of competitive advantage. Labor costs are relatively high here. I don't mind that our people have to have twenty-nine days of vacation and lots of good benefits, if that's what all the competition has to give too, which they do. We just have to manage to motivate our people a little better than the next guy, and then we've got it made. And we do motivate people better than other companies, because we've got everything else. We have the entrepreneurial spirit, right from the top. We have the know-how, we have the technology, and we have the financial resources. With the IPO, 20 percent of this company has been transferred to the public. Investors wanted to own this company and they paid handsomely for the value they saw in Waste Management International."

Nordics I: Miljøet er vor Fremdid

Businessmen everywhere agree: the point of it all is to profit from being better than the competition. No observer of Waste Management, inside or outside, disagrees. For twenty years this company has had the good fortune to see that the vision of its founder and the movement of the surrounding culture have powerfully converged. From this flowed, and continues to flow, great financial benefits. The vision has endured in time (two decades), and is now being tested in space as well. Waste Management International is the latest test. Every day, in a new place, the company must prove itself anew. "Business" may be "business," but even in the age of the "global economy" (or perhaps especially in the age of the global economy), successfully negotiating the local culture will still ultimately tell the tale.

In Denmark, Waste Management's operations are small. Renovadan is a collection and hauling company located on the edge of Copenhagen that provides residential trash collection (subcontracted from municipalities), industrial and commercial collection, and recycling. Disposal, whether landfills or incineration, still rests largely in the public sector. Privatization, while "in the air," still lies in the future, and when it comes, Waste Management would like to be part of it. Treatment (incinerators in particular) represents the new potential for value-creation. Until then, the company must learn to function and prosper in the local world as it is.

Denmark is a small country like Holland and, though less crowded, plays in the top league of "environmentally advanced" nations. For Danes, green issues are urgent. The main Copenhagen landfill was designed with a lifetime of five to six years. This has been stretched to around twenty-five years, by reducing what goes in. The city's provisions for recycling, at the point of waste generation, are radical; waste-reduction and source-separation plans are advanced and well accepted. The market end of the recycling proposition remains a great problem here as everywhere, but the popular conviction that "something must be done," and that recycling is chief among those things, is intense.

For two years, Renovadan has been in the charge of General Manager Benny Allerbring, a Swede brought in to integrate the old company into Waste Management's world. Like Peter Dessing, he is a European who has spent years working in America. His observations about the international challenge faced by the American company in Denmark are also similar:

"This is the key to the future success of Waste Management as a world company: it is that we learn how we are going to deal with the cultural differences. That's what makes international business complicated—that and no other issue."

There is a universal tendency, he continues, when going abroad to remake the world in your own national image: "If you are a Scandinavian and go to America, you try to make Scandinavians of the Americans, until you realize that that's probably not possible. And it's not possible the other way around either."

Allerbring speaks of one particular Danish situation that even he, a fellow-Scandinavian, must try to adjust to. Denmark is a well-developed welfare state that suffers from high unemployment, around 11 percent. Municipal authorities have told Renovadan that they are willing to pay to have more men on garbage trucks—part of their effort to put people back to work. For managers from an American company, "this sort of discussion is as if one were an extraterrestrial." As an American company, Waste Management focuses intensely on productivity. Danes do too, but, report the men at Renovadan, they have their own understanding about the nature of work and its rewards. Danes expect pay, plus some influence on their work situation and involvement in the decision-making process, says Klaus Petersen, who is Allerbring's Danish successor. Allerbring believes that a Dane will toss as many bags of trash as any American—under the same conditions—that is, the more he tosses, the more he earns. Productivity, in this sense, is the same in all Western cultures. If the results are different and people appear to work differently, it is because the system is different. There are scores of explanations for this. If Waste Management can comprehend and work within these different systems—can turn obstacles to strengths—then the world will be as open to it in the late-1990s as the United States was in the late-1970s.

Allerbring's command of idiomatic American speech betrays his close reading of the culture of this country, where Waste Management was born and grew up. As an example of the Old World/New World divide that must be bridged, he talks colorfully about money: "In America, it's great to make money. You work hard; you sell cars, shoes, Bibles. You make a pot full of money, and you're a hero. In most countries in Europe, you shouldn't even mention that you make money. As a Dane told me [the Swede] the other day, 'You've got to understand, this is Denmark!' If you make a lot of money, and you buy a new car, buy a car exactly like the old one, so nobody will see that you changed. Money here is something you have, but you never talk about it."

To get inside such different cultures, you need the natives on your side. Europeans bring the keys to the European markets for Waste Management. Europeans are essential to the company's operation there. Europe also brings a high level of investment in research in the technology of environmental services. (Waste

Management's WMS System of waste collection was pioneered in Germany and reworked for American use.) Combine this with America's talent for bringing good ideas commercially to life, and, Allerbring believes, the conditions are perfect for a rip-roaring trans-Atlantic partnership.

This is probably correct, if the vehicle is right, and if one is careful about the meaning of "Europe" today. Waste Management International, organized on a country basis, centrally directed, and locally operated, is beyond a doubt the sort of vehicle that will make such a partnership a true partnership, and not just another frontal "American challenge" to Europe, as the earlier forays of American corporations were perceived in the 1960s. The importance of a realistic understanding of the "new Europe" is nowhere made clearer than in Denmark, a "progressive" European country grown used to comprehensive welfare state security and with an intense environmental consciousness that only affluence makes possible.

And yet it was the Danes who, on June 2, 1992, rejected by a narrow margin the Maastricht Treaty to tighten European union. Anyone who was surprised should have another look at *Hamlet*, the story of an earlier skeptical Dane. Today's Danes have given the rest of Europe a sharp dose of realism and reminded the rest of the world that Europe is still far from united. Eurocrats in Brussels were set back on their heels, while European skeptics in Britain and elsewhere took heart. Prudent Americans trying to do business in Europe found it confirmed what the smart ones knew in their bones—the differences between nations like Denmark and Germany are of a different order of magnitude from those between states like Illinois and Florida.

Nordics II: Miljön är vår framtid

Or, it would be fair to add, between neighboring Nordic countries like Denmark and Sweden. *Fremtid / Framtid*—the languages are close, but not the same. Waste Management entered Sweden in

1988 with the acquisition of Sellbergs AB, a Swedish company more venerable than any ever brought into Waste Management anywhere. It was founded in 1884 by Amandus Zacharias Sellbergs as a transportation and construction services firm, and was run for decades as it was owned: closely, by the Sellbergs family, from an old seventeenth-century building in downtown Stockholm. Garbage collection services were added in the 1950s—another commodity that one could move with trucks (or, in the beginning, horses and wagons). Old histories are filled with pictures of Sellbergs owners and managers, and of trucks and big rigs hauling concrete, timber, just about anything anywhere in Sweden. It all fit the old company motto: "Nothing too hard to move."

Sweden is a large and relatively empty place. With 8.5 million people and an area of 450,000 square kilometers, its population density is perhaps one-tenth that of central Europe. But because of its distribution—most Swedes live in a few large cities, Stockholm, Malmo, Gothenberg—Sweden has long been awake to the waste problem and generally takes advanced positions on environmental matters. Significant environmental legislation has been in place since 1969. Sixty percent of the country's residential solid waste is treated in incinerators and converted to energy in the form of hot water or low-pressure steam for use in municipal heating systems. Landfill technology lags behind; probably a dozen modern engineered regional landfills in the country and several hundred older dumps need stricter enforcement. The government recently ended its hazardous waste monopoly by selling a controlling interest in SAKAB to Waste Management. The private sector (including Waste Management-Sellbergs) also performs certain collection services.

Recycling however is well advanced, and when Waste Management acquired Sellbergs, it acquired their proprietary BRINI system, the most advanced separation technology in the world. BRINI mechanically separates solid waste streams into three "fractions." Of the original waste, consisting of paper and plastic film, 50 to 70 percent becomes a pelletized fuel suitable for use in boilers. A "screened fraction" consisting of organic material, gravel, and glass, is processed for use as landfill cover. The "residual fraction" of everything else—metals, rubber, rigid PVC plastics—which cannot be economically recovered, is typically landfilled. Sixteen BRINI facilities, some run by public authorities, currently operate in Europe; perhaps thirty installations are worldwide. The system at the Waste Management-Sellbergs facility at Kovik, nestled in a small natural valley near Stockholm, was inaugurated in June 1982, the first in the world.

Bo Antoni is country manager for Sweden and responsible for all of Scandinavia. He is another "translator"—a European needed by Americans in order to prosper and grow in Europe. He was hired by Ed Falkman in the summer of 1990 to run Sellbergs both as part of Waste Management and as a local Swedish company. Sweden is not famous for quick management change, and aligning Sellbergs' customs with Waste Management's expectations has taken some time, which to Antoni, who knows Swedish business culture, is not surprising:

"We have perhaps a very slow management style here in Sweden, but we also have numerous labor arrangements that we must adhere to, so we just can't make things change the way you would in the States. You can't just give orders to people in Sweden. You must try to get people to agree. We have to comply with the overall goals of the group, and the business goals of the group are not to have five hundred local heroes doing whatever they want, doing business whatever way they like to do business. The problem was to transfer the culture of Waste Management to Sweden."

The few Americans sent to Sweden, like country controller Jim Long, also have had to learn to think two ways at once: to transmit their culture to the Swedes at Sellbergs and to learn the business practices of Sweden. Long has enjoyed his two years in Stockholm and has successfully managed the cultural and business challenges. One thing he would like to see more of, however, is a program of cross-cultural education for both the American and European managers thrust into these situations.

Antoni reflects on the eternal barrier of language; even when everyone speaks English, not everyone thinks it. For Americans unused to functioning in another tongue, hazards abound. Compared to Americans, Swedes travel widely abroad; half the population leaves the country every year. They are experienced in meeting different cultures, and in communicating in second, third, and fourth languages. But their apparent ease can be deceptive. "Here in this office we generally speak Swedish, but when the Americans come here we need to be precise in communicating in English. But sometimes we still need one second, or five seconds, to think how to word something, when we really know what we want to say. Sometimes this seemingly little delay can be perceived as indecision. Those who are native English speakers continue to talk during that second when the Swede is thinking. Then when we finally come up with what we wanted to say, well the conversation is already history! And then you come to the next stage when you want to say something, you lose a second again, and the conversation has gone into a new area again." He adds, with good humor: "Obviously if it were the other way around, if we all used Swedish, we [Swedes] would be exactly the same towards foreigners. But nobody speaks Swedish, so we don't have that chance!"

To his insights into the problems of transferring corporate cultures across oceans, Antoni brings historical perspective. He is forty-something, born and bred to the Swedish welfare state, and spends a lot of time with Americans. He observes that Americans seem to be taught almost from the cradle to be competitive, even aggressive. Swedes have been taught quite differently: never promote yourself over the general good of society, do not step ahead, always comply with the group consensus. "This is now part of our personality; from the very beginning we have been trained to be this sort of human being. Americans learn to compete; we learn not to compete. The only place competition has been OK is in athletics."

The management consequences of this habit of nearly half a century are very real. Wage agreements and tax philosophies for years left most working Swedes with more or less the same amount of money at the end of the day, whatever they did and however hard, or little, they worked. This is now changing, but not all at once. The world that assassinated Prime Minister Olaf Palme and his predecessors made for Sweden will linger for years to come, and it will shape the way business gets done. Foreigners must understand this. "I think the Americans think the rest of the world is very much like America," Antoni states, "and that's natural because they haven't experienced anything else. Why should they assume it is different, like we do? This is not right or wrong; it is a difference."

When Waste Management first took over Sellbergs, expectations were that changes could and would be made quickly. Change has come, but more slowly, partly because of greater difficulties in reworking local customs but also because Swedes like to know "what we shall change for."

One image of the waste business in Sweden stands out above all others to illustrate the problem, and the challenge for Waste Management. Stockholm, perched on its archipelago in the clear Baltic light, has the remarkable beauty of a three hundred-year-old city that was never bombed, and where modern development fits comfortably with the old. But where old European cities are notoriously dirty, modern Stockholm is incredibly clean. This is partly because the Swedes are careful with litter, but there is something else too. There is no garbage. This is not because Stockholmers produce no waste; it is because they do not wish to see it and can afford to hide it. In Sweden, garbage is invisible. "MSW" (municipal solid waste—garbage) is not permitted on sidewalks, streets, or alleys, not even on the day the trash collector calls. It is kept in special garbage rooms in building basements. In old buildings, old coal cellars find a new use. In new ones, special rooms, required by law, store the stuff. When the trash collectors do call, they must first haul it up to the street the old-fashioned way—on their backs—and then toss it into the truck. The rest of the world clutters the curbs with it; Sweden's curbs are clean. The service level is superior to any other country in the world. For the company that collects it, it is also extraordinarily expensive and inefficient and, measured in terms of homes-per-hour serviced, translates into extremely low productivity.

This is all ripe for change. For years Swedes wanted to have it like this and were able to pay for it. But they were able to do so only because of an historical anomaly that is now coming to an end. Until the early 1980s, Sweden enjoyed a competitive advantage over the rest of Europe. The country emerged from World War II with its productive capacity untouched and ready to meet the huge pent-up demand for goods in Europe. Customers queued up to buy. And Swedish companies could charge a great deal because they did not have to worry much about productivity, there being so little competition. It was a fat time of easy money and little work. With their lucky earnings, Swedes chose to buy for their country a uniquely high level of social services. Thus the invisible garbage in Swedish cities must be viewed in the context of pensions and sick-leaves, rich medical and educational systems, that likewise provide quite extraordinary services but at equally extraordinary costs.

Today, Sweden can no longer afford to overservice itself. "We simply cannot pay for this any more," concludes Antoni, who grew up with it and, like most Swedes, liked it while it lasted. In the last two or three years, political disaffection, turmoil in the banking system, the urgency to join the new Europe and compete, have undermined Sweden's social contentment. But it is a healthy undermining and no particular judgment on the past, only a clear signal that it is just that: past. "This is really the period when Sweden is turning from history to future." Waste Management's history of competitiveness should put it in a good position to play a part in that new Nordic future.

Six Times a Week

Spain, oddly, came with Sweden. Sellbergs had acquired several Spanish companies before it was acquired by Waste Management. They were small (approximately $35 million revenues), and they represented little more than an entry into the business on the Iberian peninsula, which is about as far geographically and culturally from Sweden as it is possible to get and still stay in Europe.

Today, the Madrid office of Waste Management (whose writ includes Iberia and the Middle East), is the domain of Vice President George Villasana, a native Cuban, an American citizen, and a twelve-year veteran of the company's international operations. Most of Waste Management's early foreign ventures—the big city-cleaning mobilizations in Saudi Arabia and South America— have felt the high energy presence of George Villasana. He came to Madrid in 1990 from Argentina, and in two years has had to deal with the "whole different set of standards" that came with the Spanish acquisitions. He wisely brought with him some familiar faces like Controller Ron Faber and Operations Manager Mark Taylor, who were with him in Buenos Aires and Jeddah. But of the approximately 1,500 other employees of the subsidiary companies Ingenieria Urbana S.A. and Saneamientos Sellbergs S.A., all are Spanish.

Villasana and his small crew work out of offices ("out of" is just the phrase; they are on the road a great deal) in Madrid that can only be described as picturesque, a word that does not leap to mind in connection with many Waste Management locales. Gran Via 61 is a pie-shaped building overlooking Madrid's main shopping street, its interior a fit of plaster moldings, dark woodwork, and leaded glass. The elevator in its central cage on any given day may or may not be working, and the rigor of the hike seven floors up is suitable preparation for the rigors of working in an office where George Villasana is in charge.

First, he had to do a lot of housekeeping. The solid waste collection, street-sweeping, and landfill operations, primarily in Murcia, all needed work. The landfills in particular were a sore issue. Several were routinely ablaze, which was not Waste Management's way. They put out the fires, put on cover, went after the rats, and took care of the leachate, none of which was required by the contracts with the municipalities and none of which earned the company a single peseta. They mended relationships, won contract extensions, and shook up operations. A common practice of the old companies, for example, was to buy nothing but old equipment—"junk." Waste Management buys new trucks. Financial reporting was reorganized, and the market was evaluated.

They concluded that opportunity in the solid waste, city-cleaning type of work, long the company's bread and butter, was very limited in Spain where perhaps 80 percent of the market is tied up by one giant company, Fomento/Constructiones. Even if more such business could be had, typical Spanish margins of 1 to 2 percent make it hardly worthwhile. It has made Villasana look for opportunity elsewhere. "Spain is one of the countries of Europe that is very far behind in environmental compliance, and as the EC standards become more enforceable, Spain will have a lot of catching up to do. This is a big market opportunity for us."

Villasana's strategy is to maintain the solid waste activity that the company now has and expand it, as possible. But the real push will come on the chemical and toxic waste side, where Waste Management's technological expertise and experience should translate into genuine advantage. "Incineration, physical and chemical treatment plants, stabilization facilities, anything in this area is the real future for us," Villasana predicts. He knows this is easier said than done, and that it requires long-term perspective and commitment. After permits are granted, for example, an incineration project is a two-year proposition in construction alone. Add in all the usual opposition to progress from Greenpeace to local NIMBYs—"all the interest groups that can make a lot of noise"—and patience is required above all.

"The name 'Waste' carries a lot of weight everywhere." Villasana speaks from the experience of a dozen years on three continents. "There is a lot of anticipation that we are going to grow over here." Yet he doesn't even like to think "multinational." "We are a national company. No matter where we go we look for a local partner, we rely on the local partner, we employ 99 percent of the people locally." Everybody knows Waste Management is an American company, but one that acts within the local environment. "We don't carry a logo and wave an American flag." In Europe, which now more than ever looks to itself and not to America, this is especially important: "We have to blend in."

"The job of a guy like me," says Villasana, "is to be the bonding between two cultures. This is never easy. If you're going to work in Spain, you have to work in the Spanish system. I can't go to the States and make people talk Chinese; the language is English, and people eat hamburgers, and I cannot change that." In Spain the thirty-day vacation in July and August is life itself. Parking places are found anywhere in Madrid. People go home at 2:30. "They do business, work hard and prosper, but they do it in their own style."

To make the point, Villasana recalls an experience with friends in Venezuela. The man was a petroleum engineer who worked for one of the big oil companies and had adjusted pretty well. But his wife never did anything but complain about Venezuela. "I finally took her aside at a party one night and asked her straight out: 'Wouldn't it be better to look on the positive side for a change, and perhaps help your husband instead of making him and everybody else miserable?' By the way," he laughed, "they got a divorce!"

Spanish cities probably get "used" harder than any in Europe. Dinner in a sidewalk restaurant at 11 P.M. is common seven days a week. On Friday and Saturday nights in Madrid, if you don't have a reservation, you don't eat. The climate is hot, the buildings crowded, the trash piles up fast. In Madrid (where Waste Management does all of $1 million of business but has an important symbolic presence), garbage gets collected six times every week. This is as extravagant, and as culturally unique, as the Swedish policy of hiding it in the cellar. The cadre of Waste Management people, like George Villasana, whose job it is to master such uniqueness in the service of Dean Buntrock's vision and the company's shareholders, have their work cut out for them.

Their reach expands quickly. In the spring of 1992 Waste Management International acquired the SPAT Group in France, consisting of four companies with municipal solid waste and demolition debris landfills near Paris. In 1991 in Britain, the company acquired a 15 percent interest in Wessex Water plc, to form Wessex Waste Management Limited (WWM), which serves as the vehicle for pursuing the waste business in the United Kingdom. WWM's first acquisition was Wimpy Waste Management Ltd., a large collection and landfill business that now operates as "UK Waste." In Argentina, Manliba S.A. and ASEO S.A. are Waste Management companies that provide collection services primarily in approximately half of Buenos Aires. Pacific Waste Management Pty Ltd. operates in all the states of Australia, while Waste Management N.Z. Ltd. serves New Zealand. In Asia, the company has formed a joint venture (Enviropace Ltd.) with two other firms (one from mainland China) to contract a hazardous waste treatment facility for the entire colony that will be operational in 1993. Negotiations advance with an Indonesian partner to provide a facility similar to the Hong Kong project in that country. Prospects elsewhere in East Asia look extremely bright as population, income, and environmental awareness increase, providing the right conditions for Waste Management's entry into those markets.

Let's Mobilize

Such moves are, and will be, the consequence of measured judgments and much planning. Other moves happen faster, the consequence of a leader's instincts or of changing world events that create needs and opportunities suddenly and in unlikely places. It is in the nature of any dynamic business for things to come and go, and in the Middle East, where the company got its international start, and in Saudi Arabia where it long had its biggest foreign presence, the business is mostly gone. But the last chapter of Waste Management's Middle Eastern involvement, in Kuwait in 1991 and 1992, illuminates a company mentality that is certain to resurface should conditions warrant.

In the Waste Management vocabulary, "mobilization" is a favorite word. It refers to the company's aptitude of bringing immense talent and resources to bear on a specific project, quickly and with great effect. The people involved would be superb in handling sudden military crises destined to have long-lasting political consequences (viz., the Berlin Airlift). "To mobilize" the cleaning of some exotic place stirs historic memories of Riyadh, when a bunch of green young Americans set off for Saudi Arabia. Fifteen years later in postwar Kuwait, some older more experienced Americans (and a Scot) proved that they still had the stuff—and felt the same old delight in it.

When Dean Buntrock saw the pictures and heard the stories of the Iraqi occupation of Kuwait—flaming wells, oil in the Gulf, a vandalized Kuwait City—he realized that this was where environmental services were most needed in the whole world. He has had his picture taken in many unusual settings, but never, until the spring of 1991, in the middle of the desert in front of a smoldering enemy tank. Here was a responsibility for Waste Management, and an opportunity. Buntrock's point man was George Villasana, whose territory this was and whom Buntrock once described as the hardest-working man he has ever known, which, given Waste Management's work habits, is no mean statement.

Commotion in the spring of 1991 about potential business in Kuwait for environmental service companies was considerable. Villasana flew off to Oak Brook for talks with Buntrock and others about the possibility of mobilizing. He conferred with Jim Range, head of the company's Washington office, and with the Army Corps of Engineers. He returned to Saudi while Saddam's SCUDS were still falling, and camped out in Dammam where the Kuwaiti government-in-exile had taken up residence. For days he chased Kuwaitis who had already signed up five Saudi companies to do the emergency clean-up once they returned home. Day and night he knocked on hotel doors, only to be told everything was already "done, done, done," that the Americans were too late.

Finally, he cornered Issa Al-Kandari and asked: "If I *could* get in there, what would you need?"

"But you *can't* get in there . . ."

"But if I *could*, what would it be?"

"Well, ten sweepers, twenty dump trucks, and a hundred men . . ."

Villasana called Buntrock who said, "Do it." He assembled the equipment from stocks already in Saudi, along with enough supplies—water, food, fuel, spare parts—to live in the desert for two months. The Kuwaitis' rooms on the twenty-first floor of the Hotel Oberoi overlooked an empty lot, which was where Villasana lined up all his trucks and men. At 11 P.M. he knocked on the door with the "Do Not Disturb" sign one more time:

"Goddam, George, not you again!"

"OK, OK, just look out the window."

"You're crazy, George!"

"OK, OK—you give me the green light and we'll help you."

"I don't need help."

"We'll do it for free."

"You're crazy!"

"We'll do it for free. If you like it, you pay me. If you don't like, you don't pay."

Two days later he got the green light. He called Buntrock, and at 6 A.M. the trucks headed north for the border with an American army escort. They stopped for the night about 100 km from Kuwait and camped on the road. Inside Kuwait, three lanes of the four-lane highway were clogged with abandoned and bombed-out tanks, guns, and armored personnel carriers. The next morning, March 10, about 5 A.M., Villasana and Crawford Ross entered Kuwait City (by then filled with American troops), met with officials, and were assigned an area to clean. They asked only one thing:

"Tell us what you want, and then just leave us alone." Trucks and men were working within two days.

Two weeks later, the Kuwaitis expanded the area. They ended up with responsibility for close to 100 km square, including the city center and all the best suburbs.

Crawford Ross is the spiritual descendant of those tough and talented Scots who a hundred years ago built bridges and laid out railways all over Victoria's empire. In Saudi and Kuwait, he is director of operations maintenance and manager (with Jim Herak, the American resident manager) of the third-country nationals from all over the Indian subcontinent who run the trucks and make the system work. For the last year, he has been in a city with something of the same "on the front line" feel that Berlin had forty years ago: the enemy, chastened but untamed, is just 80 km up the road, no doubt with a few SCUDS still ready to go. (En route from Saudi with the original truck convoy, Ross observed vast columns of allied forces heading south and wondered if he had made the right decision in saying yes to this particular "hardship" assignment.)

The Iraquis, of course, have caused no more trouble, and the military presence in Kuwait City is reduced to a few American and British officers and UN troops who control the border. What the Waste Management men found was a dirty, neglected, and vandalized city, but not the devastated one depicted by the media. What they did was to clean it up, something in which they had had much practice in other cities around the world. There is no mistaking the parts of the city cleaned by Waste Management from those that were not.

Not everything, however, worked out according to original expectations. What started with bravado ended with keen disappointment. The company invested a great deal ($30 million), at first with no contract at all, expecting a commitment of at least five years from the Kuwaitis. But after less than one year, they were told that the business was going back to local companies. Politics, not performance, was the problem (Kuwaiti personnel changed). Waste Management was not the only Western firm to get the cold shoulder. Waste management is by nature risky business, and in settings like the Persian Gulf it is especially so.

"I am looking forward to Waste Management coming back and taking me." The words are those of Prassad Bulshewar, maintenance supervisor from near Calcutta, who first came to Riyadh in

1978 and has worked for the company ever since. The sentiment is shared by many other third-country veterans of Waste Management's Middle Eastern years: S. S. Pasha, operations; Rajan Thomas, finance; Mukhtar Khaku, site service. The company has been their home and second family for their long stretches away from home and family. Their affection for it transcends "corporate loyalty" and can only be described as familial. Share a Pepsi in their quarters, an Indian meal in their "mess," and feel their closeness. "Fifteen years of my life is here," Prassad explains. "I am not in the highest status and not in the lowest status. I can provide for my family and have the opportunity every day to improve myself, and that is the gift of Waste Management to me."

Resident Manager Jim Herak is Prassad's and everyone else's boss in Kuwait. An American who came up from Jeddah, he has had the job of closing down the show, never much fun, particularly when you are not sure what comes next. In addition to the official business card in English and Arabic, he carries a playful unofficial one: "Jim Herak: Guided Hunting Service / Wars Fought / Uprisings Quelled / Governments Run / Tigers Tamed . . . And The Finest Contracting Service." In these parts, a sense of humor has always been a valuable commodity.

A certain truth lies behind the joke. Herak and the others who pulled off the Kuwait venture, only to have it pulled out from under them, could not have done so with just any other big American company. Their presence and performance—their "mobilization"—are emblems of a corporate character that one would not expect from an $10 billion behemoth with 65,000 employees and 900 divisions operating in 48 states and 24 foreign countries: the world's largest environmental services company, and growing larger every day. To many inside, who have grown up with it, Waste Management feels like a smaller company. It still has about it a certain rough-and-ready, give-us-another-campaign-to-mobilize-for style that dates to the days of its youth:

Villasana recaptured the spirit perfectly when he called the chairman from Kuwait and said, "We'll do it for free!"

Epilogue:
Family of Businesses

THE VERY earliest annual reports of Waste Management, Inc. refer to the company's desire to offer customers a "total service" answer to their waste problems. That was 1971. What then seemed rash and ambitious to Dean Buntrock, Wayne Huizenga, and the other founders, today seems simple. They wanted their company to be able to collect, transport, and dispose of the trash in a comprehensive manner: whatever the waste producer needed, they wanted to provide it. The market represented by those customer needs was still in the beginning process of formation. It represented as much the accumulation of past demands as it did of any vision of the future.

The very latest annual report of Waste Management (which is now one of the world's most valuable companies, one grown sophisticated in all the techniques of public and investor relations) charts the current manifestation of that original intention and measures off the enormous distance traveled since. "Waste Management, Inc.: A Family of Companies Offering Total Environmental Services" is how they now see themselves, and how they hold themselves forth to the world. That large phrase contains two themes that are central to this company's story. The first is how that early, simple goal became a vision capable of driving the company forward into markets unimagined a few years earlier, markets that themselves bespoke a revolution in cultural values and public policies to do with man's relationship with the natural world around him. Call it "environmentalism." The second is how the leaders of the company employed this alignment of their skills and emerging markets to achieve corporate growth and create value for their shareholders.

Today's "family of companies" represents technical sophistication and management maturity unimagined when Buntrock first cobbled together Waste Management from a few family businesses. In the best of those family firms, there were men who knew a great deal about driving trucks and moving dirt, things that thousands of other good men still do at Waste Management today. But where once they worked alone (when driving trucks and moving dirt was all there was), thousands of others now attend them: environmental engineers, analytical chemists, compliance officers, lawyers, accountants. Today, the term "total environmental services" necessarily embraces this larger, more skilled cast of characters. "Total environmental services" also continues as the vehicle toward two unchanging business goals: to serve customers and to fuel growth.

Large size (most of the numbers cited in this book will almost certainly soon be out of date) measures scope and breadth: "how much" and "how far." But what gives power to size is the quality of the pieces that make up the mass, and how well they fit and function together. In this, "family of companies," as it is applied at Waste Management, is more than a cozy annual report cliché. It is that for sure, but it is also the consequence of shrewd judgment, incalculable hard work, and considerable good fortune. The metaphor is correct: this company is a "family" and not some larger, less wieldy, less unified sort of group. It is also an old-fashioned sort of family, sensibly governed and not yet given over to disorders begotten by splintered wills and competing affections.

At Waste Management, many of the "members" still behave as their old, highly descriptive family name suggests: they manage waste. Their new family name, WMX Technologies, Inc., also describes a determination to keep the same family modern. There are two elements to this. To manage waste at the environmentally awakened end of the twentieth century is inconceivable without heavy investment in the technologies that can help us solve some of the problems that other technologies leave behind. Beyond this, however, lies an evolving field of other environmental services not directly related to waste, but that will serve a similar purpose. WMX Technologies Inc., for example, is home to the nation's third largest group of environmental engineers with capabilities in air quality control, industrial hygiene, transportation and infrastructure design services. Wheelabrator Clean Air offers a full range of air pollution control technologies and devices. Rust International ranks as one of the nation's largest design-construct contractor serving aerospace, automation, consumer products, and chemical industries, in addition to solid waste and wastewater capabilities. Today's family "members" remain steadfast as ever in the conviction that waste can be effectively managed; in addition, they are challenged as never before to explore new services whereby the environment can be practically enhanced.

In addition to universally good pay, they take from their jobs the intangible reward of believing that the world is a little better place, thanks to the difficult job they have chosen to do. No particular nobility inheres in their choice. Their jobs are jobs, like anybody else's. But they are lucky in that they feel that, similar to doctors and teachers, their work has special merit.

Waste Management's "family" is still young: one generation, in fact. Its twentieth annual report (which records continually impressive financial results despite a lingering serious recession) includes a two-page spread on the highlights of its growth. A collage of images illustrates its progress and touches on all the family members. A front-loading truck rolls toward a landfill in California. Another pulls away from a trash-to-energy plant in Connecticut. Technicians peer into colorful computer displays. Canisters of nuclear waste are deftly hoisted from tractor-trailers. Bins of plastic soft-drink bottles head for the recycler. It is also a study of contemporary political and corporate correctness; everyone is careful about these things, these days. There is a black man driving a truck, a white woman in hard hat and goggles, an Oriental woman in a lab coat. There are also smiling children in South America and workmen from India cleaning a city in the Middle East.

Three other photographs might fairly be described as "historical." There is an old, 1970s-vintage compact-truck, and a man peering through a surveyor's transit at a landfill. Both carry the company's old "pre-burgundy" straight up-and-down "WM" logo. And there is a single black-and-white image of three men, nowhere near a truck or a landfill. Dean Buntrock, Wayne Huizenga, and Harold Gershowitz, each with a hand on the ticker tape, pose (a little stiffly) on the floor of the New York Stock Exchange on the first day that Waste Management was traded (under the symbol "WMX") on the Big Board. Buntrock and Huizenga (and Larry Beck, who is not pictured) founded the company. Gershowitz came aboard close to the beginning and retires at the end of 1992. Huizenga left Waste Management in 1984 to follow other ventures. Don Flynn retired in 1991. Buntrock remains along with Phil Rooney, who was also there at the beginning and who appears with Buntrock in this, as in every, annual report next to their yearly letter to shareholders.

If the "family" has a father, it was and remains Dean Buntrock. He is a father in the old and the new style. His vision powerfully shapes corporate strategy. His values inform the behavior of thousands of employees day-to-day. He is formal but doesn't care for protocol; he and every one of his executives wear suits. He has a largish office, grand enough to intimidate longtime company truck drivers and bulldozer operators who are invited there to visit their old boss. Yet, easily and without hesitation, they still call him "Dean." Everyone does.

Look and See

Look at any Waste Management landfill or at any other waste treatment facility and chances are you will be struck not just by the character of the place itself, but by its relation to the neighborhood. This is a subjective impression, but I have seen many of these places and have found it to be so: they assume, visually, something of the character of the landscape surrounding them. If there is nothing really surprising about this, it is not immediately obvious either. You might think, automatically, that such heavy-duty facilities would not naturally meld with their settings. It is not the case.

Partly this is because of the care with which Waste Management designs these places: grassy swards and knolls, little lakes with lots of geese, tidy front offices and parking lots. But it is largely something in the eye of the beholder, as much a matter of mood as of literal likeness. The Broward County facility is sleek and modern, like the mood of its South Florida setting. The CID complex on the southeast side of Chicago seems all pipes and trucks and heavy equipment, densely packed like the industrial mass that surrounds it. If it is possible to find a landfill "lovely," almost a pleasant place to be, then that place is Waste Management's G.R.O.W.S. (Geological Reclamation and Water Systems, Inc.) Landfill in Falls Township, Pennsylvania—an immense site that serves the heavily industrialized area between Philadelphia and Trenton. Its setting takes something sylvan, even a bit elegiac, from its neighbors: the Penn Warner Fishing and Camping Club; Pennsbury Manor, William Penn's late seventeenth-century country home; the noble ruins of United States Steel's Fairless Works, now cold and abandoned. The landfill serving Kuwait City, the best part of which was until June 1992 operated by Waste Management, shares much with the bleakness of its desert surroundings and evokes, with its Iraqi scavengers, the general roughness of life in that part of the world.

The point is this. Our trash is not something "apart." On the contrary, it is part of us. As always with the garbage business, how we handle it reflects local conditions and (in this age of easy communication and no "secrets") global mandates.

From G.R.O.W.S. or Broward County to Hong Kong in South China is a journey of some 12,000 miles to a different side of the world. The neighborhood changes. The problem of waste does not. The presence of Waste Management in Hong Kong, center of the world's most populous and potentially most productive region, foreshadows large work to come and confirms Dean Buntrock's vision of the business of his company as necessarily the world's business.

The British Territory of Hong Kong, in the last five years before being returned to China, symbolizes all the wealth and enterprise of the new Asia. Among the most crowded and affluent plots of real estate in the world, it is perched on the edge of the vastness of the world's largest continent now ripe for development. Hong Kong also symbolizes a principle of sound environmentalism that will shape the global future of Waste Management: richer countries are cleaner countries.

Industrialization, for the last two centuries, has vastly enriched our world; yet in the popular imagination it is equated with pollution. The image or the cultural memory of "dark satanic mills" has proved maddeningly sturdy. Today, it is increasingly false. Mankind at the end of the twentieth century defines "development" differently from the way it did at the beginning of the nineteenth. Environmental consciousness is a big part of the difference. Never again will smokestacks (with smoke pouring out of them) symbolize "progress triumphant" as they did in old nineteenth-century prints. Quite the opposite: any "smoke" at all today means pollution, and pollution means trouble.

In those earlier times, men thought boldly in terms of "progress." In our own times, we think just as boldly in terms of "development." The words have changed, but the fundamental dynamic has not. Both speak to a process (or a "progress") whereby from the mixture of intellectual energy, physical labor, and natural resources, wealth is created—wealth which raises standards of living and enhances the range of human possibility. Once one acquires wealth, how one spends it depends on private values, public policies, and cultural fashions. In these times, all three factors dictate spending an ever-larger share of it on the environment. But make no mistake: the wealth must be there first, and it must already have provided for more fundamental requirements like food, housing, and reasonable medical care. Once such conditions are met, the environment stands to benefit mightily.

So it is in Hong Kong. The Territory has done a reasonably good job with housing, education, and health, and it has lots of money still left in the bank. Now, it is the environment's turn. Waste Management is one beneficiary of this historical evolution, its presence in Hong Kong a signpost to its future. It illustrates in general outline, if not in every particular, a process of challenge and response that summarizes the Waste Management story.

Asian and American Futures

In addition to the usual wastes produced by a city of 6 million, industrialized Hong Kong is a bedlam of chemical waste producers. Thousands of factories, packed into the tight confines of Hong Kong Island, Kowloon, and the New Territories, spew forth on the local and world markets the myriad products of Chinese enterprise. There is textile finishing, leather processing, printing, electronic components manufacturing, battery plants, metal industries, electroplating, and, yes, laundries. The list goes on and on of businesses that produce chemical wastes, and until now none of it was treated or properly disposed of. The dangers to the

327

waters of Hong Kong Harbor and the South China Sea have been obvious for years, but only relatively recently have the right conditions combined to do something about it: political initiative, financial resources, technical know-how. The gaggle of pipes and tanks and towers rising up on Tsing Yi Island in the New Territories is the result.

The Chemical Waste Treatment Facility on Tsing Yi is part of an ambitious public works program of the Hong Kong Environmental Protection Department, which includes new sewage outfalls, solid waste transfer stations, and sanitary landfills. Everything—all of the Territory's waste streams—needs urgent attention, and the project on Tsing Yi is a massive frontal assault on the most complex of them all: chemical waste. That sort of situation is tailor-made for folks who like to "mobilize." At Waste Management, "mobilization" has always made the blood race: it did in Saudi Arabia fifteen years ago; it does in Hong Kong today.

In Hong Kong, as on each new foreign field, the formulas vary. But they are only local manifestations of the "get the job done" theme that pervades the history of this company on hundreds of jobs every day, abroad and at home. Here on the south China coast the particular formula entailed formation of a consortium, Pacific Waste Management Ltd. (70 percent) with two other groups, China International Trust & Investment Corporation Hong Kong (Holdings) Ltd., an affiliate of the People's Republic (20 percent), and Kin Ching Besser Ltd. (10 percent). Enviropace Ltd. is the company they have formed exclusively for the purpose of constructing the Tsing Yi facility and operating it for fifteen years. The contract details design and performance criteria and requires Enviropace to collect and treat any hazardous (but not radioactive) wastes generated in the Territory, which were estimated in 1987 at close to 100,000 tons. Enviropace will also be a full-service operation, providing containers to store chemical waste and trucks and barges to transport it to the facility from generators throughout Hong Kong and from ships in the harbor. It will also provide free advice to industry in order to help it best determine how to meet the new regulations.

The contract with the Hong Kong government calls for Enviropace to provide the approximately $126 million development cost, and thus enables the Territory to acquire a modern chemical waste treatment facility without huge public investment. In return, the consortium will receive two forms of payment. A capital fee will constitute the Hong Kong government's payment for the facility. And a monthly operating fee will have two parts: a fixed operating fee regardless of volume, and a variable fee based on the volume of waste collected, analyzed, and treated. Bechtel Environmental, Inc. and International Bechtel, Inc. have contracted to provide detailed designs, procurement, and construction management services.

The Territory's new waste handling, treatment, and disposal rules are scheduled for full enforcement in early 1993. The plant on Tsing Yi will be ready by then to handle up to 100,000 tons of waste per year. A core group of some two dozen Pacific Waste Management staff will manage the project at start-up, but it is anticipated that within a year or two most of the expats will be gone. Chinese will therefore be in charge for thirteen of the fifteen years of the contract. For that period, and presumably into the future beyond, the plant will do everything there is to be done with chemical waste. There will be laboratories for waste analysis, bulk storage tanks, and large, drummed waste storage buildings. All of Chem Waste's major technologies will be employed here, including incineration, stabilization, the PO★WW★ER™ process, and physical chemical treatment.

It all represents a first, not just for Hong Kong, but for Waste Management worldwide. Tsing Yi will be the company's first ever, all-in-one integrated chemical waste facility, conceived and designed as such from the beginning, incorporating every process employed by the company back home. But where Chem Waste facilities back home typically grew by accretion (acquired facilities much added onto), Tsing Yi will happen all at once. It is a metaphor for East Asian economic and environmental development: everything is speeded up. Here, there is little "old and crumbling" infrastructure (that curse of many industrialized countries in the

West) to replace, only the most modern infrastructure to build for the very first time. The leap from rice paddy to electronics factory is accomplished in twenty rather than two hundred years. Wealth is created more quickly than it can be consumed. There is money to invest in the future, today.

Tsing Yi is one such dramatic investment, and Waste Management's family of companies is on hand to make it happen. Bill Grube, the crisp engineer and manager of the project, spent years at Rust International. Siuwang Chu, the technical manager, calls Brooklyn home and came from Waste Management jobs in the Midwest. Sinon Galvin, director of operations and in charge of mobilizing the 250 largely local people who will operate the plant, came out from Oak Brook. Mike Rogan, Waste Management vice president for project management in Oak Brook, who cut his international teeth dealing with Saudi money changers in the 1970s, has total responsibiity and is a regular on the eighteen-hour flights out from Chicago. Tom Smith, Waste Management's international director of corporate development for Asia, who is preparing to install the first country-manager exclusively for Hong Kong, looks with pride on the four feet of tender documents on his office shelves which will soon be transformed into the working plant on Tsing Yi.

That transformation is being accomplished with both an American and an Asian character. The process technology is pure Chem Waste. The air pollution control technology comes from Wheelabrator. The construction force is (as the operations force will be after start-up in 1993) highly skilled and largely Hong Kong Chinese. Hong Kong is a city-state whose rapid development in the last fifteen years has been literally vertical; land reclaimed from the sea is all that remains for building. Everyone lives and works in tall apartment blocks and high-rise office towers.

So it is for Enviropace on Tsing Yi. For a facility that in the States might sprawl over twenty or thirty acres, the government here allotted five, which had once been given over to a cattle-quarantine facility (its jetty still shows ramps reaching down to the water's edge to unload the bawling beasts). The abundant construction scaffolding is not, alas, quite up to Brand's standard; it is, rather, the bamboo lattice universal to building in Asia. To tour the site, you climb a lot of stairs and grow dizzy with the "vertical" activity and the international bazaar-quality of the hardware packed in before you: concrete made from Chinese cement and Hong Kong limestone; carbon steel tanks from China; structural steel from Korea; pumps from the U.S.A. You also understand engineer Grube's observation that is has been quite a challenge to compress $100 million of capital into this tight Chinese space.

Development director Tom Smith, an American who likes it "out there" and is married to a Malaysian, thinks a great deal about Asia beyond Hong Kong. The Chem Waste performance on Tsing Yi will soon be reprised in Indonesia, and as the Pacific world continues its amazing dash forward, he is convinced opportunities will abound for the environmental services company with the right combination of technical and cultural know-how. He is not alone. In the summer of 1992, yet another Asian business magazine made its debut with a disarmingly truthful title: *ASIA, INC.* It is the work of publishers in Hong Kong and Bangkok, and the premier issue lays out five essential areas that business executives must invest in if Asia's recent good fortune of "turning battlefields into marketplaces" is to continue into the next century. They are Telecommunications, Energy, Infrastructure, Skills, and the Environment: "As Asia confronts its pollution, new businesses will emerge. California universities' waste-management programs are already reportedly brimming with Asian students."

If all goes well, in Asia and elsewhere, the next century may become the age of enterprise and the environment. One without the other won't make much sense. Combining enterprise—where markets shape skills, capital, and technology into new products and services—with environmentalism—where humans rework their relation with the natural world that supports them—is a corporate job-profile that fits Waste Management like few other companies. It is a job that needs to be done close to home and far afield, as much in Chicago as in Hong Kong. It will depend both on the tangibles of technology and capital, and on the intangibles of skills and leadership. It is a subject that comes up often with Waste Management managers everywhere. Says the European or Asian country manager: "We send a lot of people back to Oak Brook for training." These Germans, Italians, Chinese, and Indonesians tread a path well worn by others from Florida, Indiana, Washington, and Ontario. They are all serious about it.

A simple graphic of the globe appears on the cover of the 1991 Waste Management annual report. The annual photograph of Dean Buntrock and Phil Rooney appears on page 4. They are posed, for the first time, at the doors of the company's new "Leadership Development Center" in Oak Brook. They share the page with an organization-chart depiction of the Waste Management "family of companies" and the jobs they do. I doubt if the page was composed deliberately with this in mind. But if one has learned anything of the history of this company, then this particular chart and photograph together reveal something of what Waste Management's story will be tomorrow. For a family to grow together and prosper, its members must partake of a common vision. They must be confident in their talents and comfortable in the work they do. They must believe that what they do serves a useful purpose, for themselves and beyond themselves.

Index